ASI REAL ESTATE SALES EXAM

LEARNINGEXPRESS

NEW YORK

Library of Congress Cataloging-in-Publication Data
ASI real estate sales exam.
     p.   cm.
   ISBN 1–57685–152–4
    1. Real estate agents—Licences—United States—Examinations, questions, etc.
2. Real estate business—Licenses—United States—Examinations, questions, etc.
I. Assessment Systems, Inc. II. LearningExpress (Organization)
HD278.A85   1998
333.33'0973—dc21

98–37854
CIP

Printed in the United States of America
9 8 7 6 5 4 3 2 1
First Edition
ISBN 1–57685–152–4

Regarding the Information in this Book
We attempt to verify the information presented in our books prior to publication. It is always a good idea, however, to double-check such important information as deadlines and application and testing procedures, as such information can change from time to time.

For Further Information
For information on LearningExpress, other LearningExpress products, or bulk sales, please call or write to us at:
    LearningExpress®
    900 Broadway
    Suite 604
    New York, NY 10003
    212-995-2566

LearningExpress is an affiliated company of Random House, Inc.
Distributed to the retail trade by Random House, Inc., as agent for LearningExpress, LLC.

ISBN 1–57685–152–4

7 85555 85152 8

An Important Note to Our Library Readers

If you have checked this book out from your school or public library, please do not write in the book itself. Instead use a separate notepad to write down your answers, so that other readers in your library can reuse the material. Thank you for your help and for your consideration of others.

Also Available from LearningExpress . . .

AMP Real Estate Sales Exam
ISBN 1–57685–150–8

PSI Real Estate Sales Exam
ISBN 1–57685–151–6

Texas Real Estate Sales Exam
ISBN 1–57685–153–2

California Real Estate Sales Exam *(January 1999)*
ISBN 1–57685–208–3

Visit your local bookstore or call 1–888–551–JOBS.

CONTENTS

LIST OF CONTRIBUTORS

The following individuals contributed to the content of this book.

Joyce L. Caughman, GRI (Real Estate Math Review), former director of Foster Institute of Real Estate, an affiliate of Long & Foster Real Estate, is a nationally respected real estate educator residing in Edgewater, Maryland.

Edith Lank (Real Estate Exams) writes a nationally syndicated newspaper column on real estate issues and has published several real estate textbooks and consumer guides. She regularly speaks on real estate and financial issues and is featured on several radio broadcasts both nationally and in her home town of Rochester, New York.

Vikki Lilly (Real Estate Exams) is director of the Fortune School of Real Estate in Myrtle Beach, South Carolina, and President-Elect of the Palmetto Real Estate Educators Association. She has developed real estate textbooks and served on exam review committees in South Carolina.

George Rink, GRI, DREI (Real Estate Exams), is founder and manager of the Mount Vernon Realty Academy of Real Estate in Virginia, where he developed the entire prelicense program. He has extensive real estate test development experience, having worked with the National Association of Realtors to establish a test bank for the Graduate Realtor Institute and with the Virginia Real Estate Board as an item reviewer.

Suzanne Staton (Real Estate Glossary) is associate editor of *Texas Realtor* magazine.

Martha R. Williams, J.D. (Real Estate Refresher Course), is editor of the Real Estate Educators Association Journal and author of several real estate textbooks. In addition to teaching prelicense and other real estate courses at the University of San Francisco Paralegal Studies Program, she has served on the review committee for the PSI real estate exam. Licensed in Texas and California, she now resides and practices in Tennessee.

C·H·A·P·T·E·R 1

THE ASI REAL ESTATE EXAM

CHAPTER SUMMARY

Congratulations! You are about to take a step that could mark your entrance to an exciting new career—real estate. This chapter provides an overview of what awaits you as you prepare for your real estate license and shows you how this book can help.

A s you probably know from your real estate studies, every state requires real estate agents to be licensed. With very few exceptions (such as for an attorney), most states require that an applicant for a real estate license take and pass one or more courses of study. Most states also require that the license applicant take and pass a comprehensive real estate examination. If you haven't done so already, you should contact the real estate office of the state in which you wish to be licensed for information on licensing requirements. You will learn how the real estate examination is administered and how you can apply to take it.

Some states prepare their own examination for prospective real estate licensees. Others rely on independent testing services to prepare, administer, and/or score real estate examinations. These tests are revised regularly to reflect current law and practice. This book will help you prepare for the Real Estate Assessment for Licensure (REAL) examination prepared by an independent testing company, Assessment Systems, Inc. (ASI).

HOW TO CONTACT ASI

Three Bala Plaza West
Suite 300
Bala Cynwyd, PA 19004-3481
610-618-2565
www.asisvcs.com

WHAT IS ASI?

ASI provides a national content-based examination to its client states. Each state's exam will also have a section of state-specific questions. ASI administers and scores the exam for its client states. Companies such as ASI make use of educational consultants and examination review committees to insure the fairness and validity of the exams they prepare. Individual states that contract with companies such as ASI can take advantage of these resources on what is, in effect, a shared basis.

You can obtain a *Real Estate Candidate Handbook* explaining your state's license application process from your state's real estate department, from your school, or directly from ASI at the address shown on the first page of this chapter.

THE ASI EXAM

The ASI REAL examination has two sections. One will be a random sampling of questions for the general (national) portion of the exam. A large bank of possible test questions for the general content portion of the exam assures that no two states' examinations will be exactly alike.

In addition, each state will have a separate bank of questions based on state-specific topics. Thus, even though the same testing service may administer exams in many different states, the exams will be individualized for each state.

All questions are in a multiple-choice format. The time allotted for the real estate salesperson's exam varies from state to state, but typically it is about three and a half or four hours. No deviation is allowed from the time limit set for the exam.

WHAT EQUIPMENT SHOULD I BRING?

A silent, battery-operated calculator without a tape printout or alphabetic keyboard is allowed, but you shouldn't plan to use a solar calculators because the interior light in the exam room may not be adequate. No books, dictionaries, note paper, mechanical recording devices, alarm watches, or other such materials are allowed in the testing room. Other requirements are noted in the *Real Estate Candidate Handbook*.

HOW OFTEN ARE NEW QUESTIONS ADDED?

The bank of test questions is large enough to insure that even repeat test-takers will rarely encounter the same question. New questions are introduced periodically, but only after undergoing thorough pre-testing. Each real estate examination will include five items (questions) that are included to assess the validity of the questions themselves. ASI will determine, based on the number of correct responses, whether a pretest item is an appropriate one to include in a future examination. Questions that are included in the exam for pre-testing are not counted in the test score.

HOW IS THE EXAM SCORED?

Each state determines the passing score for its examination. Some states, for instance, require that an applicant correctly answer at least 70 percent of the exam questions in each portion of the exam (general and state-specific). If a license applicant receives a passing score on only one part of the exam, the other part may be retaken, but the applicant must receive a passing score on both parts of the exam within the time period set by the state, such as one year. Check with your state licensing board for its exact requirements.

The exam taken by an applicant for the license given to a real estate broker (in some states, called an independent broker or employing broker) typically covers more topics, has more questions, and allows a longer time for completion, but it may require a higher passing score than the salesperson's exam.

WHAT TOPICS ARE TESTED?

Chapter 4, the ASI Real Estate Refresher Course, follows the latest ASI General Content Outline for Sales and Broker Exams, which became effective on April 1, 1998. The entire ASI General Content Outline appears at the end of this chapter as well as throughout Chapter 4. In Chapter 4, each topic on the ASI outline is highlighted so that you can follow your progress through the review material and also be assured that your study includes all of the relevant subject matter. The percentage of coverage and number of questions in each content area are shown on the content outline at the end of the chapter. There will also be five questions included for pre-testing purposes that are not counted in the test score.

HOW TO PREPARE FOR THE REAL ESTATE EXAMINATION

If you have already taken a required course in Real Estate Principles, you are well on the way to preparing to take the real estate licensing examination.

The basic course in Real Estate Principles is not long enough to cover every topic that could be included on the real estate exam in the depth necessary to understand and respond successfully to test questions on all of the topics. But, by diligently studying your course text, notes, and other study materials (such as this book), you can expect to achieve sufficient mastery of the subject matter to be able to pass your real estate exam.

RELEARNING SOME OLD SKILLS

You've already taken and passed countless quizzes, tests, and examinations of all sorts as you made your way through grade school, high school, and college-level courses. You may even have taken vocational training courses or other programs. So why should you need any tips for studying for a real estate exam?

The answer lies in your present status. Most likely, you are no longer a full-time student, so you probably are out of the habit of studying and test-taking. And not only are you out of practice in test-taking, you probably have many more responsibilities and distractions to pull you from your studies than you ever did back in the days when you had well-defined school hours and homework assignments. And, when you were a full-time student, you may never have taken an examination as comprehensive as the one you now face.

If you feel that you need help in relearning the discipline it takes to acquire the knowledge needed to successfully pass an examination, you can take comfort in the fact that you are not alone. No state can claim a licensing exam pass rate of 100 percent of all license applicants. According to the Association of Real Estate License Laws Officials (*1998 Digest of Real Estate License Laws in the United States and Canada*, published in 1998 by ARELLO, Centerville, Utah), the most recent pass rates on the salesperson's ranged from 34 percent for South Dakota to 83 percent for Texas. In other words, in some states only a third of all license applicants pass the required exam; in other states, four-fifths of applicants pass.

What these numbers mean is that many of those taking a real estate licensing examination are repeating their attempt. What can you do if you want to avoid becoming a real estate exam repeater? Or, if you have already taken the exam and failed to pass it, what can you do to improve your performance the next time?

TEST-TAKING TECHNIQUES

The EasySmart Test Prep System presented in Chapter 2 of this book will help you overcome test anxiety, set up a workable study plan, and learn test-taking skills that will enable you to use your examination time most effectively. Above all, you must set aside a regular study time. If you rely on a final-day cram session, you will only make the exam process more stressful than it needs to be.

This book also provides four complete sample examinations, based on the national portion of the ASI exam, that will give you a chance to hone your knowledge of real estate concepts, as well as provide valuable practice in exam-taking techniques. You might start with Chapter 3, the first practice exam, before going on to the review and study materials in Chapters 4, 5, and 6.

This exam will help you determine the areas on which you need to concentrate your study.

STUDY MATERIALS

Chapter 4 of this book, the ASI Real Estate Refresher Course, will help you focus on the topics and terms of greatest importance for your licensing exam. This chapter is written in outline format. Narration is deliberately kept to a minimum so that you can review more quickly and focus your attention on terminology. Each section of the outline is followed by questions that provide immediate review and reinforcement, as well as a gauge of your progress. If you answer the review questions correctly, you are making good progress.

Chapter 5 is a Real Estate Math Review that will provide you with practice in the math computations you are likely to encounter on the exam. Chapter 6 is a Real Estate Glossary that is itself an excellent review of real estate terminology.

Important Note on Using This Book

While the materials in this book include many terms, key concepts, and explanations, it would be impossible to include every possible term that could be included in the ASI exam in a single study guide. This book is designed to be an additional study aid to help you learn and remember what you need in order to pass the examination. More than that, it will give you practice in handling the terms and concepts you learned in your real estate coursework when they appear in the format of the exam questions you will be required to answer.

You will find that some of the terms that are defined in the glossary are also defined in the refresher course, some terms appear in both the refresher course and math review, and some terms appear only in the glossary. Thus, each part of this book will be of benefit to you and will also help reinforce what you have learned earlier.

THE PATH TO SUCCESS

By reading this far, you have already shown that you are serious about taking the real estate licensing examination. Now, you have to show that you are ready to do what it takes to receive a passing score on the exam. By making good use of this book, you will be well on your way to reaching your goal—and your new career.

ASI REAL ESTATE EXAMINATION GENERAL CONTENT OUTLINE

I. REAL PROPERTY CHARACTERISTICS, DEFINITIONS, OWNERSHIP, RESTRICTIONS AND TRANSFER
   20%   16 questions

   A. Definitions, Descriptions and Ways to Hold Title

      1. Elements of Real and Personal Property

      2. Property Description and Legal Description

      3. Estates in Real Property

      4. Forms, Rights, Interests and Obligations of Ownership

   B. Land Use Controls and Restrictions

      1. Public

      2. Private

   C. Transfer/Alienation of Title to Real Property

      1. Voluntary and Involuntary

      2. Deeds, Warranties and Defects in Title

II. ASSESSING AND EXPLAINING PROPERTY VALUATION AND THE APPRAISAL PROCESS
    15%   12 questions

   A. Principles, Types and Estimates of Property Value

   B. Influence on Property Value

   C. Approaches to Property Valuation and Investment Analysis

III. CONTRACTS, AGENCY RELATIONSHIPS WITH BUYERS AND SELLERS, AND FEDERAL REQUIREMENTS
     25%   20 questions

   A. Contract Elements, Types and Terminology

   B. Agency Employment Contracts, Listing and Buyer Agency Agreements, and Required Elements

   C. Purchase/Sales Contracts and Contingencies

   D. General Agency Relationships and Fiduciary Responsibilities

   E. Property Conditions and Disclosures

   F. Procedures and Laws Governing Real Estate Activities

IV. FINANCING THE TRANSACTION AND SETTLEMENT
    25%   20 questions

   A. Financing Components

      1. Financing Instruments

      2. Sources

      3. Types of Loans

      4. Financing Concepts and Terminology

   B. Lender Requirements and Obligations

   C. Settlement Procedures

   D. Settlement Documents

   E. Financing Costs, Property Taxation, Proration Calculations and Other Closing Costs

V.   LEASES, RENTS AND PROPERTY
     MANAGEMENT
     15%   12 questions

   A.   Types and Elements of Leasehold Estates, Leases,
        Lease Clauses and Rental Agreements

   B.   Lessor and Lessee Rights, Responsibilities and
        Recourse

   C.   Management Contracts and Obligations of
        Parties

C·H·A·P·T·E·R

EASYSMART TEST PREPARATION SYSTEM

CHAPTER SUMMARY

Taking the real estate licensing exam can be tough—but your career as a real estate agent depends on your passing the exam. The EasySmart Test Preparation System, developed exclusively for LearningExpress by leading test experts, gives you the discipline and attitude you need to be a winner.

F irst, the bad news: Taking the real estate licensing exam is no picnic, and neither is getting ready for it. Your future career in real estate depends on your getting a passing score, but there are all sorts of pitfalls that can keep you from doing your best on this all-important exam. Here are some of the obstacles that can stand in the way of your success:

- Being unfamiliar with the format of the exam
- Being paralyzed by test anxiety
- Leaving your preparation to the last minute
- Not preparing at all!
- Not knowing vital test-taking skills: how to pace yourself through the exam, how to use the process of elimination, and when to guess
- Not being in tip-top mental and physical shape

■ Messing up on test day by arriving late at the test site, having to work on an empty stomach, or shivering through the exam because the room is cold

What's the common denominator in all these test-taking pitfalls? One word: *control*. Who's in control, you or the exam?

Now the good news: The EasySmart Test Preparation System puts *you* in control. In just nine easy-to-follow steps, you will learn everything you need to know to make sure that *you* are in charge of your preparation and your performance on the exam. *Other* test-takers may let the test get the better of them; *other* test-takers may be unprepared or out of shape, but not *you*. *You* will have taken all the steps you need to take to get a high score on the real estate exam.

Here's how the EasySmart Test Preparation System works: Nine easy steps lead you through everything you need to know and do to get ready to master your exam. Each of the steps listed below includes both reading about the step and one or more activities. It's important that you do the activities along with the reading, or you won't be getting the full benefit of the system. Each step tells you approximately how much time that step will take you to complete.

Step 1. Get Information	50 minutes
Step 2. Conquer Test Anxiety	20 minutes
Step 3. Make a Plan	30 minutes
Step 4. Learn to Manage Your Time	10 minutes
Step 5. Learn to Use the Process of Elimination	20 minutes
Step 6. Know When to Guess	20 minutes
Step 7. Reach Your Peak Performance Zone	10 minutes
Step 8. Get Your Act Together	10 minutes
Step 9. Do It!	10 minutes
Total	**3 hours**

We estimate that working through the entire system will take you approximately three hours, though it's perfectly OK if you work faster or slower than the time estimates assume. If you can take a whole afternoon or evening, you can work through the whole EasySmart Test Preparation System in one sitting. Otherwise, you can break it up, and do just one or two steps a day for the next several days. It's up to you—remember, *you're* in control.

STEP 1: GET INFORMATION

Time to complete: 50 minutes
Activities: Read Chapter 1, "The ASI Real Estate Exam" and contact ASI or your state licensing board for details

Knowledge is power. The first step in the EasySmart Test Preparation System is finding out everything you can about your exam. Once you have your information, the next steps in the EasySmart Test Preparation System will show you what to do about it.

Part A: Straight Talk About the Real Estate Exam

Why do you have to take this exam, anyway? You've already been through your pre-license course; why should you have to go through a rigorous exam? It's simply an attempt on the part of your state to be *sure* you have the knowledge and skills necessary for a licensed real estate agent. Every profession that requires practitioners to exercise financial and fiduciary responsibility to clients also requires practitioners to be licensed—and licensure almost always requires an exam. Real estate is no exception.

It's important for you to remember that your score on the real estate licensing exam does not determine how smart you are or even whether you will make a good real estate agent. There are all kinds of things a written exam like this can't test: whether you have the drive and determination to be a top salesperson, whether you will faithfully exercise your responsibilities to your clients, whether you can be trusted with confidential information about people's finances. Those kinds of things are hard to evaluate, while whether you can fill in the right little circles on a bubble answer sheet is easy to evaluate.

This is not to say that filling in the right little circles is not important! The knowledge tested on the written exam is knowledge you will need to do your job. And your ability to enter the profession you've trained for depends on your passing this exam. And that's why you're here—using the EasySmart Test Preparation System to achieve control over the exam.

Part B: What's on the Test

If you haven't already done so, stop here and read Chapter 1 of this book, which gives you an overview of the ASI real estate exam. Chapter 1 covers the national portion of the exam. If you haven't already gotten the full rundown on the state portion of the exam as part of your prelicense course, you can contact ASI or your state licensing board.

STEP 2: CONQUER TEST ANXIETY

Time to complete: 20 minutes
Activity: Take the Test Stress Test
Having complete information about the exam is the first step in getting control of the exam. Next, you have to overcome one of the biggest obstacles to test success: test anxiety. Test anxiety can not only impair your performance on the exam itself; it can even keep you from preparing! In Step 2, you'll learn stress management techniques that will help you succeed on your exam. Learn these strategies now, and practice them as you work through the exams in this book, so they'll be second nature to you by exam day.

COMBATING TEST ANXIETY

The first thing you need to know is that a little test anxiety is a good thing. Everyone gets nervous before a big exam—and if that nervousness motivates you to prepare thoroughly, so much the better. It's said that Sir Laurence Olivier, one of the foremost British actors of this century, threw up before every performance. His stage fright didn't impair his performance; in fact, it probably gave him a little extra edge—just the kind of edge you need to do well, whether on a stage or in an examination room.

On the next page is the Test Stress Test. Stop here and answer the questions on that page, to find out whether your level of test anxiety is something you should worry about.

Stress Management Before the Test

If you feel your level of anxiety getting the best of you in the weeks before the test, here is what you need to do to bring the level down again:

- **Get prepared.** There's nothing like knowing what to expect and being prepared for it to put you in control of test anxiety. That's why you're reading this book. Use it faithfully, and remind yourself that you're better prepared than most of the people taking the test.
- **Practice self-confidence.** A positive attitude is a great way to combat test anxiety. This is no time to be humble or shy. Stand in front of the mirror and say to your reflection, "I'm prepared. I'm full of self-confidence. I'm going to ace this test. I know I can do it." Say it into a tape recorder and play it back once a day. If you hear it often enough, you'll believe it.
- **Fight negative messages.** Every time someone starts telling you how hard the exam is or how it's almost impossible to get a high score, start telling them your self-confidence messages above. If the someone with the negative messages is *you*, telling yourself *you don't do well on exams, you just can't do this*, don't listen. Turn on your tape recorder and listen to your self-confidence messages.

(continued on page 6)

Test Stress Test

You only need to worry about test anxiety if it is extreme enough to impair your performance. The following questionnaire will provide a diagnosis of your level of test anxiety. In the blank before each statement, write the number that most accurately describes your experience.

0 = Never   1 = Once or twice   2 = Sometimes   3 = Often

_____ I have gotten so nervous before an exam that I simply put down the books and didn't study for it.

_____ I have experienced disabling physical symptoms such as vomiting and severe headaches because I was nervous about an exam.

_____ I have simply not showed up for an exam because I was scared to take it.

_____ I have experienced dizziness and disorientation while taking an exam.

_____ I have had trouble filling in the little circles because my hands were shaking too hard.

_____ I have failed an exam because I was too nervous to complete it.

_____ **Total: Add up the numbers in the blanks above.**

Your Test Stress Score

Here are the steps you should take, depending on your score. If you scored:

- **Below 3,** your level of test anxiety is nothing to worry about; it's probably just enough to give you that little extra edge.
- **Between 3 and 6,** your test anxiety may be enough to impair your performance, and you should practice the stress management techniques listed in this section to try to bring your test anxiety down to manageable levels.
- **Above 6,** your level of test anxiety is a serious concern. In addition to practicing the stress management techniques listed in this section, you may want to seek additional, personal help. Call your local high school or community college and ask for the academic counselor. Tell the counselor that you have a level of test anxiety that sometimes keeps you from being able to take the exam. The counselor may be willing to help you or may suggest someone else you should talk to.

- **Visualize.** Imagine yourself reporting for work on your first day as a real estate agent. Think of yourself talking with clients, showing homes, and, best of all, making your first sale. Visualizing success can help make it happen—and it reminds you of why you're going to all this work in preparing for the exam.
- **Exercise.** Physical activity helps calm your body down and focus your mind. Besides, being in good physical shape can actually help you do well on the exam. Go for a run, lift weights, go swimming—and do it regularly.

Stress Management on Test Day

There are several ways you can bring down your level of test anxiety on test day. They'll work best if you practice them in the weeks before the test, so you know which ones work best for you.

- **Deep breathing.** Take a deep breath while you count to five. Hold it for a count of one, then let it out on a count of five. Repeat several times.
- **Move your body.** Try rolling your head in a circle. Rotate your shoulders. Shake your hands from the wrist. Many people find these movements very relaxing.
- **Visualize again.** Think of the place where you are most relaxed: lying on the beach in the sun, walking through the park, or whatever. Now close your eyes and imagine you're actually there. If you practice in advance, you'll find that you only need a few seconds of this exercise to experience a significant increase in your sense of well-being.

When anxiety threatens to overwhelm you right there during the exam, there are still things you can do to manage the stress level:

- **Repeat your self-confidence messages.** You should have them memorized by now. Say them quietly to yourself, and believe them!
- **Visualize one more time.** This time, visualize yourself moving smoothly and quickly through the test answering every question right and finishing just before time is up. Like most visualization techniques, this one works best if you've practiced it ahead of time.
- **Find an easy question.** Skim over the test until you find an easy question, and answer it. Getting even one circle filled in gets you into the test-taking groove.
- **Take a mental break.** Everyone loses concentration once in a while during a long test. It's normal, so you shouldn't worry about it. Instead, accept what has happened. Say to yourself, "Hey, I lost it there for a minute. My brain is taking a break." Put down your pencil, close your eyes, and do some deep breathing for a few seconds. Then you're ready to go back to work.

Try these techniques ahead of time, and see if they don't work for you!

STEP 3: MAKE A PLAN

Time to complete: 30 minutes

Activity: Construct a study plan

Maybe the most important thing you can do to get control of yourself and your exam is to make a study plan. Too many people fail to prepare simply because they fail to plan. Spending hours on the day before the exam poring over sample test questions not only raises your level of test anxiety, it also is simply no substitute for careful preparation and practice over time.

Don't fall into the cram trap. Take control of your preparation time by mapping out a study schedule. On the following pages are two sample schedules, based on the amount of time you have before you take the real estate exam. If you're the kind of person who needs deadlines and assignments to motivate you for a project, here they are. If you're the kind of person who doesn't like to follow other people's plans, you can use the suggested schedules here to construct your own.

Even more important than making a plan is making a commitment. You can't review everything you learned in your pre-license course in one night. You have to set aside some time every day for study and practice. Try for at least 20 minutes a day. Twenty minutes daily will do you much more good than two hours on Saturday.

Don't put off your study until the day before the exam. Start now. A few minutes a day, with half an hour or more on weekends, can make a big difference in your score.

SCHEDULE A: THE 30-DAY PLAN

If you have at least a month before you take the real estate exam, you have plenty of time to prepare—as long as you don't waste it! If you have less than a month, turn to Schedule B.

Time	Preparation
Days 1–4	Skim over the written materials from your training program, particularly noting 1) areas you expect to be emphasized on the exam and 2) areas you don't remember well. On Day 4, concentrate on those areas.
Day 5	Take the first practice exam in Chapter 3.
Day 6	Score the first practice exam. Use the outline of skills on the test given in Chapter 1 to show you which are your strongest and weakest areas.
Days 7–9	Skim through the entire "ASI Real Estate Refresher Course" in Chapter 4, concentrating on the areas that gave you the most trouble on the first exam.
Day 10	Study your real estate math in Chapter 5. You'll have another chance in this plan for more math if you need it. If you're okay on your math, spend today on the Refresher Course.
Day 11	Take the second practice exam in Chapter 7.
Day 12	Score the second practice exam. Identify *one* area to concentrate on before you take the third practice exam.
Days 13–18	Study the one area you identified for review in Chapter 4, looking up any troublesome terms in the Real Estate Glossary in Chapter 6. You may also want to go back to your course textbooks and materials.
Day 19	Take the third practice exam in Chapter 8.
Day 20	Once again, identify *one or two areas* to review, based on your score on the third practice exam.
Days 20–21	Study the one area you identified for review.
Days 22–25	Take an overview of Chapters 4, 5, and 6, as well as your training materials, consolidating your strengths and improving on your weaknesses.
Days 26–27	Review all the areas that have given you the most trouble in the three practice exams you've taken so far.
Day 28	Take the fourth practice exam in Chapter 9. Note how much you've improved!
Day 29	Review one or two weak areas.
Day before the exam	Relax. Do something unrelated to the exam and go to bed at a reasonable hour.

SCHEDULE B: THE 10-DAY PLAN

If you have two weeks or less before you take the exam, you may have your work cut out for you. Use this 10-day schedule to help you make the most of your time.

Time	Preparation
Day 1	Take the first practice exam in Chapter 3 and score it using the answer key at the end. Turn to the list of subject areas on the exam in Chapter 1, and find out which areas need the most work, based on your exam score.
Day 2	Skim through the ASI Real Estate Refresher Course in Chapter 4, the Real Estate Math Review in Chapter 5, and the Real Estate Glossary in Chapter 6.
Day 3	Review one area that gave you trouble on the first practice exam.
Day 4	Take the second practice exam in Chapter 7 and score it.
Day 5	Choose a new weak area to study today, based on your performance on the second exam.
Day 6	Take the third practice exam in Chapter 8 and score it.
Day 7	Choose your weakest area from the third practice exam to review.
Day 8	Review any areas that you have not yet reviewed in this schedule, using Chapters 4, 5, and 6 and, if necessary, your textbooks and other materials from your pre-license course.
Day 9	Take the fourth practice exam in Chapter 9 and score it.
Day 10	Use your last study day to brush up on any areas that are still giving you trouble.
Day before the exam	Relax. Do something unrelated to the exam and go to bed at a reasonable hour.

STEP 4: LEARN TO MANAGE YOUR TIME

Time to complete: 10 minutes to read, many hours of practice!
Activities: Practice these strategies as you take the sample tests in this book

Steps 4, 5, and 6 of the EasySmart Test Preparation System put you in charge of your exam by showing you test-taking strategies that work. Practice these strategies as you take the sample tests in this book, and then you'll be ready to use them on test day.

First, you'll take control of your time on the exam. Most real estate exams have a time limit, which may give you more than enough time to complete all the questions—or may not. It's a terrible feeling to hear the examiner say, "Five minutes left," when you're only three-quarters of the way through the test. Here are some tips to keep that from happening to *you*.

- **Follow directions.** If the directions are given orally, listen to them. If they're written on the exam booklet, read them carefully. Ask questions *before* the exam begins if there's anything you don't understand. If you're allowed to write in your exam booklet, write down the beginning time and the ending time of the exam.
- **Pace yourself.** Glance at your watch every few minutes, and compare the time to how far you've gotten in the test. When one-quarter of the time has elapsed, you should be a quarter of the way through the test, and so on. If you're falling behind, pick up the pace a bit.
- **Keep moving.** Don't dither around on one question. If you don't know the answer, skip the question and move on. Circle the number of the question in your test booklet in case you have time to come back to it later.
- **Keep track of your place on the answer sheet.** If you skip a question, make sure you skip on the answer sheet too. Check yourself every 5–10 questions to make sure the question number and the answer sheet number are still the same.
- **Don't rush.** Though you should keep moving, rushing won't help. Try to keep calm and work methodically and quickly.

STEP 5: LEARN TO USE THE PROCESS OF ELIMINATION

Time to complete: 20 minutes
Activity: Complete worksheet on Using the Process of Elimination

After time management, your next most important tool for taking control of your exam is using the process of elimination wisely. It's standard test-taking wisdom that you should always read all the answer choices before choosing your answer. This helps you find the right answer by eliminating wrong answer choices. And, sure enough, that standard wisdom applies to your exam, too.

Let's say you're facing a question that goes like this:

13. Alicia died, leaving her residence intown and a separate parcel of undeveloped rural land to her brother Brian and her sister Carrie, with Brian owning one-quarter interest and Carrie owning three-quarters interest. How do Brian and Carrie hold title?
   a. as tenants in survivorship
   b. as tenants in common
   c. as joint tenants
   d. as tenants by the entirety

You should always use the process of elimination on a question like this, even if the right answer jumps out at you. Sometimes the answer that jumps out isn't right after all. Let's assume, for the purpose of this exercise, that you're a little rusty on property ownership terminology, so you need to use a little intuition to make up for what you don't remember. Proceed through the answer choices in order.

So you start with answer **a**. This one is pretty easy to eliminate; this tenancy doesn't have to do with survivorship. Mark an X next to choice **a** so you never have to look at it again.

On to the next. This looks good; it's a kind of ownership that two people can share. Even if you didn't remember much about tenancy in common, you could tell it's about having something "in common." Put a check mark next to this one, meaning "good answer, I might use this one."

Choice **c** is a possibility. Joint tenants also share something in common. If you happen to remember that joint tenancy always involves *equal* ownership rights, you'll put an X here. If you don't, mark a check for "good answer" or a question mark for "well, maybe," depending on how attractive this answer looks to you.

Choice **d** strikes you as a little less likely. Tenancy by the entirety doesn't necessarily have to do with two people sharing ownership. This doesn't sound right, and you've already got a better answer picked out in choice **b**. If you're feeling sure of yourself, put an X next to this one. If you want to be careful, put a question mark.

Now your question looks like this:

13. Alicia died, leaving her residence intown and a separate parcel of undeveloped rural land to her brother Brian and her sister Carrie, with Brian owning one-quarter interest and Carrie owning three-quarters interest. How do Brian and Carrie hold title?
   ✕ **a.** as tenants in survivorship
   ✔ **b.** as tenants in common
   ? **c.** as joint tenants
   ? **d.** as tenants by the entirety

You've got just one check mark, for a good answer. If you're pressed for time, you should simply mark answer **b** on your answer sheet. If you've got the time to be extra careful, you could compare your check-mark answer to your question-mark answers to make sure that it's better. If you marked a check next to **c,** you have two check-mark answers. That gives you one-in-two odds of being right. Choose one and move on.

It's good to have a system for marking good, bad, and maybe answers. We're recommending this one:

× = bad
✔ = good
? = maybe

If you don't like these marks, devise your own system. Just make sure you do it long before test day—while you're working through the practice exams in this book—so you won't have to worry about it during the test.

Even when you think you're absolutely clueless about a question, you can often use process of elimination to get rid of one answer choice. If so, you're better prepared to make an educated guess, as you'll see in Step 6. More often, the process of elimination allows you to get down to only *two* possibly right answers. Then you're in a strong position to guess. And sometimes, even though you don't know the right answer, you find it simply by getting rid of the wrong ones, as you did in the example above.

Try using your powers of elimination on the questions in the worksheet Using the Process of Elimination beginning on the next page. The questions aren't about real estate work; they're just designed to show you how the process of elimination works. The answer explanations for this worksheet show one possible way you might use the process to arrive at the right answer.

The process of elimination is your tool for the next step, which is knowing when to guess.

Using the Process of Elimination

Use the process of elimination to answer the following questions.

1. Ilsa is as old as Meghan will be in five years. The difference between Ed's age and Meghan's age is twice the difference between Ilsa's age and Meghan's age. Ed is 29. How old is Ilsa?
    a. 4
    b. 10
    c. 19
    d. 24

2. "All drivers of commercial vehicles must carry a valid commercial driver's license whenever operating a commercial vehicle." According to this sentence, which of the following people need NOT carry a commercial driver's license?
    a. a truck driver idling his engine while waiting to be directed to a loading dock
    b. a bus operator backing her bus out of the way of another bus in the bus lot
    c. a taxi driver driving his personal car to the grocery store
    d. a limousine driver taking the limousine to her home after dropping off her last passenger of the evening

3. Smoking tobacco has been linked to
    a. increased risk of stroke and heart attack
    b. all forms of respiratory disease
    c. increasing mortality rates over the past ten years
    d. juvenile delinquency

4. Which of the following words is spelled correctly?
    a. incorrigible
    b. outragous
    c. domestickated
    d. understandible

Answers

Here are the answers, as well as some suggestions as to how you might have used the process of elimination to find them.

1. **d.** You should have eliminated answer **a** off the bat. Ilsa can't be four years old if Meghan is going to be Ilsa's age in five years. The best way to eliminate other answer choices is to try plugging them in to the information given in the problem. For instance, for answer **b,** if Ilsa is 10, then Meghan must be 5. The difference in their ages is 5. The difference between Ed's age, 29, and Meghan's age, 5, is 24. Is 24 two times 5? No. Then answer **b** is wrong. You could eliminate answer **c** in the same way and be left with answer **d.**

2. **c.** Note the word *not* in the question, and go through the answers one by one. Is the truck driver in choice **a** "operating a commericial vehicle"? Yes, idling counts as "operating," so he needs to have a commercial driver's license. Likewise, the bus operator in answer **b** is operating a commercial vehicle; the question doesn't say the operator has to be on the street. The limo driver in **d** is operating a commercial vehicle, even if it doesn't have passenger in it. However, the cabbie in answer **c** is *not* operating a commercial vehicle, but his own private car.

3. **a.** You could eliminate answer **b** simply because of the presence of the word *all.* Such absolutes hardly ever appear in correct answer choices. Choice **c** looks attractive until you think a little about what you know—aren't *fewer* people smoking these days, rather than more? So how could smoking be responsible for a higher mortality rate? (If you didn't know that *mortality rate* means the rate at which people die, you might keep this choice as a possibility, but you'd still be able to eliminate two answers and have only two to choose from.) And choice **d** is plain silly, so you could eliminate that one, too. And you're left with the correct choice, **a.**

4. **a.** How you used the process of elimination here depends on which words you recognized as being spelled incorrectly. If you knew that the correct spellings were *outrageous, domesticated,* and *understandable,* then you were home free. Surely you knew that at least one of those words was wrong!

STEP 6: KNOW WHEN TO GUESS

Time to complete: 20 minutes
Activity: Complete worksheet on Your Guessing Ability
Armed with the process of elimination, you're ready to take control of one of the big questions in test-taking: Should I guess? The first and main answer is Yes. Some exams have what's called a "guessing penalty," in which a fraction of your wrong answers is subtracted from your right answers—but real estate exams don't tend to work like that. The number of questions you answer correctly yields your raw score. So you have nothing to lose and everything to gain by guessing.

The more complicated answer to the question "Should I guess?" depends on you—your personality and your "guessing intuition." There are two things you need to know about yourself before you go into the exam:

- Are you a risk-taker?
- Are you a good guesser?

You'll have to decide about your risk-taking quotient on your own. To find out if you're a good guesser, complete the worksheet Your Guessing Ability that begins on page 16. Frankly, even if you're a play-it-safe person with lousy intuition, you're still safe in guessing every time. The best thing would be if you could overcome your anxieties and go ahead and mark an answer. But you may want to have a sense of how good your intuition is before you go into the exam.

STEP 7: REACH YOUR PEAK PERFORMANCE ZONE

Time to complete: 10 minutes to read; weeks to complete!
Activity: Complete the Physical Preparation Checklist
To get ready for a challenge like a big exam, you have to take control of your physical, as well as your mental, state. Exercise, proper diet, and rest will ensure that your body works with, rather than against, your mind on test day, as well as during your preparation.

EXERCISE

If you don't already have a regular exercise program going, the time during which you're preparing for an exam is actually an excellent time to start one. And if you're already keeping fit—or trying to get that way—don't let the pressure of preparing for an exam fool you into quitting now. Exercise helps reduce stress by pumping wonderful good-feeling hormones called endorphins into your system. It also increases the oxygen supply throughout your body, including your brain, so you'll be at peak performance on test day.

(continued on page 19)

Your Guessing Ability

The following are ten really hard questions. You're not supposed to know the answers. Rather, this is an assessment of your ability to guess when you don't have a clue. Read each question carefully, just as if you did expect to answer it. If you have any knowledge at all of the subject of the question, use that knowledge to help you eliminate wrong answer choices. Use this answer grid to fill in your answers to the questions.

ANSWER GRID

1.	ⓐ	ⓑ	ⓒ	ⓓ	5.	ⓐ	ⓑ	ⓒ	ⓓ	9.	ⓐ	ⓑ	ⓒ	ⓓ
2.	ⓐ	ⓑ	ⓒ	ⓓ	6.	ⓐ	ⓑ	ⓒ	ⓓ	10.	ⓐ	ⓑ	ⓒ	ⓓ
3.	ⓐ	ⓑ	ⓒ	ⓓ	7.	ⓐ	ⓑ	ⓒ	ⓓ					
4.	ⓐ	ⓑ	ⓒ	ⓓ	8.	ⓐ	ⓑ	ⓒ	ⓓ					

1. September 7 is Independence Day in
   a. India
   b. Costa Rica
   c. Brazil
   d. Australia

2. Which of the following is the formula for determining the momentum of an object?
   a. $p = mv$
   b. $F = ma$
   c. $P = IV$
   d. $E = mc^2$

3. Because of the expansion of the universe, the stars and other celestial bodies are all moving away from each other. This phenomenon is known as
   a. Newton's first law
   b. the big bang
   c. gravitational collapse
   d. Hubble flow

4. American author Gertrude Stein was born in
   a. 1713
   b. 1830
   c. 1874
   d. 1901

5. Which of the following is NOT one of the Five Classics attributed to Confucius?
   a. the I Ching
   b. the Book of Holiness
   c. the Spring and Autumn Annals
   d. the Book of History

6. The religious and philosophical doctrine that holds that the universe is constantly in a struggle between good and evil is known as
   a. Pelagianism
   b. Manichaeanism
   c. neo-Hegelianism
   d. Epicureanism

7. The third Chief Justice of the U.S. Supreme Court was
   a. John Blair
   b. William Cushing
   c. James Wilson
   d. John Jay

8. Which of the following is the poisonous portion of a daffodil?
   a. the bulb
   b. the leaves
   c. the stem
   d. the flowers

9. The winner of the Masters golf tournament in 1953 was
   a. Sam Snead
   b. Cary Middlecoff
   c. Arnold Palmer
   d. Ben Hogan

10. The state with the highest per capita personal income in 1980 was
    a. Alaska
    b. Connecticut
    c. New York
    d. Texas

Answers

Check your answers against the correct answers below.

1. c.	**5.** b.	**9.** d.
2. a.	**6.** b.	**10.** a.
3. d.	**7.** b.	
4. c.	**8.** a.	

How Did You Do?

You may have simply gotten lucky and actually known the answer to one or two questions. In addition, your guessing was more successful if you were able to use the process of elimination on any of the questions. Maybe you didn't know who the third Chief Justice was (question 7), but you knew that John Jay was the first. In that case, you would have eliminated answer **d** and therefore improved your odds of guessing right from one in four to one in three.

According to probability, you should get 2 1/2 answers correct, so getting either two or three right would be average. If you got four or more right, you may be a really terrific guesser. If you got one or none right, you may be a really bad guesser.

Keep in mind, though, that this is only a small sample. You should continue to keep track of your guessing ability as you work through the sample questions in this book. Circle the numbers of questions you guess on as you make your guess; or, if you don't have time while you take the practice tests, go back afterward and try to remember which questions you guessed at. Remember, on a test with four answer choices, your chances of getting a right answer is one in four. So keep a separate "guessing" score for each exam. How many questions did you guess on? How many did you get right? If the number you got right is at least one-fourth of the number of questions you guessed on, you are at least an average guesser, maybe better—and you should always go ahead and guess on the real exam. If the number you got right is significantly lower than one-fourth of the number you guessed on, you would, frankly, be safe in guessing anyway, but maybe you'd feel more comfortable if you guessed only selectively, when you can eliminate a wrong answer or at least have a good feeling about one of the answer choices.

A half hour of vigorous activity—enough to raise a sweat—every day should be your aim. If you're really pressed for time, every other day is OK. Choose an activity you like and get out there and do it. Jogging with a friend always makes the time go faster, or take a radio.

But don't overdo. You don't want to exhaust yourself. Moderation is the key.

DIET

First of all, cut out the junk. Go easy on caffeine and nicotine, and eliminate alcohol and any other drugs from your system at least two weeks before the exam. Promise yourself a binge the night after the exam, if need be.

What your body needs for peak performance is simply a balanced diet. Eat plenty of fruits and vegetables, along with protein and carbohydrates. Foods that are high in lecithin (an amino acid), such as fish and beans, are especially good "brain foods."

The night before the exam, you might "carbo-load" the way athletes do before a contest. Eat a big plate of spaghetti, rice and beans, or whatever your favorite carbohydrate is.

REST

You probably know how much sleep you need every night to be at your best, even if you don't always get it. Make sure you do get that much sleep, though, for at least a week before the exam. Moderation is important here, too. Extra sleep will just make you groggy.

If you're not a morning person and your exam will be given in the morning, you should reset your internal clock so that your body doesn't think you're taking an exam at 3 a.m. You have to start this process well before the exam. The way it works is to get up half an hour earlier each morning, and then go to bed half an hour earlier that night. Don't try it the other way around; you'll just toss and turn if you go to bed early without having gotten up early. The next morning, get up another half an hour earlier, and so on. How long you will have to do this depends on how late you're used to getting up. Use the Physical Preparation Checklist on the next page to make sure you're in tip-top form.

STEP 8: GET YOUR ACT TOGETHER

Time to complete: 10 minutes to read; time to complete will vary
Activity: Complete Final Preparations worksheet
You're in control of your mind and body; you're in charge of test anxiety, your preparation, and your test-taking strategies. Now it's time to take charge of external factors, like the testing site and the materials you need to take the exam.

FIND OUT WHERE THE TEST IS AND MAKE A TRIAL RUN

Do you know how to get to the testing site? Do you know how long it will take to get there? If not, make a trial run, preferably on the same day of the week at the same time of day. Make note, on the worksheet Final Preparations on page 23, of the amount of time it will take you to get to the exam site. Plan on arriving 10–15 minutes early so

(continued on page 22)

Physical Preparation Checklist

For the week before the test, write down 1) what physical exercise you engaged in and for how long and 2) what you ate for each meal. Remember, you're trying for at least half an hour of exercise every other day (preferably every day) and a balanced diet that's light on junk food.

Exam minus 7 days

Exercise: _____ for _____ minutes

Breakfast: _____

Lunch: _____

Dinner: _____

Snacks: _____

Exam minus 6 days

Exercise: _____ for _____ minutes

Breakfast: _____

Lunch: _____

Dinner: _____

Snacks: _____

Exam minus 5 days

Exercise: _____ for _____ minutes

Breakfast: _____

Lunch: _____

Dinner: _____

Snacks: _____

Exam minus 4 days

Exercise: _____ for _____ minutes

Breakfast: _____

Lunch: _____

Dinner: _____

Snacks: _____

Exam minus 3 days

Exercise: _____ for _____ minutes

Breakfast: _____

Lunch: _____

Dinner: _____

Snacks: _____

Exam minus 2 days

Exercise: _____ for _____ minutes

Breakfast: _____

Lunch: _____

Dinner: _____

Snacks: _____

Exam minus 1 day

Exercise: _____ for _____ minutes

Breakfast: _____

Lunch: _____

Dinner: _____

Snacks: _____

you can get the lay of the land, use the bathroom, and calm down. Then figure out how early you will have to get up that morning, and make sure you get up that early every day for a week before the exam.

GATHER YOUR MATERIALS

The night before the exam, lay out the clothes you will wear and the materials you have to bring with you to the exam. Plan on dressing in layers; you won't have any control over the temperature of the examination room. Have a sweater or jacket you can take off if it's warm. Use the checklist on the worksheet Final Preparations on page 23 to help you pull together what you'll need.

Don't Skip Breakfast

Even if you don't usually eat breakfast, do so on exam morning. A cup of coffee doesn't count. Don't do doughnuts or other sweet foods, either. A sugar high will leave you with a sugar low in the middle of the exam. A mix of protein and carbohydrates is best: cereal with milk and just a little sugar, or eggs with toast, will do your body a world of good.

STEP 9: DO IT!

Time to complete: 10 minutes, plus test-taking time
Activity: Ace the real estate exam!
Fast forward to exam day. You're ready. You made a study plan and followed through. You practiced your test-taking strategies while working through this book. You're in control of your physical, mental, and emotional state. You know when and where to show up and what to bring with you. In other words, you're better prepared than most of the other people taking the real estate exam with you. You're psyched.

Just one more thing. When you're done with the exam, you will have earned a reward. Plan a celebration. Call up your friends and plan a party, or have a nice dinner for two—whatever your heart desires. Give yourself something to look forward to.

And then do it. Go into the exam, full of confidence, armed with test-taking strategies you've practiced till they're second nature. You're in control of yourself, your environment, and your performance on the exam. You're ready to succeed. So do it. Go in there and ace the exam. And look forward to your future career as a real estate agent!

Final Preparations

Getting to the Exam Site

Location of exam site: _____

Date: _____

Departure time: _____

Do I know how to get to the exam site? Yes _____ No _____
If no, make a trial run.

Time it will take to get to exam site: _____

Things to lay out the night before

Clothes I will wear   _____

Sweater/jacket   _____

Watch   _____

Photo ID   _____

Calculator   _____

_____   _____

_____   _____

C·H·A·P·T·E·R 3

ASI REAL ESTATE SALES EXAM 1

CHAPTER SUMMARY
This is the first of the four practice tests in this book based on the ASI Real Estate Sales Exam.

L ike the other tests in this book, this one is based on the ASI Real Estate Sales Exam. See Chapter 1 for a complete description of this exam.

Take this first exam in as relaxed a manner as you can, without worrying about timing. You can time yourself on the other three. You should, however, make sure that you have enough time to take the entire exam at one sitting, at least three hours. Find a quiet place where you can work without being interrupted.

The answer sheet you should use is on the following page, and then comes the exam. After the exam, use the answer key that follows it to see your progress on each section and to find out why the correct answers are correct and the incorrect ones incorrect. Then use the scoring section at the end of the exam to see how you did overall.

1.	ⓐ	ⓑ	ⓒ	ⓓ
2.	ⓐ	ⓑ	ⓒ	ⓓ
3.	ⓐ	ⓑ	ⓒ	ⓓ
4.	ⓐ	ⓑ	ⓒ	ⓓ
5.	ⓐ	ⓑ	ⓒ	ⓓ
6.	ⓐ	ⓑ	ⓒ	ⓓ
7.	ⓐ	ⓑ	ⓒ	ⓓ
8.	ⓐ	ⓑ	ⓒ	ⓓ
9.	ⓐ	ⓑ	ⓒ	ⓓ
10.	ⓐ	ⓑ	ⓒ	ⓓ
11.	ⓐ	ⓑ	ⓒ	ⓓ
12.	ⓐ	ⓑ	ⓒ	ⓓ
13.	ⓐ	ⓑ	ⓒ	ⓓ
14.	ⓐ	ⓑ	ⓒ	ⓓ
15.	ⓐ	ⓑ	ⓒ	ⓓ
16.	ⓐ	ⓑ	ⓒ	ⓓ
17.	ⓐ	ⓑ	ⓒ	ⓓ
18.	ⓐ	ⓑ	ⓒ	ⓓ
19.	ⓐ	ⓑ	ⓒ	ⓓ
20.	ⓐ	ⓑ	ⓒ	ⓓ
21.	ⓐ	ⓑ	ⓒ	ⓓ
22.	ⓐ	ⓑ	ⓒ	ⓓ
23.	ⓐ	ⓑ	ⓒ	ⓓ
24.	ⓐ	ⓑ	ⓒ	ⓓ
25.	ⓐ	ⓑ	ⓒ	ⓓ
26.	ⓐ	ⓑ	ⓒ	ⓓ
27.	ⓐ	ⓑ	ⓒ	ⓓ

28.	ⓐ	ⓑ	ⓒ	ⓓ
29.	ⓐ	ⓑ	ⓒ	ⓓ
30.	ⓐ	ⓑ	ⓒ	ⓓ
31.	ⓐ	ⓑ	ⓒ	ⓓ
32.	ⓐ	ⓑ	ⓒ	ⓓ
33.	ⓐ	ⓑ	ⓒ	ⓓ
34.	ⓐ	ⓑ	ⓒ	ⓓ
35.	ⓐ	ⓑ	ⓒ	ⓓ
36.	ⓐ	ⓑ	ⓒ	ⓓ
37.	ⓐ	ⓑ	ⓒ	ⓓ
38.	ⓐ	ⓑ	ⓒ	ⓓ
39.	ⓐ	ⓑ	ⓒ	ⓓ
40.	ⓐ	ⓑ	ⓒ	ⓓ
41.	ⓐ	ⓑ	ⓒ	ⓓ
42.	ⓐ	ⓑ	ⓒ	ⓓ
43.	ⓐ	ⓑ	ⓒ	ⓓ
44.	ⓐ	ⓑ	ⓒ	ⓓ
45.	ⓐ	ⓑ	ⓒ	ⓓ
46.	ⓐ	ⓑ	ⓒ	ⓓ
47.	ⓐ	ⓑ	ⓒ	ⓓ
48.	ⓐ	ⓑ	ⓒ	ⓓ
49.	ⓐ	ⓑ	ⓒ	ⓓ
50.	ⓐ	ⓑ	ⓒ	ⓓ
51.	ⓐ	ⓑ	ⓒ	ⓓ
52.	ⓐ	ⓑ	ⓒ	ⓓ
53.	ⓐ	ⓑ	ⓒ	ⓓ
54.	ⓐ	ⓑ	ⓒ	ⓓ

55.	ⓐ	ⓑ	ⓒ	ⓓ
56.	ⓐ	ⓑ	ⓒ	ⓓ
57.	ⓐ	ⓑ	ⓒ	ⓓ
58.	ⓐ	ⓑ	ⓒ	ⓓ
59.	ⓐ	ⓑ	ⓒ	ⓓ
60.	ⓐ	ⓑ	ⓒ	ⓓ
61.	ⓐ	ⓑ	ⓒ	ⓓ
62.	ⓐ	ⓑ	ⓒ	ⓓ
63.	ⓐ	ⓑ	ⓒ	ⓓ
64.	ⓐ	ⓑ	ⓒ	ⓓ
65.	ⓐ	ⓑ	ⓒ	ⓓ
66.	ⓐ	ⓑ	ⓒ	ⓓ
67.	ⓐ	ⓑ	ⓒ	ⓓ
68.	ⓐ	ⓑ	ⓒ	ⓓ
69.	ⓐ	ⓑ	ⓒ	ⓓ
70.	ⓐ	ⓑ	ⓒ	ⓓ
71.	ⓐ	ⓑ	ⓒ	ⓓ
72.	ⓐ	ⓑ	ⓒ	ⓓ
73.	ⓐ	ⓑ	ⓒ	ⓓ
74.	ⓐ	ⓑ	ⓒ	ⓓ
75.	ⓐ	ⓑ	ⓒ	ⓓ
76.	ⓐ	ⓑ	ⓒ	ⓓ
77.	ⓐ	ⓑ	ⓒ	ⓓ
78.	ⓐ	ⓑ	ⓒ	ⓓ
79.	ⓐ	ⓑ	ⓒ	ⓓ
80.	ⓐ	ⓑ	ⓒ	ⓓ

1. Elderly homeowners can sometimes tap the equity in their homes without having to make monthly payments by using a
   a. wraparound mortgage
   b. reverse mortgage
   c. conversion option
   d. blanket mortgage

2. Economic or external obsolescence refers to loss of value due to
   a. wear and tear
   b. outdated design
   c. factors outside the property lines
   d. incurable defects in the subject property

3. All the salespersons in Al's brokerage firm work as independent contractors. Their office most likely provides them with which of the following?
   a. secretarial help
   b. health insurance
   c. income tax withholding
   d. paid vacations

4. A tenant applicant confined to a wheelchair is interested in renting a townhome. A request is made to the landlord to allow the tenant to have an access ramp constructed. Which of the following is true in this situation?
   a. The tenant application must be rejected.
   b. The landlord must allow the tenant to make the modification at the tenant's expense.
   c. The landlord is required to fund modifications to the property to accommodate the access problem.
   d. The landlord may collect an additional deposit to assure compliance.

5. Additions that people make to real estate are known as
   a. chattels
   b. trade fixtures
   c. parcels
   d. improvements

6. Jill Adams, a property owner, just received a bill from her local taxing authority in the amount of $2,040. Property taxes in this jurisdiction are based on 80% of assessed value and the rate is $1.50 per hundred. What value has the assessor placed on Jill's property?
   a. $136,000
   b. $170,000
   c. $163,200
   d. $190,000

7. The type of depreciation always classified as incurable is
   a. physical deterioration
   b. fictional IRS depreciation
   c. functional obsolescence
   d. economic or external obsolescence

8. A certain subdivision has a deed restriction requiring houses to be at least 2,000 square feet. The town, however, has no such restriction and gives the Smith-Joneses a building permit for a little bungalow in the subdivision. If the neighbors object, their best course of action would be to
   a. attempt to negotiate with the building inspector's office
   b. wait until a clear violation has occurred before taking any legal action
   c. request a change of the local zoning ordinance
   d. ask a court to prevent the construction or to order that the bungalow be expanded

9. A building suffers loss in value due to functional obsolescence when it is
   a. run down
   b. located near a vacant factory
   c. poorly designed
   d. next door to annoying neighbors

10. Using personal property as collateral to secure a loan while retaining the property is called
   a. mortgage
   b. encumbrance
   c. hypothecation
   d. promissory intent

11. The person who receives real property through a will is known as a
   a. testator
   b. devisee
   c. vendee
   d. legatee

12. The Civil Rights Act of 1866 prohibits discrimination and provides
   a. exceptions for some owner-occupied housing
   b. exceptions for certain apartment buildings
   c. exceptions for private clubs
   d. no exceptions

13. Credit lenders may not discriminate on the basis of age unless the prospective borrowers are
   a. parents of more than five children
   b. out-of-state buyers
   c. part-time workers
   d. minors

14. The Fair Housing Act of 1988, which addresses accessibility in new multi-family buildings for people with physical disabilities, mandates all of the following EXCEPT
   a. elevators or power lifts
   b. doors, kitchens, and bathrooms that are wheelchair friendly
   c. thermostats and lighting switches within easy reach
   d. bathroom walls strong enough to support grab bars

15. The applicant for a mortgage may NOT be asked about his or her
   a. national origin
   b. source of income used for repayments
   c. number and ages of dependents
   d. immigration status

16. In most states, no property tax is levied on land belonging to
   a. golf courses
   b. senior citizen housing
   c. churches
   d. shopping malls

17. In the relationship between principal and agent, any third party involved is properly known as the
   a. customer
   b. client
   c. principal
   d. subagent

18. The buyer of a cooperative apartment receives shares in the cooperative and a
   a. proprietary lease
   b. bargain and sale deed
   c. joint tenancy
   d. limited partnership

19. Chris Salvano is the broker hired to sell Erin Miller's house. Chris shows the house to the Martins, who want to put in an offer on it. At this point, what duties does Chris legally owe to the Martins?
   a. confidentiality and fairness
   b. fairness and honesty
   c. obedience and disclosure
   d. confidentiality and honesty

20. The appraisal principle of substitution states that
   a. the buyer is paying for expected benefits in the future
   b. some improvements have a larger payoff in increased value than others
   c. maximum value is reached where there is reasonable uniformity in the neighborhood
   d. no one will pay more if something equally desirable is available for less

21. The right to occupy a property for a specified period of time is known as a
   a. trespass
   b. prescriptive easement
   c. leasehold
   d. suit for possession

22. The real estate broker's equivalent of medical malpractice insurance is known as
   a. realty malpractice insurance
   b. liability coverage
   c. errors and omissions insurance
   d. inland marine insurance

23. In a real estate transaction, both the seller's agent and the buyer's agent are legally required to put whose interest first?
   a. their own prospect's
   b. the buyer's
   c. the seller's
   d. their principal's

24. A real estate licensee is usually presumed to be the agent of the
   a. party paying the commission
   b. party with whom a written contract has been signed
   c. owner of the real estate
   d. buyer

25. If the lease states that the landlord will provide heat, the tenant whose apartment is freezing may break the lease claiming
   a. suit for possession
   b. actual eviction
   c. constructive eviction
   d. condemnation of the premises

26. The statute of frauds requires that
   a. real estate brokers answer buyers' and sellers' questions honestly
   b. the seller of real estate provides a written disclosure about the condition of the property
   c. certain contracts, including those for the sale of real estate, must be in writing to be enforceable
   d. a mortgage borrower has three days in which to cancel the loan

27. For appraising a 20-year-old single-family residence, the best data is the
   a. probable rental figure
   b. recent sale prices of nearby houses
   c. replacement cost
   d. owner's original cost plus money spent on improvements

28. Richard Morgan wants to buy Daniel Johnson's house, but Daniel doesn't want to turn over title until he receives the purchase price. They could use either a lease option or a land contract. Richard would prefer a lease option because
   a. it will allow him to move in immediately
   b. he'll know the eventual sale price
   c. Daniel will be obligated to sell to him
   d. Richard will be free to change his mind about buying

29. Which of the following listings is illegal in many states and open to fraudulent dealings?
   a. an open listing
   b. an exclusive right to sell
   c. an exclusive agency
   d. a net listing

30. Governments have the ability to regulate the construction and use of buildings through their right of
   a. police power
   b. escheat
   c. eminent domain
   d. condemnation

31. The earnest money accompanying a purchase offer
   a. is generally 10 percent of the proposed purchase price
   b. should be held in escrow by the seller
   c. is mandated by state law
   d. is not necessary to establish a valid contract

32. The term "walk-through" refers to
   a. an appraiser's inspection of the interior of the subject property
   b. empty office buildings where the vacancy rate in the community is high
   c. a seller's check of the premises before an open house is held
   d. the buyer's final inspection of the property to check its condition

33. Which of the following would be included in a spot survey of a single lot?
   a. the location of any improvements
   b. identification of any public transit services
   c. directions to shopping areas
   d. the zoning classifications of adjacent properties

34. If during negotiations one party crosses out or changes any wording in a contract
  a. each party must initial the change in the margin for it to be valid
  b. the whole contract becomes void
  c. the document must be retyped
  d. the statute of frauds requires the document be notarized

35. The seller delivers the deed and the buyer pays the purchase price at the closing, also referred to as
  a. commitment
  b. underwriting
  c. warehousing
  d. settlement

36. Dennis Sorensen is buying land on which he plans to build a cabin. He wants 200 feet in road frontage and a lot 500 feet deep. If the asking price is $9,000 an acre for the land, how much will Dennis pay for his lot?
  a. $10,000
  b. $20,700
  c. $22,956
  d. $24,104

37. Jane Muller goes to a bank and borrows money for the purchase of her first home, thereby becoming a
  a. mortgagor
  b. mortgagee
  c. lienor
  d. lienee

38. Each "point" charged when a loan is closed represents one percent of the
  a. down payment
  b. sale price
  c. amount borrowed
  d. broker's commission

39. When real estate is purchased through a lease option, the money initially paid in return for the option can be applied to the eventual purchase price
  a. only in those states where the law allows it
  b. if it is so agreed in the contract
  c. if the lease is for a one-year period
  d. under no circumstances

40. When a mortgage borrower is required to maintain an escrow or trust account with the lending institution, money in that account is used to pay the homeowner's
  a. points
  b. utility bills
  c. property taxes
  d. life insurance

41. Lenders who deal directly with individual mortgage borrowers make up the
  a. primary mortgage market
  b. secondary mortgage market
  c. mortgage servicing industry
  d. federal reserve system

42. Ad valorem taxes are used by the local government body to provide
   a. necessary and desirable local infrastructure services
   b. entertainment funds
   c. military protection
   d. funds for long-term investments

43. In the market or sales data approach to appraisal, similar recent sale figures are
   a. assessed
   b. analyzed
   c. adjusted
   d. added

44. Nel Woodhouse wants to buy a certain condo in Florida. In order to pay for the unit, the furniture, and all the appliances, she needs a
   a. package mortgage
   b. blanket mortgage
   c. wraparound mortgage
   d. buydown mortgage

45. While listing his house, Bennet Lyons tells his agent, Will Connelly, that he doesn't want the house shown to Armenians. Will's best course of action is to
   a. take the listing, but resolve that if any Armenians want to see it, he'll show it to them without notifying Bennet
   b. take the listing but explain to Bennet that he cannot follow such instructions
   c. take the listing and obey his principal's instructions
   d. refuse the listing

46. What is the difference between MIP and PMI?
   a. PMI insures conventional mortgages, and MIP insures FHA loans.
   b. PMI is the older form of mortgage insurance.
   c. MIP is required only on VA mortgages.
   d. There is no difference; the two terms mean the same thing.

47. Gerald Fisher owns 140 acres of pasture. An oil company offers him a monthly fee plus a percentage from the sale of any oil pumped from the wells drilled on the property within the next three years. This arrangement is known as a
   a. percentage lease
   b. ground lease
   c. mineral lease
   d. variable lease

48. Mortgage insurance protects the
   a. borrower's family by paying off the loan in case of death
   b. lending institution against loss if the loan goes into default
   c. borrower in case of job loss or accident
   d. veteran by allowing no-down-payment mortgage loans

49. When the Egans applied for a mortgage, they were offered a chance to pay extra points in return for a lower interest rate, meaning they could use a
   a. cap rate
   b. buydown
   c. balloon
   d. ratio

50. Linda Robinson's offer to buy David Hendley's house has been accepted, but the actual sale will not take place for three months. Until then, their written sales contract is considered
    a. executory
    b. pending
    c. conditional
    d. voidable

51. Which of the following is an advantage of biweekly payment plans?
    a. They let the borrower pay less per month in return for a longer term.
    b. They involve the equivalent of 12 monthly payments each year.
    c. They usually carry lower interest rates.
    d. They allow the loan to be paid off sooner than scheduled.

52. Which of the following would be considered incurable depreciation?
    a. unattractive aluminum siding
    b. a roof with curled and cracked shingles
    c. regression in an area of conformity
    d. rotted fencing

53. The seller has not yet paid this year's property taxes, which are $2,400 for the period from January 1 to December 31. On July 15 the house is sold. How are the taxes adjusted at closing?
    a. credit buyer $1,300; debit seller $1,100
    b. credit buyer $1,100; debit seller $1,100
    c. debit buyer $1,300; credit seller $1,320
    d. credit buyer $1,300; debit seller $1,300

54. After paying a 7% commission to his broker, a seller receives $103,000 from the sale of his house. How much did the house sell for?
    a. $95,790
    b. $110,000
    c. $110,420
    d. $110,753

55. A commercial property is estimated to generate $5,500 in monthly net income. Using a capitalization rate of 11%, the appraiser's opinion of value would be
    a. $50,000
    b. $726,000
    c. $60,500
    d. $600,000

56. When construction of a new building has been completed in a satisfactory manner, the local building inspector issues
    a. a certificate of occupancy
    b. an environmental impact statement
    c. a restrictive covenant
    d. a variance

57. The Owens are buying a $100,000 house with 5% down and an FHA mortgage for the rest. They must pay an upfront MIP of 2.5% in addition to other closing costs that amount to $1,000. How much money will they need at the closing?
    a. $8,500
    b. $8,375
    c. $6,000
    d. $3,500

58. In a loan closing, proper signatures on the promissory note create
a. the indebtedness of the borrower
b. the lien on the property
c. the transfer of ownership to a trustee
d. recordation of the lien on the land records

59. To increase the yield on a $250,000 loan by $\frac{3}{4}$% when one point is equal to $\frac{1}{8}$%, how much would the lender collect at settlement in loan discount?

a. $2,500

b. $1,875

c. $15,000

d. $20,000

60. In the government survey system, a quarter section contains how many acres?
a. 80
b. 160
c. 640
d. 860

61. The method of financing with minimum exposure and liability to the seller is
a. purchase money mortgage
b. new financing
c. purchase subject to the mortgage
d. assumption of the existing loan

62. An investor recently paid $500,000 for a building that yields about $65,000 in annual income. The cap rate on this investment is evidently around
a. 7.69%
b. 11.5%
c. 13%
d. 32.5%

63. The source of financing for real estate with the most liberal terms and flexible procedures is
a. the seller
b. savings & loans
c. commercial banks
d. mutual savings banks

64. After the sale of the collateral property, it is determined that the net proceeds did not clear the debt. In this situation, the borrower is likely to receive a
a. notice of a deficiency judgment
b. letter of defeasance
c. certificate of liability
d. notice of foreclosure

65. Riparian and littoral rights belong to owners of
a. a homestead
b. subsurface minerals
c. land bordering bodies of water
d. remainder and reversionary interests

66. Nancy Tomsic's tenants all had several months remaining on their leases when she sold her six-unit apartment building to Chuck Dwight. Tenants in this situation typically
   a. must renegotiate their leases with the new landlord
   b. can be required to leave with one month's notice
   c. lose their leases when the new owner takes possession
   d. need do nothing and can remain until the end of their leases

67. There is a principle in valuation stating that property in a recovering area will gain value. This is the principle of
   a. anticipation
   b. competition
   c. highest and best use
   d. regression

68. Sue Addison owns an apartment building that was constructed in 1965. According to federal law, which of the following must be attached to the leases Sue prepares for prospective tenants?
   a. a report of the building's radon level
   b. a lead-based paint disclosure statement
   c. an illustration of the building's location relative to electromagnetic fields (EMFs)
   d. any known instances of groundwater contamination in the building's water supply

69. When a contract contains provisions outlining what money penalties will be levied against the party that refuses to perform, the amount specified is known as
   a. earnest money
   b. consideration
   c. specific performance
   d. liquidated damages

70. The agreement signed by the owners of House A and House B to share a common driveway is a form of
   a. encroachment
   b. party wall
   c. easement
   d. homestead

71. Property managers often make management decisions about tenant selection and budgets for their clients. In these relationships, the property manager is acting as a
   a. special agent
   b. power of attorney
   c. independent contractor
   d. general agent

72. Dave Gates, a widower, died without leaving a will or other instruction. His surviving children received ownership of his real estate holdings by
   a. adverse possession
   b. eminent domain
   c. escheat
   d. law of descent and distribution

73. Which of the following is a requirement for a valid agency relationship?
   a. written agreement
   b. compensation
   c. mutual consent
   d. brokerage license

74. Jane Doe and Richard Roe, who are not married, want to buy a house together. In order to ensure that if one dies, the other automatically becomes full owner, their deed must state that they are
   a. tenants in common
   b. joint tenants
   c. tenants in severalty
   d. tenants by the entirety

75. The duties of the property manager include all of the following EXCEPT
   a. maintaining the property while preserving finances
   b. marketing for a constant tenant base
   c. seeking interested buyers
   d. preparing budgets

76. Fred Darcy, a bachelor, sells his longtime home. How much capital gain can he realize without owing any federal income tax?
   a. $125,000
   b. $250,000
   c. $500,000
   d. An unlimited amount

77. A real estate appraiser reports a dollar amount that
   a. analyzes value
   b. determines value
   c. estimates value
   d. assesses value

78. After analyzing comparable properties that have recently sold and adjusting for differences in features, location, and amenities, the appraiser is prepared to calculate
   a. market price
   b. market value
   c. contract price
   d. option price

79. Real estate licensees are required to disclose early in a transaction
   a. for which party they are working
   b. the commission rate offered by the seller
   c. possible financial arrangements for the purchase
   d. the name of the firm's principal

80. All of the following are factors in determining whether property is real or personal EXCEPT
   a. portability
   b. original cost
   c. method of attachment
   d. intent of the owner

ANSWERS

1. **b.** With a reverse mortgage, the homeowner receives a lump sum or monthly checks, and no repayment is made until the property is sold or the owner dies.

2. **c.** External obsolescence refers to outside factors (a nearby landfill, unemployment in the community) that affect the value of the subject property.

3. **a.** An independent contractor can receive nothing that resembles an employee benefit.

4. **b.** So long as the tenant pays, there is no violation of building codes or other covenants, and the tenant agrees to restore the property to essentially its original condition, the landlord must approve the ramp.

5. **d.** Improvements, which become part of the real property, include additions that people make, like sewers, roads, and buildings.

6. **b.** $2,040 × 100 ÷ 1.5 ÷ .8 = $170,000. $2,040 ÷ 1.5 × 100 ÷ .8 = $170,000

7. **d.** Economic obsolescence is caused by factors outside the property and is considered incurable.

8. **d.** If a deed restriction is more restrictive than a local zoning ordinance, it takes precedence and can be enforced in court. The neighbors would probably win their case.

9. **c.** Functional obsolescence is due to outmoded design or construction.

10. **c.** When a borrower pledges property to secure a loan, while retaining the property's use and benefit, it is known as hypothecation.

11. **b.** The transfer of real property through a will is known as a devise.

12. **d.** The fact that no exceptions are provided for discrimination based on race is the most important aspect of this act.

13. **d.** The Equal Credit Opportunity Act was amended in 1976 to add age as a protected class, except where the would-be borrower is a minor.

14. **a.** The law does not require elevators or power lifts in residential real estate.

15. **a.** National origin is one of the protected classes under the Equal Credit Opportunity Act. Mortgage interviewers are allowed to ask about the other items.

16. **c.** Religious and charitable institutions are among the most common properties exempt from taxation.

17. **a.** The customer, while not entitled to fiduciary service, must nevertheless be treated with fairness and honesty.

18. **a.** A co-op apartment is personal property, not real estate, and no deed is involved. The owners become shareholders in the overall organization and have a proprietary lease to their apartments.

19. **b.** As customers, the Martins are entitled merely to fair and honest treatment. Chris does not owe them confidentiality or obedience to instructions.

20. **d.** Choice **a** defines the appraisal principle of anticipation, **b** the principle of contribution; and **c** the principle of conformity.

21. **c.** A lease defines the period of time during which the tenant has the right to occupy and enjoy a property. At the end of that period, the right reverts to the owner.

22. **c.** Many brokers and salespersons carry errors and omission insurance to cover their real estate practice.

23. **d.** An agent is always required to put the principal's interests first above anyone else's, including their own.

24. b. The person paying the commission is not always the principal. Often a seller will pay a buyer's broker simply to facilitate the sale.

25. c. The landlord's deliberate neglect of a duty may break a lease through the process known as constructive eviction.

26. c. Every state has adopted the statute of frauds, which requires offers, acceptances, land contracts, and other real estate documents to be in writing to be enforceable.

27. b. How much buyers have paid for similar nearby properties is the best guide to market value.

28. d. With a lease option, the potential buyer is free either to complete the purchase or to move out at the expiration of the lease.

29. d. Net listings, in which the agent keeps any part of the sale price above a given amount, are illegal in most states.

30. a. Many people are surprised to learn that the term *police power* covers all of the government's authority to protect the public's health, safety, and welfare.

31. d. A sales contract can be valid even without any earnest money; its main use is to reassure the seller and prove the buyer's good faith.

32. d. The sales contract should contain a provision allowing the buyer a walk-through within 24 hours before closing.

33. a. A spot survey discloses any improvements on a property, as well as any encroachments or easements.

34. a. Any changes should be initialed by the person making the change and the person accepting it.

35. d. The process of closing, transfer of title, and settlement is known in some states as "going to escrow" and in New England, "passing papers."

36. b. The lot will measure 200 feet by 500 feet, or 100,000 square feet in all. An acre contains 43,560 square feet, so the lot contains approximately 2.3 acres (100,000 ÷ 43,560). At $9,000 per acre, the total cost is $20,700 (2.3 × $9,000).

37. a. The borrower mortgages the property, giving the lender a claim against the real estate. As the one who does the mortgaging, she is the mortgagor.

38. c. A point is one percent of the amount borrowed, not of the full sale price.

39. b. Lease option contracts can be very flexible, and the parties may make any arrangement that suits them.

40. c. The escrow account is used to ensure prompt payment of bills including property taxes, homeowners insurance premiums, and occasionally costs for homeowners associations or flood insurance.

41. a. The primary mortgage market originates mortgages, dealing directly with borrowers.

42. a. Ad valorem taxes on real property represent the bulk of revenues generated by local governments to provide the financial resources for its infrastructure.

43. c. Sale prices of comparable properties are adjusted to match the specifications of the subject property.

44. a. A package mortgage covers both real and personal property.

45. d. While choice **b** may seem a possible answer, taking a listing with a prejudiced principal could eventually land Will in trouble.

46. a. MIP (mortgage insurance premium) is charged on FHA loans; PMI (private mortgage insurance) applies to some conventional mortgages.

47. c. An oil and gas lease is used for exploration and production of natural resources. A percentage lease is used by many commercial retail businesses. A ground lease is used for temporary use of land with the addition of removable improvements. In a variable lease, the terms are changed in reaction to a change in a common index or at a specific date.

48. b. Mortgage insurance, which protects the lender from loss, should not be confused with mortgage *life* insurance, which pays off the loan in case of death.

49. b. A buydown involves payment of additional points to lower the interest rate on the loan.

50. a. An executory contract has not yet been performed; after the sale the contract will have been executed.

51. d. Biweekly plans involve 26 half-payments a year, the equivalent of 13 full payments. The extra payment goes entirely to reduce principal, shortening the remaining term.

52. c. This is an external factor caused by the lower priced homes in the area. External factors are always incurable.

53. d. The buyer receives credit for the period the seller lived in the house: $6\frac{1}{2}$ months at $200 per month = $1,300. The buyer receives credit at closing for that amount and the seller is debited for the same amount.

54. d. The seller's $103,000 represents only 93% of the sale price (100% − 7%). The broker's commission is **not** 7% of $103,000, but rather 7% of the whole sale price. The question is: $103,000 is 93% of what figure? ($103,000 ÷ .93)

55. d. $5,500 × 12 ÷ .11 = $600,000. NOI ÷ cap rate = value

56. a. The certificate of occupancy states that the government is satisfied that the building meets local zoning and building code standards and may be occupied.

57. b. The Owens will pay at closing a total of $5,000 down payment ($100,000 × 5%) + $1,000 closing costs + $2,375 in mortgage insurance premium (2.5% of $95,000 mortgage) = $8,375.

58. a. It is the note that creates the debt in an agreement between the borrower and lender.

59. c. $250,000 ÷ 100 × 6 = $15,000. 1 point = $\frac{1}{8}$%. 6 points = $\frac{3}{4}$% increase in yield.

60. b. A section, one square mile, contains 640 acres. A quarter section contains 160 acres.

61. b. With new financing, the seller has no liability after the sale.

62. c. The question is: $65,000 gives a return of what percent on a $500,000 investment? $65,000 divided by $500,000 = 13%. The problem can be done by ratios: 65,000 is to 500,000 as what is to 100%? $\frac{65,000}{500,000} = \frac{?}{100\%}$. Cross-multiplying yields 13%.

63. a. Buyer and seller can make whatever arrangements they are comfortable with as to rate, size, frequency of payment, and other details of the loan.

64. a. If the foreclosure sale does not clear the debt, the borrower remains responsible for any moneys due, including costs and interest.

65. c. Riparian rights apply to owners of land bordering rivers and streams, littoral rights to those owning land on lakes and oceans.

66. d. A lease survives the sale, and the new landlord is in exactly the same position with tenants as the old one was.

67. a. A purchaser's belief that a future event will benefit the property adds to its value.

68. b. Federal law requires that a lead-based paint disclosure form be given to all tenants and buyers if the building was constructed before 1978.

69. d. Once the contract has agreed on whatever amount will serve as liquidated damages in case of nonperformance, no greater amount can be sought in the courts.

70. c. Each owner has the right to pass over the neighbor's half of the driveway, thus owning an easement on the adjoining property.

71. d. The general agent is empowered to make binding decisions on behalf of the principal. Approving leases and property expenditures are among those activities.

72. d. Each state has a set of laws that define the distribution of real estate owned by someone who dies without leaving written instruction. If no heirs are located, the property reverts to the state.

73. c. Of the listed suggestions only mutual consent is required. Agency is sometimes formed by the behavior of the parties; compensation is generally a result of the completion of the task assigned in the agreement; licensure is immaterial in agency.

74. b. Joint tenants are often known as "joint tenants with right of survivorship." If Jane dies, Richard will automatically receive Jane's share, no matter what her will might say.

75. c. The property manager typically is not involved in selling the property.

76. b. The $125,000 exclusion no longer applies. The Taxpayer Relief Act of 1997 set $250,000 as the exclusion for a single filer taxpayer, $500,000 for a couple filing jointly.

77. c. Even the most skilled appraisal is only an estimate of value.

78. b. The objective of the appraiser is to estimate market value. All other responses are the result of agreement between the parties.

79. a. Every state has now enacted mandatory agency disclosure laws.

80. b. Cost is not a factor in the test of personal versus real property.

SCORING

Evaluate how you did on this practice exam by first finding the number of questions you got right. Only the number of correct answers is important—questions you skipped or got wrong don't count against your score. Divide the number you got right by 80, the number of questions in the exam, to arrive at your percentage score. You may want to use the table below to check your math and find percentage equivalents for several possible scores.

ASI REAL ESTATE SALES EXAM POSSIBLE SCORES	
Number of questions right	**Approximate percentage**
80	100%
74	92%
67	84%
61	76%
58	72%
51	64%
45	56%
42	52%

Although each state sets its own passing score for the exam, if you scored 70% to 75% on this practice exam, you have a good chance of passing in any situation. Your ultimate goal, of course, is to score higher than that, so you can be *certain* of passing the real exam.

Use your percentage scores in conjunction with the EasySmart test preparation guide in Chapter 2 of this book to help you devise a study plan using the Real Estate Refresher Course in Chapter 4, the Real Estate Math Review in Chapter 5, and the Real Estate Glossary in Chapter 6. You should plan to spend more time on the sections that correspond to the questions you found hardest and less time on the lessons that correspond to areas in which you did well.

What's much more important than your overall score, for now, is how you did on each of the areas tested by the exam. You need to diagnose your strengths and weaknesses so that you can concentrate your efforts as you prepare. The five question types are mixed in the exam, so in order to tell where your strengths and weaknesses lie, you'll need to compare your answer sheet with the table on the next page, which shows which of the five categories each question falls into.

FOR REVIEW

QUESTION SUBJECT AREA	QUESTION NUMBERS
Real Property	5, 6, 8, 11, 16, 18, 30, 33, 36, 43, 56, 60, 70, 72, 74, 80
Valuation and Appraisal	2, 7, 9, 20, 27. 43, 52, 55, 62, 67, 77, 78
Contracts, Agency, Federal Requirements	3, 12, 13, 15, 17, 19, 22–24, 26, 29, 31, 32, 34, 45, 50, 69, 73, 76, 79
Financing	1, 10, 35, 37, 38, 40, 41, 44, 46, 48, 49, 51, 53, 54, 57–59, 61, 63, 64
Leases, Rents, Property Management	4, 14, 21, 25, 28, 39, 47, 65, 66, 68, 71, 75

C·H·A·P·T·E·R

ASI REAL ESTATE REFRESHER COURSE

CHAPTER SUMMARY

If you want to review real estate concepts and terminology for your ASI real estate exam, this is the chapter you need. It covers the most commonly tested concepts on the ASI exam (based on the 1998 revision), presented in an outline format. Using this chapter, you can review just what you need to know for the test. There are also sample test questions after each major section of the outline to help you hone your skills.

n April 1998, ASI (Assessment Services, Inc.) revised the national portion of its real estate licensing exam. The tests in this book and this chapter follow the new outline, which includes more material on property management, taxation, and other real estate concepts.

The most important concepts tested on the national portion of the ASI exam are reviewed in this chapter.

How you use this chapter is up to you. You may want to proceed through the entire outline in order, working through the sample test questions that come after each section. Or perhaps, after taking the Diagnostic ASI Exam in Chapter 3, you know that you need to brush up on just one or two areas. In that case, you can concentrate only on those areas.

The following are the five major sections of the ASI exam, and the page on which you can begin your review of each one.

I. Real property characteristics, definitions, ownership, restrictions, and transfer (page 2)

II. Assessing and explaining property valuation and the appraisal process (page 28)

III. Contracts, agency relationships with buyers and sellers, and federal requirements (page 38)

IV. Financing the transaction and settlement (page 52)

V. Leases, rents, and property management (page 68)

Important Reminder

This chapter presents only an outline of important concepts for the ASI exam. It doesn't replace a complete real estate pre-license course. If you need further review of particular areas after reading this chapter, be sure to go back to your textbooks and supplementary materials from your pre-license course.

I. REAL PROPERTY CHARACTERISTICS, DEFINITIONS, OWNERSHIP, RESTRICTIONS, AND TRANSFER

In some states, the terms **real estate** and **real property** mean the same thing. In other states, **real property** refers to the rights of ownership and **real estate** refers to what is ownedÑthe land (and buildings). In this outline, and in the ASI examination, the terms are used interchangeably to refer to both the land and the rights of ownership.

A. Definitions, Descriptions, and Ways to Hold Title

1. Elements of Real and Personal Property

Personal property is everything that is not **real property**. Items of **personal property** (also called **chattels**) include:

- **tangibles,** such as a car, clothing, or jewelry
- **intangibles,** such as a patent, which is considered intellectual property

Real property (real estate) is the earth itself, including:

- the surface
- what is beneath the surface (including minerals and other substances)
- the air space above the surface

The **bundle of rights** of ownership interests in **real property** includes the right to possess, use, exclude others, encumber (mortgage), and transfer title to someone else by sale, gift, will, or exchange.

Appurtenances are rights or property that ordinarily are transferred with land and used for its benefit.

Easements and other property rights may be conveyed with the land.

Fixtures are man-made additions to land, such as buildings, fences, and other improvements. Items that become **fixtures** are **personal property** before they are attached to the land.

> The five tests that courts use to determine whether or not an item is a **fixture** and thus part of the **real property** can be remembered by the word **MARIA**.
>
> Method of attachment
> Agreement of the parties, which can override all other considerations
> Relationship of the parties—in a residential sale or lease, legislatures and courts tend to favor the buyer/tenant
> Intention of the party who attached the item to land or building
> Adaptability of the item for another use or location

Trade fixtures are equipment or furnishings used in a business. **Trade fixtures** are attached to the real estate while in use but are removable by the tenant at the end of the lease term.

Growing things can be **real property** or **personal property**, depending on how they are grown.

> **Fructus naturales** are plants and trees that occur naturally or as part of the landscaping and are part of the **real estate.**
>
> **Fructus industriales** (**emblements**) are cultivated crops and are personal property.

Water rights are defined by state law and depend on the water source and use.

> On a **navigable** body of water, the property owner's boundary will extend to the water's edge or the mean (average) high water line. On a **nonnavigable** body of water, the property owner's boundary will extend to the center of the body of water.

Surface water can result in **littoral** rights for owners or property bordering a lake or other body of still water. Owners of property bordering a flowing stream may have **riparian rights**.

> According to the **natural flow doctrine**, the owner of **riparian land** is entitled to the ordinary flow of water but may not impede the use of the ordinary flow by a downstream owner. This English theory has been greatly modified by the states.
>
> According to the **doctrine of reasonable use**, individual owners of **riparian land** have the right to reasonable use of the water that does not prevent use by other owners. States following this principle usually assign a higher priority to some uses, such as domestic use (residential property).

The **doctrine of prior appropriation** has been used by many western states to give priority to the first users of water for economic reasons.

The **doctrine of beneficial use** allows the first users of a body of water to retain their priority, but imposes the limitation that the water be used for a beneficial purpose within a reasonable time.

Water permits issued by the state are used to ration scarce water resources in areas of growing population, particularly in western states.

Use of **underground (subterranean) water** is vital in many states that have insufficient water from surface sources for residential, agricultural, and commercial uses.

Percolating water drains from the surface to underground strata. The states have modified the traditional English rule that there was no limitation on the amount of water a landowner could remove.

The **doctrine of reasonable use** limits the amount of water that can be taken to the reasonable needs of the landowner.

The **doctrine of correlative rights** limits the amount of water that can be taken to a proportionate share based on each owner's share of the surface area.

Underground streams confined to well-defined channels can be difficult to establish. If the location of an **underground stream** can be determined by a noninvasive method, the type of distribution applied to surface water will be followed.

Mineral rights belong to the owner of **real property**, unless they are retained by means of a **reservation** in the deed to the landowner, or assigned to someone else by means of a **grant** from the landowner. The right to remove specified minerals can also be assigned by the landowner by means of a **mineral lease**.

Oil and gas are subject to the **rule of capture**. The surface owner has the right to remove as much oil or gas as possible from wells on the owner's land.

2. Property Description and Legal Description

In order for some or all of the rights of ownership of **real property** to be transferred, the property must be described in sufficient detail to exclude all other parcels.

The **metes and bounds system** is one of the oldest methods of land measurement and description used in this country.

The **bounds** (boundary lines) of property are measured from a specified **point of beginning** along distances called **metes**, with each change of direction marked by a compass angle. **Markers** denote each turning point; in modern descriptions, natural **monuments** (the old oak tree) have been replaced by **benchmarks** (metal pins). The description ends with the return to the **point of beginning**.

The U.S. **government survey system (rectangular survey system)** was developed to have a more uniform method of delineating property boundaries.

Property is identified by reference to the intersection of a **meridian (principal meridian)** running north-south and a **baseline** running east-west. Land is separated into rectangles called **townships** of six miles square (six miles to a side, or 36 square miles).

Townships are counted in **tiers** north or south of a **baseline** and **ranges** east or west of a **meridian**.

A **township** is divided into 36 **sections**. A **section** is one mile square (one square mile) and contains 640 **acres**.

Sections are numbered as shown in Figure 1.

Figure 1

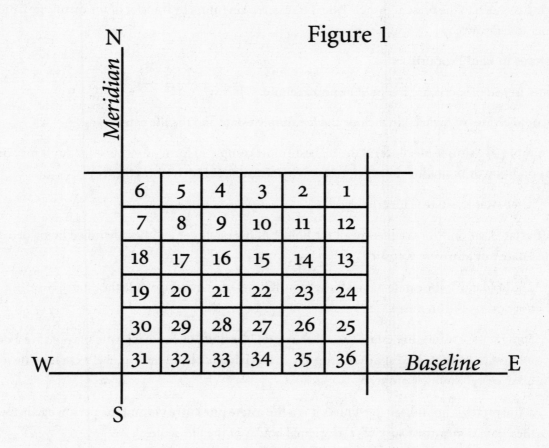

Numbered sections of the township
that is located at Tier 1 North, Range 1 East

An **acre** contains 43,560 square feet; an **acre** with four equal sides would be 208.7 feet on each side.

One **mile** is 5,280 linear feet or 320 **rods**.

One **rod** is 16.5 linear feet.

One **chain** is 66 linear feet.

The **subdivision system (lot and block system)** uses **parcel** numbers noted on a **subdivision map (plat map)**. The **deed** to each **parcel** references the book and page number in the recorder's office where the **subdivision map** can be found.

The **Torrens system** was created by Sir Robert Torrens. It is used primarily in Australia and Canada but also in Hawaii, parts of southern California, Washington, and other states. After title is cleared, a **Torrens certificate** is issued to the present owner. Title is transferred in future by transfer of the certificate from present owner to new owner.

3. **Estates in Real Property**

Estates in real property are **freehold** or **nonfreehold**.

Freehold estates of ownership include the **fee simple estate** and the **life estate**.

Fee simple (fee simple absolute) is the highest (most complete) form of ownership. But it may be subject to a condition or limitation, in which case it is a **defeasible fee (determinable fee)**.

A **fee simple estate** is inheritable.

A **life estate** lasts only for the lifetime of the holder of the estate (or another identified living person, when a **life estate pur autre vie** is created).

The holder of a **life estate** has all the responsibilities of ownership while the estate is in effect and may not destroy the premises.

Some states create a **life estate (legal life estate)** by statute. A surviving wife may receive a **dower** life interest in her deceased spouse's property; a surviving husband may receive a **curtesy** life interest in his deceased spouse's property.

A **life estate** is not inheritable unless it is a **life estate pur autre vie** and the person against whose life the estate is measured survives the original holder of the life estate.

A **life estate** is followed by a **remainder** interest in a party or parties named in the document that created the life estate. If no **remainder** interest was created, the property returns by **reversion** to the creator of the **life estate** (or that person's heirs).

Merger of a **fee** interest and **life estate** occurs when the same party owns both interests. If that happens, the **life estate** is extinguished.

Nonfreehold estates are **leasehold** interests and are considered **personal property (chattels real).**

The **lessor** (<u>owner</u> of the **leased fee**) permits the **lessee** (holder of the **leasehold** interest) to use the property for the period and under the terms specified in the **lease.**

The terms of the **lease** may allow it to be transferred during the lease term.

The types of **leasehold** interest are discussed in the last section of this outline.

4. Forms, Rights, Interests, and Obligations of Ownership

Ownership in severalty (tenancy in severalty) is ownership by one party, which can be an individual or business. (The owner's interest is *severed* from that of anyone else.)

The **owner in severalty** receives all of the benefits of ownership, such as income from space rental or sale or lease of mineral rights. In return, the **owner in severalty** is solely responsible for payment of property and other taxes and must bear the burden of property maintenance and other costs.

Concurrent ownership is ownership by more than one party. The rest of this section discusses forms of **concurrent ownership.**

A **tenancy in common** has the following attributes.

- Individual interests can be acquired at different times.
- Ownership interests can be equal or unequal. **Benefits** (income) and **burdens** (expenses) of ownership are divided in the same proportion.
- Each owner has an undivided right to use of the entire property, unless the parties agree otherwise.
- Each owner can transfer, **encumber,** or will his/her interest without affecting the rights of the other owners. The new owner will be a **tenant in common** with the other owners.
- A **partition action** can be brought to terminate the tenancy and divide the property (or the proceeds of a sale of the property) according to each co-owner's proportionate share.
- A creditor may force a sale of a co-owner's interest to satisfy a debt. The new owner of that share will be a **tenant in common** with the other owners.

A **joint tenancy** has the following attributes.

- Individual interests must be acquired at the same time (**unity of time**).
- Individual interests must be acquired by the same document (**unity of title**).
- Ownership interests are always equal (**unity of interest**), as are each co-owner's share of the **benefits** (income) and **burdens** (expenses) of ownership.
- Each owner has an undivided interest; that is, the right to use of the entire property (**unity of possession**).

The **four unities** of **time, title, interest,** and **possession** are what make a **joint tenancy** unique.

A properly created **joint tenancy** will carry with it the **right of survivorship**. This means that a **joint tenant** cannot will his/her ownership interest; when a co-owner dies, the surviving co-owners share equally in the deceased owner's interest.

A **partition action** can be brought to sever a **joint tenancy** and divide the property (or the proceeds of a sale of the property). In some states, a recorded document, such as a will, can be used to sever a **joint tenancy** as to that co-owner's share.

Creditors may force a sale of a share of jointly owned property to reach an individual owner's interest. If there were more than two co-owners in the **joint tenancy**, the share that is sold is held in a **tenancy in common** and the remaining shares are still held in **joint tenancy** as to those interests only.

A **tenancy by the entirety** has the following attributes.

- It is allowed in some states as a form of **joint tenancy** that is available only to married couples.
- It is terminated by agreement of both spouses, dissolution (divorce) or death.
- A transfer of property held in **tenancy by the entirety** requires the agreement of both spouses.
- Creditors of only one spouse may be unable to reach property owned in **tenancy by the entirety**.

Community property is recognized in Arizona, California, Idaho, Louisiana, Nevada, New Mexico, Texas, and Washington. Other states (such as Michigan and Wisconsin) have adopted similar forms of marital property ownership.

- **Community property** is an ownership option only for a married couple. It is the option that will be assumed if no other choice is specified when spouses take title to property.
- **Community property** usually includes all property (both **real** and **personal**) acquired during marriage with the exception of property acquired by gift or inheritance to one spouse only, or by the sale of one spouse's **separate property** (noncommunity property).
- **Separate property** that is **commingled** with **community property** (combined with, as occurs with funds held in a joint checking or savings account) may be treated as **community property**.

- Both spouses usually have the right to manage **community property**. A transfer of **real estate** held as **community property** will require the signature of both spouses.
- Creditors' rights depend on state law.

A **tenancy in partnership** is the way in which property is owned by a **partnership** created to conduct business for profit.

In a **general partnership**, all of the following occur.

- All **partners** are entitled to actively participate in **partnership** business.
- All **partners** are equally liable for **partnership** debts.
- All **partners** have equal right of control of **partnership** property.
- All **partners** must agree to transfer of **partnership** property. (Sale of real estate also requires signatures of spouses of **partners**.)
- **Partnership** income is taxed to individual **partners** and not the **partnership**.
- Personal creditors of the **partners** cannot reach **partnership** property.

In a **limited partnership**, all of the following occur.

- One or more **general partners** actively manage the business and have the full responsibility of **partners**, as listed above.
- One or more **limited partners**, as defined by state law, are inactive (not involved in day-to-day business management), in exchange for which they are not liable for **partnership** obligations beyond the amount invested.
- **Partnership** income is taxed to individual **partners** and not the **partnership**.

A **joint venture** is similar in form to a **general partnership**, but created to carry out a single project. Individuals or firms may contribute their work product, rather than money.

A **corporation** is an artificial entity created by state law.

- **Shareholders** are owners of stock in the **corporation**.
- **Bylaws** grant authority to specified officers to transact business.
- **Shareholders** are not personally liable for corporate debts.
- A **shareholder's** interest is inheritable.
- The **corporation** is taxed, as are individual **shareholders** when they receive stock **dividends**, so double taxation results.

An **S corporation** is created under **Subchapter S of the Internal Revenue Service Code.**

- It can have no more than 35 **shareholders**.
- It allows **corporate** income to be taxed only to individual owners (**shareholders**), thus avoiding double taxation.

A **limited liability company** (**LLC**) is defined by state law.

- It offers the limited liability of a **corporation**.
- Its income is taxed directly to its owners, thus avoiding double taxation.

A **syndicate** is a group formed by a **syndicator** to combine funds for **real estate** investment. The form of ownership may be a **partnership**, **corporation**, **limited liability company**, **tenancy in common**, or other arrangement.

A **trust** may be created to hold and manage real estate.

- A **real estate investment trust** (**REIT**) is defined by both federal and state law.
- A **REIT** must have more than 100 investors.
- A **REIT** allows ownership **shares** to be publicly traded.

REVIEW QUESTIONS—DEFINITIONS, DESCRIPTIONS, AND WAYS TO HOLD TITLE

1. The right of survivorship will accompany a properly created
   a. tenancy in common
   b. joint tenancy
   c. tenancy in severalty
   d. corporation

2. Ernie's Ice Cream Parlor is closing after 30 years in business. Ernie is removing his property from the leased building. Which of the following statements is true?
   a. Ernie is entitled to remove his ornate fittings, including the counter and refrigerators.
   b. Ernie can remove anything that is not attached in some manner to the floor, walls, or ceiling.
   c. Ernie is relieved of responsibility for any damage he may have created during his occupancy, or during the move.
   d. Ernie is the lessor.

3. Which of the following is the largest parcel that is larger than a parcel of 40 acres?
   a. 2 million square feet
   b. 1.8 million square feet
   c. 1.6 million square feet
   d. 174,240 square feet

4. Reference to a book and page number in the recorder's office is part of a legal description using the
   a. U.S. government survey system
   b. rectangular survey system
   c. subdivision system
   d. metes and bounds system

5. The kind of business that subjects its income to double taxation is the
   a. limited liability company
   b. corporation
   c. S corporation
   d. limited partnership

6. Polly owns a cottage on Lake Cicada. Polly can use water from the lake because of
   a. littoral rights
   b. riparian rights
   c. the rule of capture
   d. mineral rights

7. The rule of capture applies to removal of
   a. growing crops
   b. water
   c. oil and gas
   d. solid minerals

8. If you travel from the township located at T4N, R2W to the township located at T4N, R2E, both referenced to the Mt. Diablo Baseline and Meridian, in what direction are you traveling?
   a. north
   b. south
   c. east
   d. west

9. Aria, Barb, and Carol own Greenacre as joint tenants. Carol dies, naming her nephew David as her heir. This means that now:
   a. Aria, Barb, and David own Greenacre as joint tenants.
   b. Aria and Barb own Greenacre as joint tenants.
   c. Aria, Barb, and David own Greenacre, with Aria and Barb being joint tenants and Carl being a tenant in common.
   d. Aria, Barb, and David own Greenacre as tenants in common.

10. A division of land that is one mile square is called a
   a. township
   b. acre
   c. range
   d. section

ANSWERS

1.	b	**4.**	c	**7.**	c	**9.**	b
2.	a	**5.**	b	**8.**	c	**10.**	d
3.	c	**6.**	a				

B. Land Use Controls and Restrictions

1. Public

The **police power** of government is its right to regulate for the benefit of the public health, safety, morals, and welfare. Exercise of their **police power** by the states in the context of land use generally is passed on to local governing bodies (counties, cities) by **enabling acts**. Federal regulations also exist.

Planning is used to establish permissible land uses in defined areas.

A region, county and/or municipality may be required by state law to formulate a **master plan** that sets the pattern for future land development.

Establishment of a **master plan** is a time-consuming process that involves recommendations of consultants as well as public review and comment.

The **master plan** can be revised, but each change requires further public review and comment.

A **planning commission** may carry out a continuous process of review and enforcement.

Zoning is the primary method of carrying out the goals of the **master plan**. When an area is **zoned**, designated parcels are limited to specific property uses. Deviation from those uses requires petition to a **board of zoning adjustment** (**board of zoning appeals**, **zoning appeals board,** or **zoning hearing board**). Further appeal usually is to the local governing body, such as the city council. Appeal beyond the local level will be to the designated state court and then to higher levels of the state court system. The ultimate arbiter of an appeal on constitutional grounds (such as an unlawful taking of property without payment of just compensation) is the **U.S. Supreme Court**.

A **nonconforming use** is one that was in existence before the **zoning** regulation went into effect. Such property improvements typically will be allowed to remain, though subject to strict rules regarding future modifications.

A **variance** will be granted for a minor deviation from a **zoning** requirement, if to do otherwise would deny a property owner a use expected by owners of comparable properties. An example would be a steeply sloping residential building lot that requires the house to be placed closer to the front property line than would ordinarily be permitted.

A **conditional use (special use) permit** allows a property use that is not specified for the **zoned** area but is nevertheless considered of sufficient benefit to property owners to be allowed. An example would be a child care center located in an area **zoned** for residential use.

Rezoning is a change in permitted uses that may be the result of a revision of the **master plan** or consent of the governing body. **Downzoning** is a change to a more limited range of property uses, such as a change from multifamily residential to single-family residential. **Upzoning** is a change to a broader range of uses, such as a change from residential to commercial.

Spot zoning is a change of **zoning** that affects only one or a few properties and is generally not permitted.

Subdivision development usually is subject to specific state regulations on the formation, marketing, and sale of parcels. Intended to protect consumers, such regulations typically require that prospective purchasers be fully informed of the type of property and amenities that are being marketed, including indication of the financial stability of the developer and proposed date of completion of improvements.

The **Interstate Land Sales Full Disclosure Act** applies to interstate offerings (marketing of parcels to buyers in other states) of 25 or more parcels of less than five acres each.

This federal law requires disclosure to prospective purchasers of the nature and extent of the ownership interest they will acquire. The disclosure must include:

- the type of title that will be transferred
- findings of soil and other reports
- the number of parcels in the finished development
- the amenities that will be provided (from utilities to clubhouse and other facilities)
- the proximity of the development to necessary services, such as police and fire departments

Building codes adopted by state and local jurisdictions are minimum construction standards for building framing, plumbing, electrical wiring, and other systems. They are usually based on regional or national standards such as the **Uniform Building Code** established by the **Building Officials and Code Administrators International, Inc. (BOCA).**

A **building permit** is issued when plans are approved for either new construction or a remodeling. A plan must conform with **setback** (minimum distance from property boundaries or other buildings), **dimension** (length, width, height), **size** (square or cubic footage), **design**, and applicable state as well as local requirements (such as installation of sprinkler systems in high fire-risk areas). A **building permit** is required no matter who performs the work. Building contractors are licensed by the state.

When work is underway, the local **building inspector** or **codes director** will examine the construction project at various stages of progress for compliance with the minimum standards.

A **certificate of occupancy (CO)** is issued on completion only after all requirements have been satisfied.

Manufactured homes (formerly called **mobile homes**) are subject to construction requirements of the **Department of Housing and Urban Development (HUD).** The structural integrity and components of *HUD-code homes*, as they are called, are not subject to local requirements. But such homes are subject to local rules regarding building placement as well as the grading of the site, foundation work, and manner of installation of the home, plumbing and electrical connections, and other site-related features.

Most states define the type of housing that will be considered **manufactured (mobile) homes**, and regulate the **mobile home parks** and other developments set aside solely for their use.

There may be special requirements for sales and rental agents who deal in new or used **manufactured homes** on a regular basis, including disclosures that must be made to prospective purchasers or lessees.

Environmental regulations exist at both federal and state levels. Federal laws include the **Clean Water Act, Clean Air Act, National Environmental Policy Act**, and others.

The **Comprehensive Environmental Response, Compensation, and Liability Act (CERCLA)**, enacted in 1980, is the **Superfund Law** and is enforced by the **Environmental Protection Agency (EPA).**

The **EPA** has identified more than 30,000 inactive hazardous waste sites, and placed the most dangerous of these (those requiring immediate attention) on a **National Priority List (NPL)**.

Expenses of cleanup work are paid in part by the **Hazardous Substances Response Fund (Superfund)**, which is financed by taxes on industries (such as oil and chemical companies) with the greatest likelihood of causing contamination. Other federal as well as private funds are also used in this effort.

Other inactive industrial sites that may or may not be contaminated are described as **brownfields**. The **EPA** estimates that there are 450,000 such sites throughout the country. Documentation of such sites has begun in 40 state and regional jurisdictions.

Some states, such as California and New Jersey, have their own hazardous waste remediation laws. In the event of a property transfer, state law may require disclosure by the property owner of known or suspected contamination. In addition, a property transfer may require inspection and/or remediation.

The federal **Toxic Substances Control Act** has resulted in recommendations from the EPA on detection and remediation or containment of:

- **asbestos** insulation fibers
- naturally-occurring **radon** gas that seeps into a building foundation
- **urea-formaldehyde (UF)** gas that may be released by some glues, resins, preservatives, and bonding agents found in plywood and other building products and furnishings

The **Safe Drinking Water Act** was amended in 1986 to prohibit use of materials containing **lead** in public water supplies as well as in residences connected to public water supplies. In 1988, the use of **lead-based solder** in plumbing applications within buildings was prohibited. Homes built before 1988 may still have pipe connections made with **lead-based solder**.

The **Residential Lead-Based Paint Hazard Reduction Act of 1992** requires disclosure of the possible presence of **lead-based paint** in all houses built before 1978.

- Houses and other buildings built before 1978 are likely to have ceilings, walls, and other surfaces painted with **lead-based paint**.
- The **EPA** enforces the law.

Throughout the United States, **taxation** of **real property** is the primary method of financing schools, police and fire departments, and other amenities and services provided by state and local governments.

Real property taxes usually are **ad valorem** taxes. This means that they are based on the value of the property taxed.

State law specifies when and how often real property is to be **assessed** or **reassessed** to determine its value for tax purposes. A property owner who disagrees with an **assessed valuation** can present an independent **appraisal** as the basis for an appeal.

An **assessment ratio** often is applied to the **assessed valuation**, reducing it for purposes of computing the tax owed. Homeowners may be entitled to a **homestead exemption**, which further reduces the **assessed valuation**. There also may be special exemptions for elderly, low income, or disabled homeowners, or homeowners who are veterans.

The state or local jurisdiction (typically, the county) sets the **tax rate** to be charged and the deadline for payment of each year's tax owed.

A **tax lien** is placed on all property taxed and is enforced if taxes remain unpaid for the period set by law.

Net proceeds from the sale of **real estate** in excess of the property's tax **basis (book value)** are subject to federal income tax and may also be subject to state income tax. The **basis** of **real estate** for purposes of calculating tax owed (or deductible loss) is:

- the **acquisition cost** of the property (or **market value** at the time title passes if acquired by inheritance, gift, exchange, or other nonsale transaction)
- *plus* any amount spent on capital improvements (additions to the property, such as a new room, but not maintenance expenses, such as a new furnace)
- *minus* any depreciation taken on the property

In order to encourage homeownership and home affordability, Congress has provided several important benefits for home owners. For purposes of the tax law, a **residence** is any habitation that has living space as well as cooking and toilet facilities. Thus, a motor home or houseboat can qualify as a **residence.**

The **mortgage interest deduction** is available for interest paid on:

- loans secured by the **principal residence** and one other residence
- in an amount no greater than a total of $1,000,000 of **acquisition indebtedness** (loan amount at the time of purchase) and $100,000 of other indebtedness (the **home equity loan**)

It is important to note that, if a home mortgage loan is **refinanced**, only the interest paid on the loan balance remaining from the original loan will be deductible. Additional loan amounts may be designated as **home equity** indebtedness, to take advantage of the $100,000 **home equity loan mortgage interest deduction**.

The **mortgage interest deduction** is also allowed for interest paid at the time of financing in the form of **points (discount points)**.

- **Points** paid at the time of purchase are deductible from that year's income.
- **Points** paid in a **refinancing** are deductible on a pro rata basis over the life of the loan. For example, on a 20-year loan refinancing, 5% of the amount paid in **points** is deductible in each full year.

The Taxpayers Relief Act of 1997 established the **exclusion rule for gain on sale of the principal residence**. Previously, gain on the sale of the **principal residence** could be deferred as long as a new residence of equal or greater value was purchased within two years before or after the sale; persons aged 55 or over were allowed a once-in-a-lifetime exclusion of up to $125,000 of gain.

The new rule allows single individuals to exclude up to **$250,000** of gain on the sale of the **principal residence**. A married couple is allowed to exclude up to **$500,000** of gain on the sale of the **principal residence**.

The **principal residence** usually is the home in which the taxpayer lives most often and from which the taxpayer works, votes, and pays taxes. But each spouse is allowed to have a different **principal residence** (for instance, when they work in two different cities), in which case each will be entitled to a separate $250,000 exclusion.

The home must have been occupied as the **principal residence** for at least two of the five years preceding the sale.

The new rule applies to sales on or after **May 7, 1997**.

There is no limit to the number of times that the exclusion may be taken, but it may be taken only **once every two years**. A portion of a residence used for business (say, a home office) will be considered part of the residence for the purpose of the exclusion if that portion of the home is converted back to residential use for at least two years prior to the sale.

If the property is used as the **principal residence** for less than two of the five years preceding a sale, the exclusion is still available, but only up to the percentage of two years that the taxpayer used the home as the **principal residence**. For example, if a home has been occupied for 18 months by a single taxpayer, and all other conditions are met, the percentage of the exclusion to which the taxpayer is entitled is 18/24, or 75% of $250,000, which is $187,500. For a married couple in the same circumstance, the exclusion would be $375,000.

Use of the exclusion is **optional**; that is, the taxpayer may elect to pay tax on the gain.

The **residence replacement rollover rule** is no longer in effect. Whether or not they take advantage of the exclusion, homeowners can no longer defer taxation on any gain by purchasing a new home of equal or greater value.

The **once-in-a-lifetime exclusion** of up to $125,000 of gain for a home seller aged 55 or older is no longer in effect. If a homeowner has already taken advantage of that exclusion, it is no impediment to taking advantage of the new $250,000/$500,000 exclusion on the sale of a subsequent principal residence.

There is no longer any deduction for **fixing-up expenses** incurred in the sale of a home.

As in the past, the amount paid for **property taxes** is a deduction from income. The amount paid for **special assessments** (for improvements such as sewers) is not deductible from income, but can be added to the **cost basis** of the property.

Owning **real estate** as an investment has several important tax consequences.

In general, **active** management of real estate provides greater tax benefits than does **passive** ownership. **Active** management involves regular participation on a continuous basis in the operation of the investment; the level of involvement required will vary depending on the demands of the property.

Active losses (losses from property actively managed) are deductible from **ordinary income** no matter what the source.

Passive losses (losses from property in which the taxpayer is a passive investor) are deductible only from **passive income** (such as income received as a limited partner).

Adjusted gross income is the total potential income to be received from a property, less an allowance for expected vacancy and collection losses. **Net income** is what remains after deducting actual expenses of ownership, including estimated annual **depreciation** of buildings and other depreciable assets.

Depreciation is computed at the time of property acquisition by the **straight-line method**. The cost attributable to an improvement is divided by the number of years of its **economic life (remaining useful life)**. Thus, a building with a cost of $200,000 and a **remaining useful life** of 40 years can be estimated to depreciate at the rate of $5,000 per year ($200,000 divided by 40).

The Tax Reform Act of 1986, which took effect on January 1, 1987, increased the minimum period of years over which **depreciation** may be taken from 19 years to $27\frac{1}{2}$ years for residential property and from 19 years to $31\frac{1}{2}$ years for commercial property.

Prior to January 1, 1987, investors had the option of using various forms of **accelerated deprecia-tion** in which a greater amount of **depreciation** could be claimed in the early years of the invest-ment. This method is no longer available, but may continue to be used for properties acquired before January 1, 1987.

At-risk rules limit the amount that an investor may deduct from any investment to the amount of the investment plus any **recourse financing** (loan amount for which the investment is liable).

As of **May 7, 1997**, the maximum tax rate on **long-term capital gains** (profits from the sale of capital assets) is:

- **10%** for taxpayers in the 15% bracket
- **20%** for all others

As of **January 1, 1998**, the special tax rates for **long-term capital gains** apply to property held for at least **12 months**. Before that date the holding period for eligibility for **long-term capital gains** treatment was one year.

An **installment sale** can be used by an investor to spread out the receipt of taxable income from a sale.

As of **May 7, 1997**, the maximum tax rate on installment income (even for transactions originated before that date) is:

- **10%** for taxpayers in the 15% bracket
- **20%** for all others

A **land contract** (**contract for sale**) is an **installment sale** in which the seller retains title for at least one year following the date of sale, even though the buyer takes possession of the property.

The parties to a **tax-free exchange** under **Internal Revenue Code Section 1031** trade like-kind proper-ties. Taxation is avoided at the time of the trade unless **boot** (cash or equivalent) is received in addition to title to the traded property. The party receiving the **boot** must pay tax on that amount to the extent that it represents a profit on the value of the property traded.

A **tax lien** is available to federal, state, and local taxing authorities. Enforcement usually is by **tax sale** fol-lowing which the purchaser receives a **tax deed**. **Tax liens** take precedence over all other liens.

A **federal tax lien** is imposed by the **Internal Revenue Service** for nonpayment of federal income, gift or other tax.

A **state tax lien** is imposed for nonpayment of state income, sales, use, or other tax.

A **property tax** or **special assessment tax lien** is imposed for nonpayment of state or local tax.

Property used in the commission of a drug-related crime is subject to **forfeiture** and sale.

2. Private

Private controls of land use have been around longer than public controls. The most common form of private control is a limitation referenced in the **deed** from **grantor** to **grantee**. By accepting the **deed**, the **grantee** agrees to be bound by the limitation.

Subdivision restrictions typically are listed in a **Declaration of Restrictions** that is recorded with the **subdivision map** and referred to in the **deed** to every individual lot buyer in the subdivision. Each landowner thus becomes bound by the listed obligations.

Restrictions are also termed **conditions, covenants**, and **restrictions (CC&Rs)**. In practice, the term **restriction** can refer to any of these:

A **condition** stipulates an action that a property owner must perform, or refrain from performing.

A **covenant** is a promise of a property owner.

A **restriction** stipulates a forbidden activity or property use.

Many **subdivisions** make use of a **homeowners' association** to enforce **deed restrictions** and maintain common areas.

An **encumbrance (cloud on the title)** is anything that affects title to real estate. It is **voluntary** if it is imposed with the consent of the titleholder. It is **involuntary** if it can be imposed without the consent of the titleholder.

A **lien** is a claim to property to enforce payment of a debt.

The **voluntary** use of **real estate** as **security** for payment of a debt is discussed in Section IV of this outline, "Real Estate Finance."

A **mechanic's lien** is an example of an **involuntary** use of **real estate** to secure payment of a debt. State law specifies the requirements for creating and enforcing a **mechanic's lien**.

In general, a **mechanic's lien** is available to anyone who provides material or labor for an improvement to **real estate**, including design services. An architect, surveyor, contractor, carpenter, plumber, electrician, landscaper, and many other participants in the construction process are all entitled to a **mechanic's lien** if they have not been paid for their services or materials.

There are statutory time periods for:

- providing **notice** to the property owner of the right to file a **mechanic's lien**
- **filing** the **lien**
- **foreclosing** on the **lien** in the event that the underlying debt is not repaid

When a **mechanic's lien** is properly created, it takes priority over all other subsequent **liens**, except for **tax liens**.

Foreclosure (sale) of the real estate may be postponed by the property owner during a court hearing on the merits of the case, provided the property owner posts a **bond** to ensure payment to the claimant.

A **judgment** is a determination of a court that may impose an obligation for payment on a property owner.

A **lis pendens** is a document that can be recorded to warn anyone examining the title to the specified real property that the property is the subject of a legal action.

If a **judgment** is made in favor of a claimant, and the **judgment** is not satisfied (paid off) in timely fashion, a **writ of attachment** can be requested of the court. The **writ of attachment** specifies the property that is to be sold to satisfy the **judgment** and prevents any transfer of the property.

If further action is necessary, the court issues a **writ of execution** directing the sheriff to sell the specified property to satisfy the **judgment**.

An **easement** is a right to use land for a limited purpose, such as the right to travel over a shared driveway. An **easement** may be acquired by **deed** or as described below. (Don't confuse an **easement** with a **license**, which is a temporary permission to come onto someone's land. The holder of a concert ticket has a **license** to enter the concert hall for the performance.)

The **dominant tenement** is a parcel of land that benefits from an **easement** over an adjoining parcel. An **easement appurtenant** is one that *runs with the land* because it is transferred when title to the **dominant tenement** is transferred.

The **servient tenement** is the parcel of land that is burdened with the easement; that is, the parcel over which the owner of the **dominant tenement** is allowed to travel.

An **easement in gross** is a personal right and exists apart from ownership of any parcel of land. A **utility easement** is an example.

An **easement by implication of law** is created when an owner of land sells a parcel that would otherwise be landlocked except for a route over other adjoining land still owned by the seller of the landlocked parcel.

An **easement by necessity** is created when a parcel is landlocked and there is no method of ingress or egress other than over someone else's land. In that case, the most efficient route must be taken.

An **easement by prescription** is obtained in a manner similar to that of **adverse possession**. The right to be obtained is a right of use rather than ownership, but the use must be without the permission of the property owner and must continue for the statutory period. Property taxes need not be paid, however.

An **easement** can be terminated by **deed** from the owner of the **dominant tenement** to the owner of the **servient tenement**.

An **easement** is extinguished by **merger** if the same party acquires both the **dominant** and **servient tenement**.

An **encroachment** occurs when a property improvement extends onto an adjoining parcel of land.

An **encroachment** may be so slight as to be unnoticeable or unobjectionable, as with a fence line that deviates by only one or a few inches from the defined property boundary.

Though usually occurring at ground level, there may be an **encroachment** into an adjoining property owner's air space by the roofline or other part of a building.

The remedy may be removal of the **encroachment** or money damages. But if no legal action is taken (or permission granted) by the owner of the burdened land, the owner of the encroaching building or other improvement may acquire title to the encroached-upon space by **adverse possession**.

REVIEW QUESTIONS—LAND USE CONTROLS AND RESTRICTIONS

1. A change in an area's permitted land use from commercial to residential is an example of
a. upzoning
b. downzoning
c. spot zoning
d. special use

2. Frank is in court seeking to enforce his mechanic's lien on Nelson's new house. In order to protect his interest, Frank should record a
a. writ of attachment
b. writ of execution
c. judgment
d. lis pendens

3. Frank was successful in his action to enforce his mechanic's lien claim against Nelson for the work he did on Nelson's new house. In order to protect his interest, Frank should record the
a. writ of attachment.
b. writ of execution
c. judgment
d. lis pendens

4. The order that directs the sheriff to sell Nelson's house in order to pay Frank for the work he did on it is the
a. writ of attachment
b. writ of execution
c. judgment
d. lis pendens

5. Zoning is an exercise of the government's
  a. right of escheat
  b. power of condemnation
  c. right of eminent domain
  d. police power

6. A property use that is allowed to continue despite zoning that prohibits such use is an example of a
  a. conditional use
  b. variance
  c. nonconforming use
  d. special use

7. A benefit of home ownership is the
  a. depreciation deduction
  b. mortgage interest deduction
  c. at-risk rule
  d. residence replacement rollover rule

8. A principal residence is the home
  a. identified by the taxpayer
  b. in which the taxpayer lives at least 50 weeks of the year
  c. on which the taxpayer pays the highest property tax
  d. located where the taxpayer works and votes

9. Carl and Erika, a married couple, have sold Pine Hollow, their home for the last three years. The maximum amount of profit that they will be allowed to exclude from taxation is
  a. $0
  b. $250,000
  c. $500,000
  d. $1,000,000

10. The maximum amount that a single person may exclude from taxation on sale of the principal residence is
  a. $100,000
  b. $250,000
  c. $500,000
  d. $1,000,000

ANSWERS

1.	b	4.	b	7.	b	9.	c
2.	d	5.	d	8.	d	10.	b
3.	c	6.	c				

C. Transfer/Alienation of Title to Real Property

Alienation is the conveyance (transfer) of all or part of the ownership interests in **real property**.

1. Voluntary and Involuntary

A property transfer is **voluntary** when it is made with the consent of the owner.

A **deed** from the present owner is the principal method used to transfer title to **real property**.

A **will** can identify the recipient of property to be transferred on the death of the owner, who is said to die **testate**. To be valid, a **will** must comply with state law. In general:

- A **will** must be signed by the **testator** and witness(es).
- A **codicil** that contains an addition or change can be added to a **will** at a later date, but it must also be signed and witnessed.
- A new **will** cancels any prior **will**.
- A transfer of **personal property** by will is called a **bequest** or **legacy**.
- A transfer of **real estate** by will is called a **devise**.

Transfer of title to all or part of a parcel of **real estate** without the consent or action of the owner is considered **involuntary**. Remember the types of **involuntary** transfer by the acronym **INAFEE**.

Intestate succession is the manner of distribution of property by state law when property owner has died without leaving a valid **will** (died **intestate**).

Natural forces may diminish property boundaries or destroy improvements.

Avulsion is the sudden action of a body of water that washes away part of a parcel of land.

Erosion is the gradual wearing away of surface soil by action of rain or wind.

Adverse possession may be used to acquire title to property by someone who occupies it for the period required by state law. The occupancy must be **ONCHA**—open, notorious (not secretive), continuous, hostile (without permission), and adverse to the interests of the true owner. Most states also require that the adverse possessor pay all property taxes during the period of occupancy. In some states, paying taxes is not required but doing so shortens the required period of **adverse possession**.

The required period of possession may be accomplished by **tacking** (adding together) the occupancy periods of successive adverse possessors.

Some states require that an adverse possessor have **color of title**—a deed that appears on its face to be valid.

Clear title may be established by the adverse possessor by bringing a **quiet title action** in court.

Foreclosure is the loss of secured property following default on the underlying debt. Some states provide **homestead** protection that prohibits sale of a residence for the benefit of nonsecured creditors in certain circumstances.

Eminent domain is the right of the government (federal or state) to take private property for a public purpose.

Condemnation is the action taken by the government. If necessary, there is a trial in which the right to take the property is established and the **fair market value** of the property is determined in order to provide just compensation to the owner.

In an **inverse condemnation** action, a property owner brings suit for compensation against the government, claiming that a nearby public use has, in effect, diminished the right to the owner's full use of affected property.

Escheat is the state's right to ownership of property for which no heirs can be found.

2. Deeds, Warranties, and Defects in Title

A **deed** is a written document that conveys property from the **grantor** (owner) to the **grantee**. State law dictates the form that a **deed** must take. The requirements for a valid **deed** are as follows.

- It must be in writing.
- The **grantor(s)** must be of sound mind (legally capable).
- It must identify the parties, preferably by full name and marital status (single, married, widow, and so on).
- It must identify the property adequately, preferably by full legal description.
- It must contain a **granting clause** that contains the appropriate words ("I hereby grant and convey").
- It must be signed by the **grantor(s).**
- It must be delivered to the **grantee** *and* accepted by the **grantee**. A deed held by a third party until the **grantor** dies, for instance, will have no effect during the **grantor's** life and on the **grantor's** death will be invalid. Even after a valid delivery, the fact that the **deed** is in the hands of the **grantee** does not mean that it is accepted. Many charitable donations of real estate have ultimately been rejected because of the high cost of their maintenance or remediation (as in the case of contaminated property).

In most states, a **deed** must be **acknowledged** (signed before a notary public or other official) in order to be **recorded** (made a part of the public records of the county in which the property is located).

A **recorded deed** provides **constructive notice** (assumed notice) of the conveyance.

There are different types of **deeds**.

A **bargain and sale deed** states the consideration paid by the **grantee**. There may or may not be a warranty that the **grantor** actually has an interest in the described property.

A **gift deed** requires no consideration to be paid by the **grantee**.

A **grant deed** (using the words "I grant and convey" or similar) carries three implied promises of the **grantor**:

- The **grantor** has good title.
- There are no **encumbrances** other than those noted.
- The **grantor** will convey any after-acquired title (ownership interest received after the **grant deed** is delivered) to the **grantee**.

A **quitclaim deed** conveys whatever interest the **grantor** may own, but does not warrant that the **grantor** actually has any interest in the described property.

A **sheriff's deed** conveys title to property sold at public auction following a foreclosure or other court action.

In some circumstances, the former owner has a **right of redemption** for the stated period after a forced sale in which to reclaim the property on payment of amounts owed, including court costs.

A **tax deed** conveys title to property sold at public auction to cover unpaid taxes.

The former owner may have a **right of redemption** for a statutory period following the sale during which the property may be reclaimed on payment of amounts owed plus court costs.

A **trust deed (deed of trust)** is used to make real estate security for the repayment of a debt. The **trust deed** conveys title from the **trustor** (property owner) to the **trustee** to be held for the benefit of the named **beneficiary** (the lender).

In the event of default by the **trustor**, and in conformance with state law, the **trustee** will sell the property at public auction in order to repay the underlying debt. After the sale, a **trustee's deed** is used to convey title from the **trustee** to the purchaser.

In the event the debt is repaid, the **trustee** returns title to the **trustor** by a **reconveyance deed**.

A **general warranty deed** carries the **grantor's** express or implied assurances (called **warranties** or **covenants**).

The **covenant of seizin** and **right to convey** promises that the **grantor** is the rightful owner of the property as described in the **deed**.

The **covenant against encumbrances** promises that there is no **encumbrance (cloud on the title)** other than what may be stated in the document.

The **covenant of quiet enjoyment** promises that no one will object to the conveyance and that the **grantee's** possession will not be interfered with in future.

The **covenant of further assurance** promises that the **grantor** will take whatever action is necessary in future to correct any title defect.

The **covenant of warranty forever** promises that the **grantor** will defend the **grantee's** title (pay for legal expenses) in any dispute brought by a third party.

A **special warranty deed (limited warranty deed)** carries the **grantor's** assurances only as to the state of the title after the **grantor** acquired ownership.

REVIEW QUESTIONS—TRANSFER/ALIENATION OF TITLE TO REAL PROPERTY

1. A transfer of real estate by will is called a
a. bequest
b. legacy
c. devise
d. deed

2. The sudden loss of land by the action of a body of water is called
a. avulsion
b. erosion
c. reliction
d. reversion

3. Samuel died intestate. If no heirs can be located, Samuel's property will become the state's by the right of
a. escheat
b. condemnation
c. inverse condemnation
d. eminent domain

4. A legal action brought by a property owner, claiming that a public action has diminished her property value, is
a. escheat
b. condemnation
c. inverse condemnation
d. eminent domain

5. Able began a period of adverse possession on Baker's land. Able died, leaving the property to Charlie, who moved onto the land. Charlie's claim to the land may ultimately succeed because of
a. eminent domain
b. escheat
c. law of intestate succession
d. tacking

6. A grantor does not warrant any interest in the property described in a
a. grant deed
b. quitclaim deed
c. trust deed
d. special warranty deed

7. The grantor of title to real estate claims to be the rightful owner of the described property by the express or implied
a. covenant of seizin
b. covenant against encumbrances
c. covenant of quiet enjoyment
d. covenant of further assurances

8. The grantor of title to real estate promises not to interfere with the grantee's property rights by the express or implied
a. covenant of seizin
b. covenant against encumbrances
c. covenant of quiet enjoyment
d. covenant of further assurances

9. The grantor of title to real estate promises to correct any defect in the title conveyed that may arise in future by the express or implied
a. covenant of seizin
b. covenant against encumbrances
c. covenant of quiet enjoyment
d. covenant of further assurances

10. Another term for the special warranty deed is
a. standard warranty deed
b. limited warranty deed
c. extended coverage warranty deed
d. title commitment

ANSWERS

1.	c	4.	c	7.	a	9.	d
2.	a	5.	d	8.	c	10.	b
3.	a	6.	b				

II. ASSESSING AND EXPLAINING PROPERTY VALUATION AND THE APPRAISAL PROCESS

The **Financial Institutions Reform, Recovery, and Enforcement Act of 1989 (FIRREA)** requires most appraisals in **federally related transactions** to be performed by state licensed or certified appraisers. Examples of **federally related transactions** are those involving:

- a lender chartered or insured by an agency of the federal government
- a loan funded, insured, or guaranteed by any federal agency
- a loan sold to a federal or quasi-federal organization

The **Appraisal Foundation** is a nonprofit corporation established in 1987 to assist in setting minimum standards for:

- appraisals
- appraiser education and training

Licensing is required in valuations of one- to four-unit residential property unless the property is of unusual size or complexity. Licensed appraisers also can handle appraisals of nonresidential property and complex residential property valued at less than $250,000.

Certification is required for appraisal of property valued at more than $1 million or complex one- to four-unit residential property valued at more than $250,000.

A **certified residential appraiser** is allowed to appraise one- to four-unit properties of any size or complexity.

A **certified general appraiser** is allowed to appraise any type of real property within the appraiser's qualifications.

The **Appraisal Standards Board** of the **Appraisal Foundation** has produced the **Uniform Standards of Professional Appraisal Practice (USPAP)**. These standards set the minimum requirements for appraisals. Some useful definitions are:

Appraisal—the act or process of estimating value; an estimate of value.

Cash flow analysis—a study of the anticipated movement of cash into or out of an investment.

Departure provision—section of **USPAP** that allows the appraiser to perform an assignment that will vary from the specific guidelines set by **USPAP**. The guidelines are not intended to be binding, but any variations should be undertaken only after:

- appropriate determination by the appraiser that the deviation is warranted
- notification to the client that the appraisal will vary from recommended guidelines
- agreement of the client to the stated limitations on the work to be performed

Feasibility analysis—a study of the cost-benefit relationship of an economic endeavor.

Mass appraisal—the process of valuing a universe of properties as of a given date utilizing standard methodology, employing common data, and allowing for statistical testing.

Report—any communication, written or oral, of an appraisal, review, or consulting service that is transmitted to the client upon completion of an assignment. The types of report include the:

- **Self-contained appraisal report**—the most complete report, with a detailed presentation of the data collected and the valuation process.
- **Summary appraisal report**—a more concise presentation of the data and analysis.
- **Restricted appraisal report**—a report providing minimal data and analysis and limited to the use(s) specified.

Review—the act or process of critically studying a report prepared by another.

A. Principles, Types, and Estimates of Property Value

An appraisal will specify the type of value sought. The elements that establish value can be remembered by the word **DUST:**

Demand for the type of property

Utility (desirable use) the property offers

Scarcity of properties available

Transferability of the property to a new owner (lack of impediments to a sale)

Appraisals most often are used to estimate a property's **market value. Market value** can be defined as the **most probable price** that a buyer is willing to pay, and a seller is willing to accept, when:

- both parties are aware of the condition of the property
- neither party is acting under duress
- financing for the transaction is typical of what is available locally

Market value is an *estimate* of value only. The estimate is not necessarily what a property will actually sell for.

A property's **cost** is the expense to its owner of buying or improving it. A property's **sales price** is what someone else pays for it. The **sales price** frequently is less than the **cost** of the land and improvements. This happens when a property owner over-customizes or over-improves a property, failing to take into account the likely needs of a prospective purchaser.

Other values that may be sought include the following.

Assessed value—determination for property tax purposes.

Book value—depreciated cost basis used for accounting and tax purposes.

Insurance value—the maximum amount that an insurer will be willing to pay for an insured loss.

Investment value—what an investor is willing to pay for the right to receive the **cash flow** produced by the property.

Loan value—the maximum loan that can be secured by the property.

Salvage value—what the component parts of a building or other improvement will be worth following demolition or removal.

The principles of value that underlay the appraisal process include the following.

Anticipation—the expectation that property value will rise over time.

Assemblage (plottage)—bringing a group of adjoining parcels under the same ownership, which may make them more valuable for a particular purpose, such as construction of a residential or commercial development.

Change—forces to which all property is subject, including:
- **physical**—the action of the elements, which can occur gradually or in a brief period of time
- **political**—regulations that affect property use
- **economic**—employment level, business start-ups, expansions and failures, and other factors that influence the level of prosperity of a region
- **social**—demographic and other trends that affect the demand for property

Conformity—individual properties in a residential neighborhood tend to have a higher value when they are of similar architecture, design, age, and size. The same principle applies generally to commercial properties.

Competition—a result of increasing demand as well as a creator of increasing demand. For example, even though a regional mall may offer many stores selling similar products, it will benefit all store owners by bringing more shoppers to the area.

Highest and best use—the legally allowed property use that makes maximum physical use of a site and generates the highest income.

Law of decreasing returns—in effect when property improvements no longer bring a corresponding increase in property value.

Law of increasing returns—in effect as long as property improvements bring a corresponding increase in property value.

Progression—the benefit to a property of being located in an area of more desirable properties. The small, plain house on a street of mansions will benefit from proximity to them.

Regression—the detriment to a property of being located in a neighborhood of less desirable properties. The large, over-improved house on a street of small, plain houses will have a lower value than it would in a neighborhood of comparable houses.

Substitution—the principle underlying appraisal practice that the typical buyer will want to pay no more for a property than would be required to buy another, equivalent property. This principle, when applied to income-producing property, is called **opportunity cost**. An investor will want to pay no more for **real estate** than another investment offering the same likely risk and potential reward.

Theory of distribution—consideration of the contribution to value of each of the four factors of production—**land** (rent), **labor** (salaries), **capital** (interest), and **management** (profit). When these factors are in **balance**, property value will be at its highest.

B. Influences on Property Value

Environmental—any factor in the climate, terrain, or other natural feature of an area that affects value. Effects can be local or global, such as high pollution from fires following a drought.

Externalities—effect on value of factors outside a property. An example is any government action taken to increase housing affordability and thus purchases, such as the mortgage interest deduction for homeowners.

Life cycle—applies to an individual property as well as a neighborhood.

The initial period of **development (growth** or **integration)** becomes a period of **equilibrium** (when properties are at their highest and best use) followed by **decline (disintegration)**, when property values go down as maintenance requirements increase and are not met.

In areas that warrant the substantial expense of building renovation, there may then be a period of **revitalization**.

Supply and demand—as the number of properties available for sale goes up relative to the number of potential buyers, prices will fall. As the number of properties declines while the number of potential buyers remains the same or increases, prices will rise.

C. Approaches to Property Valuation and Investment Analysis

Following are the steps in the appraisal process.

- **State the problem.** The nature of the appraisal assignment must be clearly understood. The assignment may be to find the **market value** of the subject property. If so, that should be stated.
- **Determine the kinds and sources of data necessary**. The appraiser must ask:

  What are the characteristics of the subject property?
  What economic or other factors will play a role in determining property value?
  What approach(es) will be most appropriate in this appraisal and what kind of data will be necessary?

- **Determine the highest and best use of the site.**
- **Estimate the value of the site**.
- **Estimate the property's value by each of the appropriate approaches (market data, cost, and/or income)**.
- **Reconcile the different values reached by the different approaches to estimate the property's most probable market value**. This process is called **reconciliation** or **correlation.**
- **Report the estimate of value to the client.** There are several types of documents that may be prepared.

  The **narrative appraisal report** provides a lengthy discussion of the factors considered in the appraisal and the reasons for the conclusion of value.

  The **form report** is used most often for single-family residential appraisals. The **Uniform Residential Appraisal Report** (**URAR**) is required by various agencies and organizations. Computerized appraisal generation and delivery by modem is possible and is increasingly expected by banks and other lenders.

  The **self-contained report** defined by **USPAP** will be as complete as the **narrative appraisal report**. Use of either the **summary report** or **restricted report** defined by **USPAP** will require the consent of the client.

An appraiser uses one or more of three approaches to reach an estimate of value.

The **market data (sales comparison) approach** makes use of data on sales of nearby, comparable properties to estimate the likely value of the property being appraised (subject property). This process of **paired data (paired sales) analysis** is the best method for valuing most residential property.

The **sales price** of a comparable property (comp) is adjusted down to compensate for the market value of a desirable feature that is present in the comp but not the subject property.

The **sales price** of a comp is adjusted up to allow for desirable features that are present in the subject property and not the comp.

Example: The house at 1230 River Road is being appraised. A comparable house at 1142 River Road sold last month for $230,000. The comp has a detached garage and the subject property does not. The estimated value of the garage is $9,600, which is subtracted from the sales price of $230,000 to derive an adjusted sales price for the comp of $220,400. After analyzing the sales prices of five comps in this way, and comparing the resulting adjusted figures, the appraiser estimates the value of the subject property as $220,000.

Land, whether or not it has any improvements (buildings) is often valued separately by using the **market data approach.**

The **cost approach** uses the following formula: reproduction cost of improvements minus depreciation on improvements plus land value equals property value. If a property (such as an older building) has features that could not be economically duplicated today, the replacement cost of a functionally equivalent structure will be found.

Building reproduction cost typically is found by one of the following methods.

- **Square-foot method**—the current cost per square foot of comparable construction is multiplied by the number of square feet in the subject building.
- **Index method**—a factor representing the change over time in construction prices is applied to the original cost of the building.
- **Unit-in-place method**—current price of each component part (foundation, framing, roofing, and so on) is added.
- **Quantity survey method**—detailed cost breakdown of each element of construction, including direct (labor, materials) and indirect (permit, profit) costs.

Depreciation for appraisal purposes is not the same as that used for tax purposes. The appraiser estimates the actual effect on value of **depreciation** from all causes, termed **accrued depreciation**. **Depreciation** can be **curable** or **incurable**; it is **curable** if the defect is one that could be corrected at a reasonable expenditure of time and money. Causes of **deterioration** include:

Physical deterioration—the effect of the elements and ordinary wear-and-tear. Can be **curable** or **incurable.**

External obsolescence—economic, locational, or environmental influences that may have a negative effect on value. Generally **incurable.**

Functional obsolescence—features that are no longer considered desirable, in design, manner of construction, or layout. A house with four bedrooms and only one bathroom suffers from **functional obsolescence.** Usually **incurable** (that is, it usually cannot be remedied easily).

Depreciation can be estimated by using the:

- **age-life method (straight line method)**—the rate of annual depreciation is determined by dividing the number 1 by the number of years of the building should be useful for its intended purpose, then multiplying the resulting percentage by the building's **effective age**. For example, a building with a total estimated useful life of 50 years depreciates at the rate of $\frac{1}{50}$, or 2% per year. If the building is 20 years old, but has been well maintained, the appraiser may decide that it shows an effective age of only 15 years. Its accrued depreciation would then be calculated as 30% (2% × 15 years).

- **observed condition method**—each category of building component is separately considered and the effective appreciation of each is noted. For example, a roof that will need replacement within the next few years may be considered to have depreciated 90%. This approach requires that each component be separately valued and then separately depreciated.

The **income approach** is also called the **income capitalization approach**.

The simplest way to use property income to estimate market value is to use a **gross income multiplier (GIM)**.

Income produced by comparable properties is compared to their sales prices. A factor is created for each property by dividing the property's sales price by its annual gross income. Then, a factor is derived that can be applied to the **market rent** of the subject property—the rent the property would be capable of producing at today's going rates.

Example: Building A produces annual gross income of $20,000 and sold recently for $200,000. Building B produces annual gross of $32,000 and sold recently for $300,000. The **GIM** for Building A is $200,000 divided by $20,000, or 10. The **GIM** for Building B is $300,000 divided by $32,000, or 9.375. After analyzing several more properties, the appraiser concludes that a **GIM** of 10 is appropriate for the subject property. Applying that multiple to the subject property's annual market rent of $28,000, the appraiser reaches an estimate of value by this method of $280,000.

A **gross rent multiplier (GRM)** based on monthly market rent typically is used in the appraisal of a house.

A much more detailed income valuation can be made using **direct capitalization**.

Market rent—the property's potential income if available for a new occupant at current rates—is estimated by analysis of comparable properties.

Effective gross income is found by totaling income from all sources and subtracting an allowance for vacancy and collection losses.

Net operating income is found by subtracting **operating expenses** from **effective gross income**.

For appraisal purposes, **operating expenses** include **variable expenses** (such as salaries and utilities), **fixed expenses** (such as real estate taxes and insurance), and **reserves for replacement** (such as set-asides for a new roof and furnace) but not costs of financing, income tax payments, depreciation deductions, and capital improvements.

Net operating income is divided by the **capitalization rate** (the desired return on the investment) to arrive at an indication of **value** (what an investor would be willing to pay for the **income stream** generated by the property).

The **capitalization rate (cap rate)** is found by building its component parts. An investor expects to receive a profit (interest rate) on the capital invested, as well as to have the capital itself returned by the time the investment is unusable. For example: Mary wants to purchase an apartment building that has a **remaining economic life** of 40 years. She wants interest of 10% annually on her investment, as well as the return of the amount invested. The building's **net operating income** is $120,000 annually. Thus, each year the investment will have to have a **cap rate** of 10% plus $2\frac{1}{2}$% (100% divided by 40 years), or $12\frac{1}{2}$%. If we divide the income of $120,000 by the $12\frac{1}{2}$% **cap rate**, the value of the property to this investor can be estimated at $960,000.

The **break-even point** (the point at which a property begins to generate profit) is found by adding **operating expenses** and the **debt service (mortgage payment)** on the property, and then dividing that total by the property's **potential gross income**.

Example: A property has **operating expenses** of $50,000 per year and requires **debt service** of $120,000 for the same period. The property can be expected to produce **gross income** of $190,000 per year. The property's **break-even ratio** is the total of all expenses of property ownership divided by the total income the property is expected to produce.

In this example, the **break-even ratio** is created by adding $50,000 and $120,000 to arrive at $170,000, and then dividing $170,000 by $190,000. The resulting percentage is the **break-even point**—in this case, 89.5%.

This means that, when the property has an occupancy level of 89.5%, the expenses of owning it equal the income it generates. Below that point, the property has a **negative cash flow** (it costs more to own than it earns). Above that point, the property generates **profit**.

Discounted cash flow is another way to determine value by analyzing income projections. The income expected in each year of ownership is **discounted** to its present worth. The annual income figures are then added together to find the property's total present value.

REVIEW QUESTIONS—ASSESSING AND EXPLAINING PROPERTY VALUATION AND THE APPRAISAL PROCESS

1. A federally related transaction involving a 16-unit apartment building valued at over $1 million will require the services of a
   a. licensed appraiser
   b. certified general appraiser
   c. certified residential appraiser
   d. federally licensed appraiser

2. A study of the cost-benefit outcome of a project is a
   a. feasibility study
   b. marketing study
   c. demographic study
   d. cash-flow analysis

3. House X sold recently for $175,000 and has been rented at $1,075 monthly. What is the GRM for this property (rounded to the nearest whole number)?
   a. 6
   b. 11
   c. 163
   d. 175

4. The effect of the law of supply and demand is that, if the market for entry-level housing increases, and the number of homes available does not increase to meet that demand
   a. the cost of entry-level housing is unaffected
   b. the cost of entry-level housing goes up
   c. the cost of entry-level housing goes down
   d. the cost of all housing goes down

5. One of the oldest neighborhoods in Big City, very near the business area, is undergoing a number of changes as new owners remodel and update homes. This is an example of
   a. development
   b. equilibrium
   c. decline
   d. revitalization

6. A house of 3,000 square feet with a galley kitchen that is 9 feet by 12 feet is an example of
   a. physical deterioration
   b. locational obsolescence
   c. economic obsolescence
   d. functional obsolescence

7. Gary's house, a modest three-bedroom ranch, is in a neighborhood of mostly large two-story homes on double lots. Gary's house has a higher market value than it would have in a neighborhood of homes just like his. This is an example of
   a. progression
   b. regression
   c. conformity
   d. substitution

8. Depreciation for appraisal purposes is
   a. the same as depreciation for tax purposes
   b. based on a remaining useful life of 40 years
   c. computed as part of the cost approach
   d. found by use of a standard formula

9. The Uniform Standards of Professional Appraisal Practice are to be followed
   a. rigidly, with no deviation from any standard
   b. at the appraiser's convenience, as they are not mandatory
   c. whenever possible, unless in compliance with the Departure Provision
   d. by real estate agents as well as those with appraiser licensing or certification

10. The four elements of value are
    a. demand, utility, supply, transferability
    b. desire, utility, supply, title
    c. demand, utility, scarcity, transferability
    d. progression, regression, conformity, balance

11. The most complete type of appraisal report mentioned in the Uniform Standards of Professional Appraisal Practice is the
    a. form report
    b. self-contained report
    c. limited report
    d. restricted report

12. Potential income minus an allowance for vacancy and collection losses is
    a. effective gross income
    b. gross income multiplier
    c. net operating income
    d. contract rent

13. For appraisal purposes, all of the following expenses are taken into account EXCEPT
    a. salaries
    b. mortgage interest
    c. real estate taxes
    d. reserves for replacement

14. A detailed breakdown of every element of the construction process, including both direct and indirect costs, is made using the
    a. square foot method
    b. index method
    c. unit-in-place method
    d. quantity survey method

15. A capitalization rate takes into account the fact that an investor expects to receive
    a. interest and the return of the investment
    b. maximum profit and appreciation
    c. a risk-free investment
    d. a mortgage-free property at the end of its useful life

16. A broken window would ordinarily be considered an item of
    a. curable external obsolescence
    b. curable physical deterioration
    c. incurable functional obsolescence
    d. incurable economic obsolescence

17. The market value of a parcel of real estate will tend to be the price that is being paid for similar properties because of the principle of
   a. conformity
   b. contribution
   c. substitution
   d. anticipation

18. To the nearest percentage point, what is the break-even point of a property that has operating expenses of $25,000 per year, requires debt service of $120,000 per year, and produces gross annual income of $170,000?
   a. 71%
   b. 75%
   c. 81%
   d. 85%

19. The process by which a final estimate of market value is made is called
   a. correlation
   b. averaging
   c. depreciating
   d. capitalization

20. The four factors of production are
   a. political, economic, locational, and functional
   b. earth, sky, wind, and water
   c. book value, loan value, insurance value, and salvage value
   d. land, labor, capital, and management

ANSWERS

1. c	6. d	11. b	16. b
2. a	7. a	12. a	17. c
3. c	8. c	13. b	18. d
4. b	9. c	14. d	19. a
5. d	10. c	15. a	20. d

III. CONTRACTS, AGENCY RELATIONSHIPS WITH BUYERS AND SELLERS, AND FEDERAL REQUIREMENTS

In a **real estate agency** relationship, there will be many contracts and other documents used to initiate various steps in the transaction process and bring a transaction to a successful conclusion.

A. Contract Elements, Types

A **contract** is a promise between two or more legally competent parties to do or refrain from doing some legal act. In exchange for the promise, each party gives the other something of value, called **consideration. Consideration** can be money, goods, or services. In the case of a **real estate** transaction, it can also be another parcel of **real estate**, as in an exchange.

The elements of a **valid contract** are:

- **legal capacity** by both parties
- an **offer** by one party that is **accepted** by the other party
- a **lawful** activity or subject
- payment of **consideration**
- a written agreement, as the parties choose or as required by law

Persons with **legal incapacity** include a **minor** (usually, anyone under the age of 18) and a person who is judged **incompetent** by a court.

A **legal representative** (attorney, guardian, or estate executor or administrator) can act on behalf of a **minor**, a person who is judged **incompetent,** or the estate of a deceased individual.

An **offer** can be revoked before **acceptance**.

An **offer** is made when received.

According to the **mailbox rule**, an **offer** is **accepted** when it is given over for delivery, or when actual notice of **acceptance** is given.

Any change to the terms of an **offer** is a **counteroffer** and has the effect of rejecting the initial **offer** and making a new **offer**.

The **offer** and **acceptance** must both be made voluntarily (without coercion) and without misrepresentation.

Actual fraud can be an act or omission with the intent to deceive.

Constructive fraud is an act or omission made without intent to deceive, but with a disregard for the truth of the action or omission that goes beyond mere negligence.

The obligation of both parties to pay **consideration** as part of the agreement is termed **mutuality of contract**.

The **Statute of Frauds** that is part of state law requires most **contracts** dealing with **real estate** to be in writing. The only exception typically is for **leases** that will terminate *within one year of the date of agreement*. Even then, it is in the best interests of both **landlord** and **tenant** to have a written agreement.

If a written agreement is required, the **parol evidence rule** will prevent oral testimony as to the contract terms (from discussions in the period before the writing was signed) from being admitted in any future contract dispute.

A **contract** is **executory** when it has not yet been fully performed.

A **contract** is **executed** when all **contract** terms have been met and the transaction is completed. (The word **executed** can also refer to the **signing** of a **contract** or other document by the necessary parties.)

A **contract** is **express** when its terms are stated in a written or oral agreement.

A **contract** is **implied** when its terms are understood by the conduct of the parties (acting as if a contract exists).

A **bilateral contract** is one in which both parties promise to do or refrain from doing something.

A **real estate** sales contract is **bilateral** because both sides have an obligation to perform—the turning over of title to the property in exchange for money or other **consideration.**

A **unilateral contract** is one in which one party makes a promise and the other party does not promise, but can make the **contract** a binding agreement by taking some action.

A **voidable contract** is one that appears valid but is subject to cancellation by one of the parties.

If one of the parties is acting under a fraudulent misrepresentation by the other party, the misrepresentation will give the deceived party the option to perform the **contract** or to cancel it.

A **void contract** is one that fails to meet all of the requirements for a **valid contract**.

When all the terms of a **contract** have been fulfilled, the **contract** is **discharged**.

A **novation** is a redrafting of the agreement, substituting the new one for the old one.

A **rescission** is a mutual agreement to cancel the agreement.

A **reformation** is a mutually agreed change to some **contract** term to remove an ambiguity or to correct a mistake.

An **assignment** is a transfer of the **contract** rights and obligations of one of the parties to another person. Some **contracts**, by the nature of the obligation imposed, cannot be assigned. Examples are **contracts** offering a **personal service** and **contracts** for the sale of a particular parcel of **real estate**.

A **breach of contract** is a failure by one of the parties to fulfill the agreed-upon terms. Because every parcel of **real estate** is considered unique, if a seller refuses to complete a sale of **real estate**, the buyer may bring a **suit for specific performance** requesting that the court enforce the **contract**. The same remedy may be available in an **exchange, lease,** or **option** agreement, if the property owner refuses to complete the transaction.

B. Agency Employment Contracts, Listing and Buyer Agency Agreements, and Required Elements

In most states, a **real estate broker** is someone licensed to act as a **real estate agent**, representing one of the parties to a **real estate** transaction (sale, lease, exchange, and so on).

A **real estate salesperson** or **real estate sales associate** can be licensed to perform the activities of a **real estate agent**, but only under the supervision of an **employing broker**.

The **real estate salesperson** can be hired by the **real estate broker** as an **employee** or as an **independent contractor** for tax and some liability purposes.

The written agreement between **real estate broker** and **salesperson** will list the responsibilities and obligations of each.

(Other terms used to describe the role of the **real estate agent** appear in part D of this section of the outline.)

The **listing agreement** is the contract that establishes the **agency relationship** of property owner and **real estate agent**. The object of the **listing agreement** usually is the sale of the described property.

An **open listing (nonexclusive listing)** results in payment of a commission to the **listing agent** only if that person is the **procuring cause** of the sale. If the property is sold by any other agent, the **listing agent** is not entitled to a commission.

An **exclusive agency listing** prevents the property owner from listing the property with any other agent. This means that, in the event of sale, the **listing agent** will receive at least part of the commission even if another agent was the **procuring cause** of the sale. The owner is still entitled to sell the property to someone without the agent's assistance and avoid paying any commission.

An **exclusive authorization and right-to-sell listing** provides the greatest protection to the **listing agent**, who will be paid the commission no matter who sells the property.

An **option listing** gives the **listing agent** the right to purchase the property. This kind of agreement requires disclosure by the **listing agent** of the details of any planned subsequent transaction, including the agent's profit, and agreement of the property owner.

A **net listing** offers the property owner a guaranteed sales price, with the **listing agent** taking any part of the purchase price over that amount. This arrangement is frowned upon as it opens the agent to charges of misrepresentation of the true value of the property at the time the agreement is initiated.

The **listing agreement** will include:

- identity of the parties
- description of the property
- object of the agreement (property sale, exchange, lease)
- term (length of time) of the agreement
- definition of the agent's role and list of agent's obligations
- statement of compensation to which agent is entitled on fulfilling the agent's obligations
- **safety clause** stipulating that agent's compensation is to paid if a sale is transacted with a buyer who was introduced to the property owner by the agent, within a stated period after termination of the **listing agreement**
- authorization for the agent to use the local **multiple listing system**, Internet listing system or other marketing forum
- authorization for the use of subagents
- authorization to hold key or to use **lock box** or other means of property entry in owner's absence
- authorization to receive deposit or other funds on behalf of the buyer, and stipulation as to how those funds are to be handled
- **arbitration** or **mediation** provision to be enforced in the event of a **contract** dispute
- statement of compliance with all applicable **fair housing** laws
- any other provision required by law
- **signature** of seller and **signature** of agent

A **listing agreement** can be **terminated** by:

expiration of the time period specified in the agreement

performance—a successful transaction or other fulfillment by the agent of the terms of the agreement

mutual consent of the parties (**rescission**)

revocation by property owner, who may be liable for damages (advertising expenses, and so on) to the agent

abandonment (inaction) by the agent

death or **adjudicated incompetency** of either owner or agent

destruction of the property

A **buyer agency (buyer broker) agreement** will establish the terms under which the agent will find property that meets the buyer's specifications and work to complete the transaction. The **buyer agent's** compensation must be specified. It can be a flat fee, an hourly rate, or (most often) a percentage of the purchase price to be paid at the time of **closing**.

The **real estate listing agent** owes the property owner the duties of a **fiduciary**. The agent must act in the owner's best interests.

The **buyer's agent** owes the same responsibilities to the buyer.

The agent's duties include:

> **Loyalty**
> **Good faith** (fair dealing with all parties to the transaction)
> **Honesty**
> **Full disclosure** of material facts concerning the transaction
> **Due diligence** in carrying out the terms of the agreement
> Avoidance of any **conflict of interest**

The agent may not make any **secret profit** as a result of the transaction.

The property owner owes the **real estate agent** and buyer honesty and disclosure of material facts concerning the property. The buyer also must pay the agreed-upon compensation on completion of a transaction.

C. Purchase/Sales Contracts and Contingencies

The **real estate sales contract** begins as an **offer** from buyer to seller and typically will include the following.

- Identity of all parties to the transaction.
- Full legal description of the **real estate** as well as a listing of any **personal property** to be included.
- **Sales price**, including amount of down payment and indication of how the remainder of the price will be paid at closing.
- **Financing contingency** giving details of the type of financing the buyer hopes to obtain and stipulating a deadline for release of the **contingency**.
- Statement that the transaction is **contingent** on a sale of other property of the buyer. (The seller will want a deadline for release of the **contingency**, particularly if a **noncontingent offer** is made while the transaction is pending.)
- **Escrow agent** for the transaction and by whom the fee for this service will be paid.
- **Property inspections** to be made and by whom, including deadlines for the inspections as well as the appropriate notifications to buyer and/or seller. (The seller will want a limit on expenditures for any pest control treatment or necessary repairs.)
- List of applicable categories of **disclosure** required by state and federal law, which may include location in a flood, earthquake or other zone, and the presence of hazardous materials, such as **lead-based paint**.
- **Arbitration** or **mediation of disputes**.
- **Liquidated damages** in the event of breach by one of the parties.
- Compliance with the federal **Foreign Investment in Real Property Tax Act (FIRPTA)**.

- Statement of compliance with all applicable **fair housing** laws.
- Compliance with any other state or federal law not already mentioned.
- **Final walk-through** by the buyer to insure that the property has been adequately maintained before **closing**.
- Statement of who will bear the risk of loss in the event of property damage or destruction between the time the **contract** is signed and the transaction is **closed**.
- Statement of the **agency representation** and commission owed.
- Statement of how long the offer will be left open.
- **Signature** of the buyer(s) and space for **signature** of the seller(s).
- Statement that the **agent** has received the indicated deposit, and **signature** of the **agent**.

An **offer** will **expire (end)** if it is not accepted by the deadline specified in its terms. If no deadline is specified, a reasonable time period will be implied.

The purchase **offer** can be **terminated** by:

- **revocation** of the **offeror (buyer)** before **acceptance**
- **rejection** by the **offeree (seller)**
- **counteroffer** by the **offeree**

If it is accepted by the seller, a **real estate sales contract** can be **terminated** by:

- completion of the terms of the **contract**
- mutual consent of the parties (**rescission**)
- **breach** by one of the parties
- **destruction** of the property

D. General Agency Relationships and Fiduciary Responsibilities

In many states, the role of the **real estate agent** is being examined and, in some cases, redefined. Following are some of the ways in which the function and responsibilities of those in the **real estate** sales profession are currently viewed.

Agent—the traditional definition is that the **agent** represents the interests of another person, called the **principal**, in dealings with third persons. In a **real estate** sales transaction, the traditional view is that:

- the **real estate agent** of the seller (**listing agent**) acts as a **fiduciary** to the seller
- in the absence of an agreement to the contrary, any **cooperating agent** who brings a buyer to the transaction acts as a **subagent** of the **listing agent** and thus is also owed the duties of a **fiduciary** to the seller

Dual agent—an agent who represents both parties to a transaction. A **dual agent** is always required to have the consent of both parties before acting in that capacity. In some states this type of representation is prohibited. State law will define the relationship of two sales associates working under the same broker and separately representing both parties to a transaction. They may or may not be considered **dual agents**.

Subagency—the traditional view that a **cooperating agent (selling agent)** is the **subagent** of the **listing agent** and thus represents the seller. Some states retain this presumption, some states have eliminated it and other states consider the **cooperating agent** to be the agent of the buyer.

Transaction broker—a nonagent role for the **real estate** practitioner created by law in some states. As defined, the **transaction broker** assists the parties to a **real estate** transaction but is neither agent nor advocate for any party. Nevertheless, the statutory duties of the **transaction broker** are comparable to those of the agent, such as the obligation to exercise reasonable care and skill, to account for all monies held, and to make the numerous disclosures required by both state and federal law.

For **in-house transactions** in which both listing and sale are generated by the same firm, some states allow the **transaction broker** to appoint separate **designated agents** to represent seller and buyer exclusively.

E. Property Conditions and Disclosures

Disclosures to be made by property owners as well as **real estate agents** to each other as well as the other parties to a transaction increase in number every year. The listing below is not meant to be inclusive but to serve as a guide to the type of information that must now be revealed.

The recent move toward **disclosures** began with **property condition disclosures**. Many states now require the following.

Seller disclosure—completion of a form summarizing various property features, noting their condition and also pointing out other known defects in the property. The form is presented to a prospective buyer at the stipulated time, usually within a number of days after an offer to purchase is accepted.

Agent disclosure—an experienced **real estate agent** will be aware of many property defects that even the owner may not have noticed. In some states, the agent is now legally obliged to conduct a property inspection and indicate the results of that inspection to seller and buyer. In other states, courts are increasingly recognizing this responsibility.

In many states, the relationship of any agent involved in a **real estate** transaction must be discussed with and consented to by the applicable parties.

An **agency relationship disclosure form** will list the forms of representation possible and allow the party and agent to indicate their desired form of representation.

The state may require signed documentation confirming the relationships of all agents in the transaction to be a part of the **closing** process.

Concerns over the presence of toxic materials in home building materials and furnishings, as well as geological and other conditions affecting property use, have led to numerous **disclosures** required by both federal and state law.

- Location in a **special flood hazard area**—required by the **Federal Emergency Management Agency (FEMA)**.
- Location in a **fire hazard area**—may be required by state law.
- Location in a **geologic, seismic, or earthquake hazard area**—may be required by state law.
- Possible presence of **lead-based paint**—in a transaction involving residential property constructed prior to 1978, the buyer and seller are required to sign a **lead-based paint disclosure form**. There is a similar requirement for rental units. In addition, the buyer/tenant is to be provided a copy of a booklet prepared by the Environmental Protection Agency (EPA) entitled "Protect Your Family from Lead in Your Home," available from state environmental agencies or regional EPA offices.

F. Procedures and Laws Governing Real Estate Activities

Federal fair housing laws are supplemented in many states by state regulations. If the two cover the same subject, the more stringent will apply. In other words, it is not possible to ignore a federal provision if the state law is more lenient, and vice versa. All of the laws mentioned next are federal.

The **Civil Rights Act of 1866** prohibits discrimination on the basis of race in the sale, lease, or other transfer of **real** or **personal property**.

The **Civil Rights Act of 1866** has no exceptions. It applies to individual home sellers as well as to **agencies** that represent sellers and/or buyers. The law was upheld by the U.S. Supreme Court in **Jones v. Mayer** (1968).

The **Civil Rights Act of 1964** prohibited housing discrimination in transactions involving loans insured by the **Federal Housing Administration (FHA)** or guaranteed by the **Department of Veterans Affairs (VA)**.

The **Federal Fair Housing Act (Title VIII of the Civil Rights Act of 1968)** broadened the prohibitions against discrimination in housing to include national origin, race, color, and religion.

With the **Housing and Community Development Act of 1974**, Congress increased the range of protected classes to include sex (gender). The law was amended in 1988 to include protection against discrimination on the basis of handicap and familial status. There is to be no discrimination against:

- children (those under age 18)
- families with children (whether headed by a parent or guardian)
- persons who are in the process of obtaining custody of a child
- pregnant women

Families with children may not be offered only certain units in an apartment complex and must be allowed full access to facilities unless rules limiting or prohibiting access to children are nondiscriminatory.

An exception to compliance with the law regarding familial status is allowed if either one of the following is true:

- the housing is intended for and solely occupied by persons age **62 or older**
- at least 80 percent of units are occupied by at least one person age **55 or older**

A complaint alleging a violation of the law may be filed with **HUD** or the office of the **U.S. Attorney General**.

A **real estate agent** must display an **Equal Housing Opportunity** poster in the agent's principal place of business.

The **Americans with Disabilities Act of 1990 (ADA)** prohibits discrimination by employers and businesses against persons with a physical and/or mental disability.

An individual with a disability is defined as:

- anyone with a physical or mental impairment that substantially limits a major life activity (walking, seeing, hearing, speaking, performing manual tasks, caring for one's self, and so on)
- anyone who has had such an impairment
- anyone who is perceived as having such an impairment

ADA covers both temporary and chronic conditions, including vision loss, mental retardation, AIDS, HIV infection, cancer, heart disease, and others.

ADA does not cover such categories as homosexuality or bisexuality, gender identity disorders, compulsive gambling, kleptomania, pyromania, and psychoactive substance use disorders stemming from illegal use of drugs.

An employer must make **reasonable accommodation** for known impairments, but the employer is not expected to accept an **undue hardship** to the business in doing so.

Businesses involved in **public facilities, goods, and services** must make those sites, products, or services accessible to customers with disabilities. *Responsibility for compliance rests with any person who owns, leases, leases to, or operates a place of public accommodation.*

Architectural barriers must be removed whenever **readily achievable** (possible without undue expense or difficulty).

Company policies, practices, or standards must be changed to provide equal access to persons with disabilities, provided the changes are reasonable and would not:

- impose an **undue burden** on the business
- make a **fundamental change** in the goods and services of the business
- cause a **direct threat to the health or safety of others**

The only exceptions to the rules regarding public accommodations are for religious organizations and exclusive private membership clubs.

The **Sherman Antitrust Act** prohibits certain business practices that could place unfair restrictions on free competition in the marketplace. Prohibitions against **restraint of trade** that directly effect the **real estate** industry include the following.

- There can be no **price fixing**. **Agency** fees or commissions are always subject to negotiation between **principal** and **agent** before an **agency relationship** is established. **Agents** for different companies are not allowed to agree to predetermined fees, or to agree on a range of fees for specific services. Even discussion of such matters could subject **agents** to civil and criminal penalties that could result in fines and/or imprisonment.
- **Agencies** cannot agree to provide service only in a designated geographic area.
- **Agencies** cannot agree to **boycott** certain companies or other **agencies**.
- **Agents** are not to form exclusive organizations (such as property listing services) that arbitrarily prevent nonmembers from gaining access to sales and marketing information. Membership criteria must be designed so as not to unfairly exclude otherwise qualified **agents** from participation.

REVIEW QUESTIONS—CONTRACTS, AGENCY RELATIONSHIPS WITH BUYERS AND SELLERS, AND FEDERAL REQUIREMENTS

1. A contract in which both parties promise to do something is
   a. unilateral
   b. bilateral
   c. conforming
   d. nonconforming

2. A contract that appears valid but is subject to cancellation by one of the parties is
   a. implied
   b. void
   c. voidable
   d. revoked

3. Mutual agreement to cancel a contract is called
   a. rescission
   b. reformation
   c. novation
   d. breach

4. Failure of one of the parties to perform a requirement of a contract is a
   a. rescission
   b. reformation
   c. novation
   d. breach

5. Rita makes an offer on Sam's condominium. Sam considers the offer, then sends his acceptance to Rita by overnight delivery service, scheduled to arrive in Rita's office before the offer expires. The next day, before the acceptance arrives, Rita sends a fax to Sam canceling her offer. At this point
   a. there is a valid offer contingent on Sam's ratification of Rita's counteroffer
   b. there is no agreement because Rita beat the deadline for acceptance
   c. there is a valid offer and acceptance because the mailbox rule applies
   d. Sam is entitled to a suit for specific performance

6. The law that requires that certain contracts be written is the
   a. Parol Evidence Rule
   b. Statute of Frauds
   c. Law of Intestate Succession
   d. Law of Contracts

7. Melanie is applying for work as a truck driver. Because Melanie suffers from narcolepsy, she can fall asleep without warning at any time of the day. Which of the following is true?

a. In her job interview, Melanie need not mention her condition because she is protected under ADA.

b. Her condition prevents Melanie from qualifying for work as a truck driver.

c. Melanie's prospective employer is not allowed to ask her if she is able to drive a truck.

d. If she is hired, Melanie's employer must accommodate her condition by providing her with a specially equipped truck that will stop the motor when she begins to doze off.

8. Sam is habitually late for work and is fired. He sues his former employer, claiming that his tardiness is the result of his diagnosed depression and that, under ADA, he should be allowed to keep his job. The court is likely to find that

a. Sam's tardiness was not sufficient reason to fire him.

b. Sam's employer should accommodate Sam's special needs.

c. Sam's tardiness makes him unqualified for the job.

d. Because Sam is undergoing treatment, he should be sympathized with and not turned away.

9. An agent can insure that the seller doesn't wait until the listing agreement expires, then enter into a transaction with someone contacted by the agent during the listing period, by means of a(n)

a. estoppel certificate

b. safety clause

c. arbitration clause

d. mediation clause

10. Tom signed a six-month listing agreement with real estate agent Vicky. After four months, Tom decided to take his house off the market and notified Vicky that he was canceling the agreement. At this point

a. Tom has no further obligation to Vicky.

b. Vicky can sue Tom for specific performance.

c. Tom's attempt to cancel the agreement is ineffective because the listing term hasn't expired.

d. Vicky can sue Tom for damages.

11. The Civil Rights Act of 1866

a. applies only to investment properties

b. provides no exception for owner-occupied property

c. has no exceptions

d. prohibits discrimination on the basis of race and religion

12. An agent who represents both parties in a transaction is a
   a. cooperating agent
   b. subagent
   c. dual agent
   d. nonagent

13. Methods of settling a contract dispute without going to court include arbitration and
   a. mediation
   b. remediation
   c. conciliation
   d. specific performance

14. Federal fair housing laws protect against discrimination based on all of the following EXCEPT
   a. religion
   b. sex
   c. handicap
   d. income

15. An act or omission with intent to deceive is
   a. actual fraud
   b. constructive fraud
   c. criminal negligence
   d. mere negligence

16. A counteroffer has the effect of
   a. holding the original offer in reserve before its expiration date
   b. rejecting the original offer
   c. giving the offeree an option
   d. leaving the original offer open to an assignee

17. The Loyal Order of Hummingbirds, a private club, has no wheelchair access to its meeting hall. This is
   a. acceptable under ADA
   b. a situation that will subject the club to a heavy fine
   c. acceptable until a prospective member in a wheelchair tries to enter the hall
   d. criminal conduct

18. William, who is 15 years old, went through a model home and signed a purchase contract with the agent on duty. This agreement is
   a. valid
   b. void
   c. voidable by William
   d. enforceable by William

19. A contract that has not yet been fully performed is
   a. executory
   b. executed
   c. voidable
   d. discharged

20. In an exclusive agency listing, in order to receive a commission the agent must be the
   a. first to sign a listing agreement with the seller
   b. first to appear at closing
   c. procuring cause of the sale
   d. person identified on the For Sale sign

ANSWERS

1.	b	6.	b	11.	a	16.	b
2.	c	7.	b	12.	c	17.	a
3.	a	8.	c	13.	a	18.	b
4.	d	9.	b	14.	d	19.	a
5.	c	10.	d	15.	a	20.	c

IV. FINANCING THE TRANSACTION AND SETTLEMENT

The most important factor in the increasing number of homeowners in this country is the availability of **long-term financing** at **reasonable cost**.

A. Financing Components

The components of the typical transaction can be put together efficiently with the **Computerized Loan Origination (CLO)** available at many real estate or mortgage brokerage offices.

1. Financing Instruments

Separate documents establish the fact that:

- a debt is owed (the **note**)
- the debt is **secured** by **real estate** (the **mortgage** or **deed of trust**)

The **promissory note** from borrower to lender records the amount borrowed and the terms of payment.

When it meets legal requirements, a **promissory note** can qualify as a **negotiable instrument**. This means that it is as acceptable as a check to a future buyer. To qualify as a **negotiable instrument**, a **promissory note** must be an unconditional promise to pay a specified amount of money (sum certain) at a definite time or on demand (whenever payment is requested), to the identified party or the bearer of the **note**, and be signed by the maker of the **note**.

Someone who buys a **negotiable instrument** will be termed a **holder in due course (HDC)** if that party takes the **note** as an innocent transferee who has no business relationship with the party from whom the document was received. A **holder in due course** is one who takes a **negotiable instrument**:

- for value
- in good faith
- without notice that it has been dishonored, is overdue, or that there is any defense against it or claim to it by anyone else

Principal is the amount borrowed. **Interest** is the cost of a loan.

With a **straight note**, only the **interest** is paid over the term of the loan, with the entire **principal** due at the end of the loan term.

With an **installment note**, periodic payments of **principal** are made in addition to payments of **interest**.

When an **installment note** is **amortized**, payments (usually monthly) are equal and include both **interest** for the payment period and some of the **principal** owed. In the beginning of the loan term, payments are mostly for **interest**. As more of the **principal** is repaid, **interest** decreases. By the last required payment, the entire amount owed has been repaid.

With a **fixed-rate note**, the **interest rate** is the same over the life of the loan.

With an **adjustable-rate note**, the **interest rate** will vary over the life of the loan depending on changes in an agreed-upon **index**.

The **margin** is a rate added to the **index** rate.

There will be a **cap** (maximum amount of increase) in the allowable rate increase for a stated period. There may also be a **cap** on the amount of the payment.

The required payment may increase or decrease as the **interest rate** rises or falls. If the **interest rate** goes up but payments do not, there may be **negative amortization**—that is, if the payment isn't sufficient to cover both **interest** and some of the **principal** owed, the amount of the debt will be increased.

A **balloon payment**, typically the final payment, is one that is at least twice the amount of any other payment. A short-term loan (say, three to five years) may have payments calculated on a 30-year loan term, but with the entire remaining balance due in the final **balloon payment**. This device can be useful when:

- the borrower knows that the period of occupancy will be temporary and the property will be sold before the **balloon payment** is due
- **interest rates** are high and the borrower expects to **refinance** at a lower rate in a few years

Purchase money mortgage is a term used to describe:

- any loan that is used to finance the purchase of **real estate**
- a credit from the seller for all or part of the purchase price (**seller financing**)

A **blanket mortgage** is one in which more than one parcel of **real estate** is used as collateral.

An **open end mortgage** allows the borrower to increase the amount of the loan up to a predetermined limit.

A **reverse annuity mortgage** is one in which the borrower *receives* monthly payments from the lender in exchange for a lien on the specified property. The borrower must own the home outright or have substantial **equity** in it. Interest on the amount borrowed is added to the amount owed. The loan will be paid off when the property is sold, the borrower dies or the loan period ends. This type of loan is used to allow elderly homeowners to benefit from the **equity** in their property without having to sell it.

The term **mortgage** is used to refer to any instrument used to **secure real estate** in payment for a debt. In practice, the **security instrument** may take the form of either a **mortgage** or **deed of trust**. There are separate requirements for the creation and enforcement of the two forms of **security instrument**.

The requirements for a **mortgage** are established by state law.

The **mortgage** creates a **security interest** in the identified **real estate**.

The **mortgagor** is the property owner and the **mortgagee** is the lender.

A **mortgage** must be **recorded** in the county clerk's or recorder's office in the county where the property is located in order to establish its priority.

A **first mortgage (senior mortgage)** takes priority over every other **encumbrance** filed after it.

A **second mortgage (junior mortgage)** will be satisfied on default of the borrower only after the **first mortgage** debt has been repaid. There may even be a **third mortgage** or more. Each successive lien takes a weaker position.

On repayment of the loan by the borrower, the **mortgagee** executes a **release of mortgage (satisfaction of mortgage** or **discharge of mortgage)** that can be recorded to indicate that the lien is no longer effective.

On a **default** by the borrower, the traditional remedy for the holder of a **mortgage** was **strict foreclosure** in which the property could be sold immediately. The modern requirement is a **foreclosure** action that must be brought in court following statutory notice and other requirements.

If the **security instrument** is a **mortgage with power of sale**, the property may be sold without a court hearing, but state law still applies and there will be specific notice and other requirements. Even after the property has been sold at public auction, there may be a **right of redemption** for the borrower within the statutory time period.

What if the **sales price** at the **foreclosure sale** does not cover the amount owed on the loan?

Some states allow the lender to obtain a **deficiency judgment** against the borrower. This means that other assets can be claimed by the lender to satisfy the remaining indebtedness.

Other states provide homeowners with **anti-deficiency** protection in the event that the proceeds of sale on loan default do not cover the amount owed. This means that the lender has no recourse except the **real estate**.

The **contract for deed (land contract)** is a form of seller financing in which title to the **real estate** is not given to the purchaser for a year or longer following the date of sale.

This type of financing is often used in rural areas for purchases of vacant or improved land when the buyer doesn't want to deal with a conventional lender or when the buyer has difficulty finding or qualifying for any other form of financing.

Because of former abuses of the **contract for deed** in which defaulting buyers lost all equity in the property, even when payments had been made for a substantial period of time, the states have strict rules regarding the formation and enforcement of this type of instrument.

Even when **legal title** is still held by the seller, a defaulting buyer may be found to have **equitable title** to the property and thus be entitled to an ownership (**equity**) interest in the proceeds of any **foreclosure sale**.

In many states, the **deed of trust** is the preferred **security instrument** because in the event of default in payment of the underlying debt it does not require a **judicial (court-ordered) foreclosure**.

The **deed of trust** executed at the time the loan is originated actually transfers title from the **trustor** (owner) to a **trustee** (third party), who holds title in trust for the benefit of the **beneficiary** (lender).

The **trustor** remains in possession of the **real estate** while the **deed of trust** is in effect.

If the underlying debt is repaid, the **trustee** is notified by the **beneficiary** and title is returned to the **trustor** by means of a **reconveyance deed** from the **trustee**.

In the event of a **default** in payment of the underlying **note** by the **trustor**, the **trustee** is authorized to sell the property to pay off the remaining debt. When the property is sold a **trustee's deed** is given to the new owner.

As with a **mortgage foreclosure**, state law will dictate whether or not the lender is entitled to a **deficiency judgment** in the event that the proceeds of a forced sale do not cover the amount owed.

In the case of an owner-occupied dwelling, there may be **anti-deficiency** protection, which means that the lender will not be able to sue the borrower for any indebtedness remaining after the sale of the **secured real estate**.

2. Sources

Conventional loans are those made without any form of government-backed **insurance** or **guarantee**. The lender looks to the borrower and the security (the property) for assurance that the loan will be repaid by the borrower (or by forced sale of the property). **Conventional loans** are made by a variety of lenders.

Savings and loan associations (S&Ls) at one time made the majority of residential loans. Today, the number of **S&Ls** has been so greatly reduced that their share of the home mortgage market has dropped dramatically.

- Most transactions that would formerly have been handled by an **S&L** are now handled by **commercial banks**.
- **S&L** deposits are now insured by the **Federal Deposit Insurance Corporation (FDIC)**, the agency that has always insured **bank** deposits.

Commercial banks are currently the dominant residential lenders.

- They may be chartered by either the state or federal government, although the trend is toward federally chartered institutions.
- Their deposits are insured by **FDIC**.

Mutual savings banks are owned by their depositors.

Mortgage companies (mortgage bankers) make loans that are then resold.

- The **mortgage company** typically will retain the **loan servicing** function.
- **Mortgage bankers** must be distinguished from **mortgage brokers**, who serve as middlemen between borrowers and lenders.

   Licensing requirements for **mortgage brokers** vary from state to state. Some states allow licensed **real estate agents** to act as **mortgage brokers**, while other states require separate licensing.

Life insurance companies have become important sources of investment funds for commercial and development properties. They are subject to regulation of the state in which they are authorized to do business.

Credit unions may make home loans, particularly **home equity loans**, to their members.

The **primary mortgage market** consists of lenders who deal directly with borrowers to make loans. The lender may or may not retain ownership of the loan after it is made.

A loan will be kept in the lender's **portfolio** if it is not sold to someone else.

Even when a lender sells a loan, it may retain the **loan servicing** function. The borrower's payments will continue to be made to the originating lender, who will charge a fee to the new owner in exchange for carrying out the collection function.

The right to payment on most residential loans is resold by the lender who originated the loan as part of what is termed the **secondary mortgage market**. When funds are returned to lenders, more loans can be made, interest rates kept down and property ownership encouraged.

The originating lender may retain the **loan servicing** function.

Loans that are sold often are treated as **mortgage-backed securities (MBS)**. This means that they are sold individually or bundled into **pools (blocks)** for sale to an organization such as those listed below.

The **Federal National Mortgage Association (FNMA or Fannie Mae)** is the largest purchaser of all types of home loans. **FNMA** was originally a government agency, then was converted to entirely private ownership and control. **FNMA** sells **stock, bonds,** and **notes**.

The **Government National Mortgage Association (GNMA or Ginnie Mae)**, originally part of **FNMA** but now a division of **HUD**, is a major purchaser of government-backed mortgage loans. **GNMA** sells **pass-through certificates** that pass on mortgage payments of principal and interest (less **servicing** fees).

The **Federal Home Loan Mortgage Corporation** (**FHLMC or Freddie Mac**) is a subsidiary of the **Federal Home Loan Bank** and primarily purchases **conventional loans**. **FHLMC** sells **bonds** and **participation certificates**.

The **Federal Agricultural Mortgage Corporation (FAMC or Farmer Mac)** is a part of the **Farm Credit System** and helps expand the availability of funds for agricultural lending. **FAMC** serves as a co-insurer (with the original lender) of pools of such loans.

Privately formed companies also buy **pools** of loans; ownership of the loans ultimately belongs to holders of the company's **stock**.

When **real estate** is used as **security** for a loan, it is said to be **hypothecated** (it remains in possession of the borrower). When **personal property** is used as **security**, it is **pledged** (it is held by the lender until the debt is repaid).

The states differ in how they view the effect of using **real estate** to secure a loan.

In **lien theory** states, a debt **secured** by **real estate** is considered to impose a **lien** on the **real estate**.

In **title theory** states, a debt **secured** by **real estate** is considered to constructively transfer title (termed **bare legal title**, because it does not include the right of possession) to the lender.

A **bridge loan** (**gap loan** or **swing loan**) is a temporary, short-term, relatively high-interest loan used before a longer-term loan can be made. Typical use of a **bridge loan** is to finance construction of improvements.

A **hard money loan** is one that is made by a private (noninstitutional) lender, usually for a term of no more than three to five years, and usually at an **interest rate** that is higher than the market rate. It is usually a **second** or **junior** loan, meaning that it is subject to the **security interest** of another lender.

Concerns about **seller financing (creative financing)** can arise at any time, but particularly when the supply of properties available is much greater than the number of qualified purchasers.

There may be specific state laws providing protection to homebuyers when **seller financing** is used, including preparation of a **seller financing disclosure form**, to be given to the buyer by the seller, in which all terms and conditions of the financing are stated.

Federal tax requirements for creation and reporting of an **installment sale** may apply.

In some states, **mortgage loan foreclosure consultants** are strictly regulated to prevent consumer fraud.

3. Types of Loans

Conventional loans are those available from one of the lending institutions mentioned above, such as S&Ls and **commercial banks**.

Conventional loans typically are **conforming loans**. This means that they meet the borrower and property qualification requirements of **FNMA** and are eligible for resale on the secondary market.

Borrowers who make a down payment of less than 20% of the sales price may be required to purchase **private mortgage insurance (PMI)**. The insurance premium usually is a monthly charge added to the loan payment. It can be eliminated (with the lender's approval) when the borrower's **equity** in the home is at least 20% of the home's value.

Government-backed loans are those that receive some form of assurance of payment from an agency of the government.

FHA-insured loans are those that the **Federal Housing Administration (FHA)** insures.

- A one-time insurance payment is made by the purchaser at the time of the closing of the sale.
- **FHA** sets maximum loan amounts that it will lend depending on the state or county in which the property is located.
- The borrower of an **FHA-insured loan** must meet the financial qualifications set by **FHA**.
- The property being purchased must be appraised by a **licensed appraiser**.
- The **interest rate** to be paid is subject to negotiation between borrower and lender.
- **Discount points** can be charged and can be paid by either buyer or seller, as they agree.

- Because of the **FHA** insurance, a lower-than-usual down payment can be made.
- **FHA** no longer allows any part of the borrower's down payment to be made with borrowed funds.
- **FHA-insured loans** made before December 15, 1989 are assumable without buyer qualification. **FHA-insured loans** made on or after December 15, 1989, require the new owner to qualify before the loan can be assumed.

VA-guaranteed loans carry the assurance of the **Department of Veteran Affairs (VA)** that the lender will be protected in the event of default by the borrower.

- **VA-guaranteed loans** are available to veterans of the U.S. Armed Forces or a U.S. ally who meet certain minimum service requirements.
- The **certificate of eligibility** is the VA's statement that the veteran is eligible for the loan guarantee program.
- The **VA** sets the loan amount that it will guarantee. The property purchased may be a greater amount, but the guarantee will not increase.
- The **interest rate** is subject to negotiation between the veteran and lender.
- The property must be appraised and the VA will then issue a **certificate of reasonable value (CRV)** based on that estimate.
- The funding fee depends on the category of veteran and the amount of the down payment, which can range from zero to 10% or more.
- The property may be sold and the VA loan assumed, but the veteran must receive a written **release of liability** from the VA to be relieved of obligation in the event of a future foreclosure.
- The veteran's entitlement can be reused on a subsequent home purchase, although the amount of the entitlement will be reduced if there has been an assumption of a prior loan guarantee.

The **Farmer's Home Administration (FmHA)** actually makes loans to purchase rural property. It also guarantees loans made by private lenders.

There may also be **state-sponsored programs** (such as programs benefiting low-income home buyers, veterans, or rural property buyers) that make loans or provide loan insurance or guarantees.

4. Financing Concepts and Terminology

Some of the contract provisions that may be included in a **promissory note** are listed below.

The **due-on-sale clause (alienation clause)** allows the lender to demand full payment of the remaining indebtedness if the property is sold.

An **impound account (escrow account)** may require the borrower to make regular payments to be used to pay property taxes and insurance.

Late charges will be incurred if the borrower is late in making a payment.

A **prepayment penalty** provides an additional charge if the borrower makes any early loan payment. Most current loans allow prepayment of all or part of the loan balance without penalty.

A **release** clause will benefit the borrower if the loan is secured by more than one lot or parcel. As the loan is paid off, the lender will **release** its **security interest** as to individual lots or parcels.

B. Lender Requirements and Obligations

Borrower qualification is the first concern of the lender.

Compliance with **FNMA's** qualification requirements is vital for a **conforming loan** that will be sold on the **secondary mortgage market**.

The **Uniform Residential Loan Application** form was created by **FNMA** and **FHLMC** to provide consistent data for evaluating the credit-worthiness of prospective borrowers.

Factors to be considered in the loan application process include income, employment history, and other financial obligations.

The **loan-to-value ratio** (percent of the property's value that will be borrowed) will determine whether or not **private mortgage insurance** (**PMI**) will be required.

The **Equal Credit Opportunity Act**, a federal law that has been in effect since 1975, prohibits discrimination in the granting of credit on the basis of age, sex, race, color, marital status, religion, or national origin.

Factors that can legitimately be considered are the applicant's income, stability of the source of the income, total assets and liabilities, and credit rating (past history of use of credit).

A loan applicant must be notified of the lending decision within three days.

Property qualification is also a concern of the lender. Is there sufficient **collateral** to back the loan value sought? This question is answered by an **appraisal** of the property that will be the **security** for the loan.

The **Truth in Lending Act** was passed by Congress and became effective on July 1, 1969. It was amended in 1982 and 1991. **Regulation Z** of the **Federal Reserve Board** carries out the provisions of the **Truth in Lending Act**.

The law applies to **creditors (lenders)** involved in either one of the following:

- more than 25 consumer credit transactions per year
- more than five transactions per year with a dwelling used as **security**

Unless they involve property that is the borrower's principal residence, the law exempts:

- loans for business, commercial or agricultural uses
- loans for more than $25,000

In general, loans to acquire owner-occupied rental property of two of more units, or to improve or maintain owner-occupied rental property of four or more units, fall within the business purpose classification and thus are exempt from the law. All loans on rental properties that are not owner-occupied also are exempt from the law.

The required **truth in lending disclosures** must be made in a **disclosure statement** that highlights certain information in a box or by using boldface type, a different type style or a different background color. The **disclosure statement** must be presented to the borrower before the transaction is completed. Information to be disclosed includes (in addition to other items) the:

- **amount financed**
- **finance charge**
- **annual percentage rate (APR)**
- **total amount** that will be paid over the life of the loan
- **prepayment penalties**, if any
- **late-payment charges**

There is no **right to rescind** when a loan involving a consumer's **principal dwelling** is one of the following:

- a **purchase money first mortgage** or **trust deed** loan
- a **refinancing** of a **purchase money** loan in which no new funds are received by the borrower

On all other transactions involving a consumer's **principal dwelling**, the consumer has a **three-day right** to rescind the transaction. **This right may be waived in writing by the consumer if compliance would delay funding**. Unless waived in writing, the rescission period ends at midnight of the third business day following the *latest* to occur of:

- delivery of the **truth-in-lending disclosure statement**
- delivery of notice of the **right to rescind**
- completion of the transaction

Advertisements for covered loans must give the **APR** and provide other payment terms.

C. SETTLEMENT PROCEDURES

The culmination of the **real estate** sale is the **closing**, when the purchase funds are transferred to the seller and title is transferred to the buyer. A **closing** is also used for an exchange, refinancing, lease, or other type of transaction.

In some states, it is the practice for all of the parties to be present for the final execution and transfer of documents.

In other states, or when necessitated by difficulties in getting all of the parties together at the same time, the parties will execute documents at separate times for transfer at a stipulated future date.

Settlement procedures vary from state to state, as well as within individual states. The details of the **closing** may be handled by on of the following:

- an **attorney** for either the buyer or seller
- a **real estate agent** (as allowed by state law)
- an agent of a **title company**
- an agent of an **escrow company**

Throughout the rest of this section we refer to the **escrow agent**, who can be any of the above individuals.

An **escrow** is the possession by a third party of the funds and documents necessary to **close** a transaction.

Although the **escrow agent** should be a disinterested third party, state law may allow a **real estate agent** or **attorney** for one of the parties to act as the **escrow**.

The **escrow agent** is not allowed to carry out the terms of the underlying agreement (such as the transfer of funds and title in a sales transaction) until all of the contract requirements of all of the parties have been met.

The legal requirements for a valid **escrow** include:

- a **binding contract** between the parties to the transaction
- **conditional delivery** of the necessary documentation and funds

The **escrow agent** is given **escrow instructions** (including a copy of the transaction agreement) to know what is to be accomplished.

- When all of the requirements (conditions) of the transaction have been met, the transaction can be **closed.**
- If there is any disagreement of the parties or other impediment to a **closing**, the **escrow agent** may bring a legal action called **interpleader** against the parties to the transaction.

The **escrow agent** asks the court to determine the action that should be taken.

It is not a function of the **escrow agent** to settle disputes or determine the rights of the parties, but merely to carry out the **escrow instructions**.

D. Settlement Documents

The **escrow agent** makes sure that all of the necessary paperwork is on hand before the **closing** takes place. The number of documents will vary depending on the nature of the transaction, state and federal law, and unique requirements of the agreement. A sales transaction may include the following.

- Escrow instructions
- Transaction agreement
- Agency relationship disclosure statement
- Preliminary title report (discussed below)
- Property condition disclosure statement
- Other disclosures required by federal or state law, such as the **Lead Paint Disclosure Statement**
- Property inspection reports—pest control (termite), well, septic system, and other reports
- Statement from each of the present lenders
  Demand for payoff will indicate the remaining balance to be paid at closing in order to satisfy the seller's debt and release the lender's **lien** on the property
  Beneficiary statement indicating loan balance as of the date of **closing**, if the buyer will assume the existing loan
- Paperwork from new lender(s)
  If the source of funds for the purchase is a new lender, there will be a new **note** and **security instrument** to be executed before the funds will be released at **closing**.
- Fire, flood, and other insurance policies
  The new lender will require necessary insurance in order to protect the value of the collateral.
- Property tax and assessment statements
  Depending on the date of the transaction and the date that taxes and assessments are due:
    the seller may owe taxes that will be a debit to the seller and credit to the buyer *or*
    the seller may have prepaid taxes, in which case there will be a credit to the seller and debit to the buyer.
- **Settlement statement** prepared by the **escrow agent** indicating how funds are to be disbursed
- Other documents required by the sales contract, such as **notes** and **deeds**

The primary responsibility of the property seller is to convey **marketable title**—an ownership interest that a well-informed buyer can reasonably be expected to accept and that the buyer can transfer in a future transaction. There are several ways in which the buyer is assured of acceptable title.

A **certificate of title** is an opinion of the condition of the title as of the date specified.

An **abstract of title** accompanied by an **attorney's opinion of title** is a cumbersome method. It provides a complete history of the recorded documents affecting the title, called the **chain of title**. Although once used for all types of transactions, today it is used mainly for large commercial properties.

Title insurance has become the most common method of protecting the buyer.

A **title company** issues a **preliminary title report** or **title commitment.** It will indicate the present condition of the title based on examination of the documents maintained by the **title company** as well as any exceptions to the coverage that the **title company** is willing to provide.

The **title company** will defend the purchaser's title in a title dispute covered by the policy.

If an insured claim is paid out by the **title company** to the policy holder, the **title company** will be entitled by its right of **subrogation** to take the policy holder's place in seeking compensation from the party who caused the loss.

Standard policy of title insurance does not protect purchaser against defects actually known to the purchaser, claims of parties in possession of the property, defects in the survey or any other item noted as an exception. It does protect against monetary loss due to:

- forged documents
- mistakes in the public records
- incapacity of the **grantor(s)**
- improperly delivered **deeds**

Extended coverage policy of title insurance does not protect against defects actually known to the purchaser or any other item noted as an exception. It does protect against monetary loss stemming from any of the four categories noted above for the **standard policy**, plus:

- defects revealed by examination of the property survey
- encumbrances or unrecorded claims that would be revealed by an inspection of the property
- unrecorded liens that were not known to the purchaser

The **Real Estate Settlement and Procedures Act (RESPA)** is the federal law that requires disclosures by lenders in **federally related** transactions involving the sale or transfer of a dwelling of one to four units. As noted earlier in the section on financing, a **federally related** transaction is a loan that involves *one* of the following:

- a federally chartered or insured lender
- a loan made with funds or with insurance or guarantees of any federal agency
- a loan to be sold on the secondary mortgage market

The **Real Estate Settlement Procedures Act (RESPA)** took effect on June 30, 1976; amendments were effective on December 2, 1992.

- The lender must provide the borrower with a copy of the **Special Information Booklet** prepared by **HUD.**
- The lender must provide the borrower with a **good-faith estimate of closing costs**.
- If there are two or more loan applicants, the information needs to be given to only one of them.

- A **Uniform Settlement Statement** (see below) must be given to the borrower and seller by at least the day of **closing**.

  The borrower can waive the right to receive the **Uniform Settlement Statement** by the day of **closing**.

  If the borrower does so, the information must be delivered as soon as possible after the **closing**.

- The lender is not allowed to charge a fee for preparing any of the documents required by **RESPA** or by the **Truth-in-Lending Act**.

- Fees, kickbacks, or other such payments to persons who do not actually provide loan services are strictly prohibited.

- A fee may be charged by someone who counsels a borrower or who assists the buyer in entering information into a **Computerized Loan Origination (CLO)** program.

E. Financing and Other Closing Costs

Many expenses reported at **closing** are paid by either buyer or seller, some are shared equally, and others are divided on a proportionate basis (**prorated**). All expenses are subject to negotiation of the parties.

Local custom or the agreement of the parties can dictate the party responsible for expenses incurred on the day of **closing**.

Because the transfer of funds and title occurs on the day of **closing**, the buyer usually is responsible for that day's expenses.

By the same reasoning, the buyer is also entitled to receive whatever benefit may accrue from ownership that day, such as the day's income if the property is a rental unit.

The **Uniform Settlement Statement** will indicate how each expense is to be apportioned.

- Unless the parties have agreed otherwise, the **escrow agent** will follow local custom as to the number of days in a year or month.

- For ease of calculation, a **year of 360 days** and **standard month of 30 days** may be assumed.

- *Unless you are instructed otherwise, you should use a 360-day year and 30-day month for proration problems in the licensing examination.*

  Example: Property taxes on Graycastle are due on July 1 for the year beginning on that day and ending on the following June 30. Harold has paid $1,800 in property taxes for the current tax year on the home he is selling. The sale is to close on September 15. What amount will be credited to Harold and what amount will be debited to Jane, the buyer, for property taxes?

  Jane is responsible for paying property taxes on $9\frac{1}{2}$ months of ownership (half of the month of September and the months from October through the following June). At the rate of $150 per month ($1,800 divided by 12 months), Jane must pay $1,425 ($150 multiplied by 9.5).

See Chapter 5, the Real Estate Math Review, for more help with proration problems.

REVIEW QUESTIONS—FINANCING THE TRANSACTION AND SETTLEMENT

1. The documents necessary to use real estate as collateral for a debt are the
   a. mortgage and deed of trust
   b. installment note and deed of reconveyance
   c. note and security instrument
   d. loan application and deed

2. A loan that provides equal payments that include interest owed as well as some principal in each payment is
   a. an installment note
   b. a balloon note
   c. insured
   d. amortized

3. The Truth in Lending Act is implemented by
   a. the Equal Credit Opportunity Act
   b. Regulation Z
   c. local real estate associations
   d. Fannie Mae

4. On loans to which the Truth in Lending Act applies, there will be a
   a. 48-hour right of rescission
   b. three-day right of rescission
   c. five-day right of rescission
   d. 30-day right of rescission

5. Fannie Mae and Ginnie Mae are part of the
   a. first mortgage market
   b. second mortgage market
   c. primary mortgage market
   d. secondary mortgage market

6. All of the following terms are used to describe a temporary short-term loan at a high interest rate EXCEPT
   a. bridge loan
   b. swing loan
   c. gap loan
   d. bank loan

7. An investor interested in receiving payments of principal and interest from a pool of mortgages may purchase
   a. certificates of reasonable value
   b. computerized loan originations
   c. pass-through certificates
   d. certificates of eligibility

8. The security instrument in which title to the secured property is transferred to a third party is called a
   a. mortgage
   b. deed of trust
   c. pledge
   d. release of mortgage

9. The mortgagor is the
   a. borrower
   b. lender
   c. mortgage banker
   d. mortgage broker

10. The provision that allows the lender to demand full payment of the remaining loan balance when the secured property is sold is the
   a. deficiency clause
   b. mortgage with power of sale
   c. alienation clause
   d. contract for deed

11. A real estate transaction is finalized
   a. on the date an escrow agent is selected
   b. at the closing
   c. on receipt of the good faith estimate
   d. on the day title is recorded

12. The lender gives the borrower the
   a. escrow instructions
   b. preliminary title report
   c. good-faith estimate of closing costs
   d. Uniform Settlement Statement

13. A valid escrow requires
   a. a binding contract and conditional delivery of documents and funds
   b. a listing agreement and contract of sale
   c. a preliminary title report and structural pest control report
   d. escrow instructions and a good faith estimate of closing costs

14. The Uniform Settlement Statement indicates
   a. how title is to be taken by the buyer
   b. the condition of the property title
   c. how funds are to be disbursed
   d. the conditions of sale

15. If the buyer is not assuming the seller's loan, the seller's lender will issue a
   a. beneficiary statement
   b. right of redemption
   c. reverse mortgage
   d. demand for payoff

16. If there is a dispute between the parties, an escrow agent can bring a legal action called
   a. a partition action
   b. interpleader
   c. suit to quiet title
   d. release of lien

17. If a loan involves a dwelling of one to four units, the lender must give the borrower a
   a. Special Information Booklet prepared by HUD
   b. Uniform Settlement Statement
   c. preliminary title report
   d. Computerized Loan Origination application

18. If no other information is provided, the escrow agent usually will assume a
   a. 365-day year and actual number of days in each month
   b. 360-day year and 30-day month
   c. 360-day year and actual number of days in each month
   d. 365-day year and 30-day month

19. Lou is selling his house to Moe. There has been a delay in the paperwork, but Moe has already delivered cash for the purchase to the escrow agent. Lou assures the escrow agent that the documentation is on its way and asks to have part of the funds released to him. The escrow agent

a. should comply with the request because the funds are available

b. should comply with the request but make Lou sign a receipt for the money

c. cannot release any funds until all the conditions of the escrow have been met

d. cannot release any funds because this is not an installment contract

20. Nell is selling her house to Olive. Property taxes of $3,650 for the calendar year are due on March 1 and the closing is set for February 17. What is the required proration using the actual number of calendar days?

a. Nell is credited $480 and Olive is debited $470.

b. Nell is debited $480 and Olive is credited $480.

c. Nell is credited $470 and Olive is debited $470.

d. Nell is debited $470 and Olive is credited $470.

ANSWERS

1. c	6. d	11. b	16. b
2. d	7. c	12. c	17. a
3. b	8. b	13. a	18. b
4. b	9. a	14. c	19. c
5. d	10. c	15. d	20. d

V. Leases, Rents, and Property Management

A. Types and Elements of Leasehold Estates, Leases, Lease Clauses, and Rental Agreements

The **lessor** (owner of the **leased fee**) permits the **lessee** (holder of the **leasehold** interest) to use the property for the period and under the terms specified in the **lease**.

An **estate for years** (**tenancy for years**) is a **leasehold** with a specified termination date.

A **periodic tenancy** specifies a lease term that is renewed automatically.

A **tenancy at will** has no definite termination date and may be terminated by notice of either **lessor** or **lessee.**

A **tenant (tenancy) at sufferance** is created when a tenant's possession of leased premises is no longer lawful. If the **lessor** accepts rent from the **holdover tenant**, a new lease term is created; otherwise, the **tenant at sufferance** may be evicted.

In most states, the **Statute of Frauds** requires that a **lease** that will terminate *one year or more from the date of its signing* must be in writing.

State law governs many of the provisions in a **residential lease,** also referred to as a **rental agreement.** The typical **lease** will include the following.

- identity of the **lessor** (**landlord**) and **lessee** (**tenant**)
- description of the premises to be leased
- **term** of the lease, including beginning and ending times
- **rent** to be paid and when payment is due—a grace period is usually specified, as well as the **penalty for late payment** due after that time
- obligations of the **lessor**, which will include compliance with an express or implied **warranty of habitability**
- obligations of the **lessee**, which will include payment of the stated **rent** as well as maintenance of the premises
- **arbitration** or **mediation clause** to be enforced in the event of a dispute in the terms of the agreement
- **signature** of the **lessee** and **signature** of the **lessor** (or agent)

Other terms are used to refer to **commercial leases.**

With a **percentage lease (participation lease)**, the **lessee** pays part of the proceeds from operation of the business on the leased premises. The terms of the **percentage lease** may indicate a base rent as well as a **percentage** that varies depending on the level of income achieved, usually per month.

With a **gross lease**, the **lessor** is responsible for paying all expenses of property ownership, such as property taxes.

With a **net lease**, the **lessee** pays rent but is also responsible for paying some or all of the expenses of ownership. Under the terms of a **triple net (net, net, net) lease**, the **lessee** pays all of the expenses of ownership, in addition to the required **rent**.

A **sale and leaseback** may be used by a company that wants the advantages of receiving the proceeds of a sale, while still retaining the use of the property under the terms of a **lease**.

B. Lessor and Lessee Rights, Responsibilities, and Recourse

The **lessor** (property owner, or **landlord**) of residential property will have certain obligations imposed by the terms of the **lease**, or by state law. The **lessor's** obligations can also be termed the **lessee's** (**tenant's**) rights.

There will be a limitation on the amount and disposition of any **security deposit**.

The **landlord** will not be allowed to interfere with the **tenant's quiet enjoyment** of the leased property. This means that the **landlord** must recognize the **tenant's right of possession** of the property. The **landlord** cannot enter the property without the **tenant's** permission, except:

- in an emergency
- to provide services or make repairs that were agreed to, or that are necessary to maintain the habitability of the property (after giving reasonable notice to the **tenant**)
- to show the property to prospective **tenants**, purchasers or service providers (after giving reasonable notice to the **tenant**)
- if the **tenant** has abandoned or surrendered the property
- if a court orders or permits an entry

An express or implied **warranty of habitability** will require the **landlord** to keep the property in livable condition. This includes:

- structural integrity of the building, including weatherproofing of roof, walls, windows, and doors
- provision of utilities, including water (hot and cold), sewage disposal, electricity and gas or other source of heat, all in compliance with state and local laws
- maintenance and cleanup of common areas, such as halls and stairways
- federally mandated disclosure of the possible presence of lead-based paint in new and renewal leases on property built before 1978
- other state and local requirements, such as installation of a smoke detector, dead-bolt lock or sprinkler system

If the **landlord** fails to meet these obligations, the **tenant** can usually do one of the following:

- withhold rent up to a certain amount
- abandon the property with no further obligation under the lease

In turn, the **tenant** is obliged to:

- keep the leased property clean and dispose of trash in a sanitary manner
- use fixtures and appliances in a safe and sanitary manner, and in the rooms designated for their use
- not damage, deface or otherwise destroy the property, or permit anyone else to do so

If the **tenant** fails to meet these obligations, the **landlord** can evict the **tenant** by one of the methods described later in this section of the outline.

In a **commercial lease**, the **lessor** owes fewer obligations to the lessee unless specifically set out in the **lease**. In general, the **commercial tenant** will bear a greater responsibility for maintenance and repair of the property.

Liability for injuries on leased property may belong to **lessor, lessee,** or both, depending on state law.

In general, if a dangerous condition or property defect is due to the negligence or deliberate act of the **lessee**, the **lessee** will be liable to an injured party.

If the property is residential, and the **lessor** was negligent (the **lessor** knew or should have known of the condition or defect, and did not act to correct it), the **lessor** will be liable, as well.

Termination of a **lease** can be accomplished in the following ways.

- notice as required by the **lease** agreement or by law
- destruction or condemnation of the leased property
- breach of an express or implied condition or covenant
- illegal use of the property
- in a **tenancy at will** or **tenancy at sufferance**, death of the **lessor** or **lessee**
- **merger** of property rights, which occurs if the **lessor** acquires the **leasehold** interest, or the **lessee** acquires the **leased fee**
- bankruptcy of the **lessee**, at the court's discretion, or, in some cases, bankruptcy of the **lessor**

Unlawful detainer is the legal action that is the usual method of ousting a defaulting **lessee**. Statutory notice and other procedural requirements must be met by the **lessor**.

An **action in ejectment** is a holdover from the common law, and is a lengthier court proceeding used by a **lessor** to evict a **lessee**.

C. Management Contracts and Obligations of Parties

Management of investment (rental) property increasingly is placed in the hands of professional **property managers**. State law may require that the **property manager** (individual or firm) have a **real estate** or other license.

In some states, residential rental property of a minimum number of units must have a **resident property manager** on the premises. In that case, the **property manager** usually is the **employee** of the property owner.

The agreement between the property owner and **property manager** usually will provide the following.

- identity of the parties
- description of the property to be managed
- **term** (time period) during which the agreement will be in effect, including specified beginning and ending times
- responsibilities of the **agent**, including **agent's** authority to arrange for building maintenance, market vacancies, execute leases, serve notice on tenants when necessary, and hire an attorney for necessary legal services
- financial limitation on **agent's** authority to order repairs, materials, or services on behalf of the property owner
- **agent's** authority to use rents and other property income to make authorized payments
- responsibilities of the property owner, including payment of specified compensation to the **agent**
- **signature** of owner and **signature** of **agent**

REVIEW QUESTIONS—LEASES, RENTS, AND PROPERTY MANAGEMENT

1. The person who rents an apartment is the
 a. lessor
 b. lessee
 c. mortgagor
 d. mortgagee

2. Another term for landlord is
 a. lessor
 b. lessee
 c. offeror
 d. offeree

3. The law that requires that certain leases be written is the
 a. Parol Evidence Rule
 b. Statute of Limitations
 c. Best Evidence Rule
 d. Statute of Frauds

4. The lessor pays all expenses of property ownership under a
 a. gross lease
 b. net lease
 c. triple net lease
 d. percentage lease

5. Liquidity may be the primary concern of a company that makes use of a
 a. gross lease
 b. net lease
 c. sale and leaseback
 d. arbitration clause

6. A tenant who is no longer lawfully in possession of leased premises has created a
 a. periodic tenancy
 b. tenancy at will
 c. tenancy at sufferance
 d. tenancy for years

LEARNINGEXPRESS

20 Academy Street, P.O. Box 7100, Norwalk, CT 06852-9879

FREE!

TEN TIPS TO PASSING ANY TEST

To provide you with the test prep and career information you need, we would appreciate your help. Please answer the following questions and return this postage paid survey. As our Thank You, we will send you our "Ten Tips To Passing Any Test"—surefire ways to score your best on classroom and/or job-related exams.

Name: _____

Address: _____

_____

Age: _____   Sex: ☐ Male   ☐ Female

Highest Level of School Completed: ☐ High School
                                      ☐ College

1) I am currently:
   A student—Year/level: _____
   Employed—Job title: _____
   Other—Please explain: _____

2) Title of the book this card came from:
   _____

3) Jobs/careers of interest to me are:
   1. _____
   2. _____
   3. _____

4) If you are a student, did your guidance/career counselor provide you with job information/materials? ____
   Name & Location of School: _____

   _____

   _____

5) What newspapers and/or magazines do you subscribe to or read regularly? _____

   _____

6) Do you own a computer? _____
   Do you have Internet access? _____
   How often do you go on-line? _____

7) The last time you visited a bookstore, did you make
   a purchase? _____
   Have you purchased career-related materials from
   bookstores? _____

8) Which radio stations do you listen to regularly
   (please give call letters and city name)?

   _____

   _____

9) Do you subscribe to Cable TV? _____

10) How did you hear about this LearningExpress book?
    An ad?_____
    An order form in the back of another book? _____
    A recommendation?_____
    A bookstore?_____
    Other? _____

11) Please check (or rank) your reasons for purchasing
    this book:

Content _____   Price _____

Recommended to you ____   Only book available ____

LearningExpress books are also available in the test prep/study guide section of your local bookstore.

LearningExpress

The new leader in test preparation and career guidance!

LearningExpress is an affiliate of Random House, Inc.

7. The landlord's responsibility to provide acceptable living conditions when leasing residential property is called the
a. covenant of quiet enjoyment
b. warranty of habitability
c. covenant of seizin
d. special warranty

8. The most efficient legal way to take back leased premises from a defaulting tenant is
a. a partition action
b. an action in ejectment
c. suit to quiet title
d. unlawful detainer

9. A lease may be terminated by all of the following EXCEPT
a. illegal use of the property
b. a lock-out
c. condemnation of the leased property
d. the death of the lessee

10. A property management agreement will usually stipulate
a. age of the lessor
b. Federal Reserve requirements
c. responsibilities of the agent
d. agent's right to a mechanic's lien

ANSWERS

1.	b	**4.**	a	**7.**	b	**9.**	b
2.	a	**5.**	c	**8.**	d	**10.**	c
3.	d	**6.**	c				

C·H·A·P·T·E·R
REAL ESTATE MATH REVIEW
5

CHAPTER SUMMARY

Contrary to rumor, there is no "mathematics" on the real estate exam. All you will find there is basic arithmetic, which can be acquired by study of the elementary principles, some good common sense, and a whole lot of "cool."

Learning three basic types of problems can give you 90% of the arithmetic on the real estate licensing test:

- Percentages
- Measurement
- Miscellaneous Real Estate Concepts

These three types of problems are easy to learn. There are many roads to follow in solving arithmetic problems, but in this chapter you will find the simplest, most mechanical method employed. If you already know how to do the problem, go ahead and do it your way. There is only one correct answer, and it doesn't matter how you get it.

TYPES OF PROBLEMS

Problems can (and should) be classified into types:

- Percentages
  Commissions
  Interest
  Taxes
  Insurance
  Capitalization
- Measurement
  Distance and area
- Miscellaneous Real Estate Concepts
  Appraisal
  Financing
  Proration

FOOLPROOF STRATEGIES FOR MATH QUESTIONS

ANSWER EVERY QUESTION

You should answer every single question, even if you haven't a clue to the answer. There is no penalty for a wrong answer, and the lowest odds are 4–1. If one or two answers are ridiculous on the face of it, the odds may be even higher on selecting the correct one.

CALCULATORS

A word about calculators: *Bring one*, and an extra battery. (Check with the testing agency about the type of calculator that is allowed.) It will speed up your whole test. These problems are not really hard but they are sometimes long. What is needed for long problems is perseverance and a good calculator.

Pitfalls

However, be aware that there are some pitfalls to the use of a calculator. First of all, you should know how to use it and how to read it. It should have a floating decimal and a large clear display of at least eight digits, but it should not be too complicated. A "constant" for multiplying and dividing is handy, but square roots are not needed. The simpler, the better.

Practice working arithmetic problems with the calculator you plan to use on the examination.

Hot Tip

Don't expect all the answers to come out exactly. They may not, owing to differences in calculators. Carry to three decimal places throughout and round off at the end. If the third number is 5 or more, round the second number up; if not, drop it. (Example: .056 = .06; .051 = .05)

Do One Step at a Time

The main pitfall with calculators is the temptation to work the problem all the way through to the end on the calculator. At this point, if none of the answers provided is correct, there is no way to know *where* the mistake lies. You then whip through the whole problem a second time. Still not finding the answer, you continue to wildly punch around on the calculator, hoping to find an answer something like the correct one.

Label

Resist the temptation to "save time" by doing all your work on your calculator. Use your scratch paper. Label each step before you work it out, and put the steps down on paper as you do them, in the order in which you do them. Labeling problems is always a good practice, and in the long run it will save you time.

Prove

Proving or checking your problems is always good practice, and it's usually quite simple. If you're taking your test on computer, you will need to do your proof before you move on to the next problem. If you're working on paper, you can use any time you have left after taking the exam to check your work.

BASIC ARITHMETIC FUNCTIONS

Here's a quick review of some of the equivalences and formulas you will need to answer the arithmetic questions on your exam.

PERCENTAGE

Percent (%) means *per hundred*. If you think of *per* as meaning *divided by*, you will understand that 50% means "50 divided by 100."

Converting Percents to Decimals

1. To change a percent to a decimal, you divided it by 100. The easiest way to do this is to move the decimal point 2 places to the *left*.

   $25\% = .25$ $\qquad$ $5\% = .05$ $\qquad$ $130\% = 1.30$

2. Change decimal fractions to percent by doing the opposite—move the decimal point 2 places to the right (multiplying).

   $.45 = 45\%$ $\qquad$ $.07 = 7\%$ $\qquad$ $2.60 = 260\%$

Converting Percents to Fractions

1. To change a percent to a common fraction, show as hundredths and reduce to lowest terms.

   $40\% = \frac{40}{100} = \frac{2}{5}$ $\qquad$ $75\% = \frac{75}{100} = \frac{3}{4}$ $\qquad$ $90\% = \frac{90}{100} = \frac{9}{10}$

2. To change common fractions to a percent, change to decimal fractions (hundredths), and then show as a percent.

$$\frac{1}{2} = \frac{50}{100} = .50 = 50\% \qquad \frac{3}{5} = \frac{60}{100} = .60 = 60\%$$

Another way of doing this is to divide the numerator by the denominator.

$$\frac{1}{2} = 2\overline{)1.00}^{.50} = 50\% \qquad \frac{3}{5} = 5\overline{)3.00}^{.60} = 60\%$$

DECIMALS
Addition

To add decimals, place the decimal points in the numbers to be added directly over one another, and the decimal point in the answer directly under that in the numbers being added.

```
    3.75          4.00
     .05          6.87
     .5        + 10.825
   24.7          21.695
+ 324.50
  353.50
```

Subtraction

As with adding, place the decimal points in the numbers to be subtracted directly underneath the other decimals.

```
  71.275        26.27
 − 5.10       − 4.27
  66.175        22.00
```

Multiplication

In multiplying decimals, it is not necessary to align the points. Simply write the numbers to be multiplied as you would any other multiplication problem and multiply. When you have the answer, count the total number of places to the *right* of the decimal in *both* numbers multiplied and then count off that total number of places from the right in the answer.

```
    500                 .1005 (4 places)
 ×  .07 (2 places)    ×  7.5 (1 place)
  35.00 (2 places)      5025
                        7035
                       .75375 (5 places)
```

Division

When dividing by a decimal, change the divisor to a whole number, and then move the decimal point in the dividend to a corresponding number of places to the right. Align the decimal point in the answer with the *new* decimal point in the dividend.

$$7.60\overline{)8.75}$$

$$\begin{array}{r} 1.151 = 1.15 \\ 760.\overline{)875.000} \\ \underline{760} \\ 1150 \\ \underline{760} \\ 3900 \\ \underline{3800} \\ 1000 \\ \underline{760} \\ 240 \end{array}$$

FRACTIONS

Addition

Find a *common denominator*. For instance, to add $\frac{1}{2} + \frac{1}{6} + \frac{1}{4}$, convert all three fractions to twelfths, the common denominator.

$$\frac{1}{2} = \frac{6}{12}$$
$$\frac{1}{6} = \frac{2}{12} \qquad \frac{(6 + 2 + 3)}{12} = \frac{11}{12}$$
$$\frac{1}{4} = \frac{3}{12}$$

Subtraction

Again, find a common denominator.

$$1\frac{1}{2} - \frac{3}{16} \qquad \frac{24}{16} - \frac{3}{16} = \frac{21}{16} = 1\frac{5}{16}$$
$$\frac{25}{35} - \frac{3}{10} \qquad \frac{50}{70} - \frac{21}{70} = \frac{29}{70}$$

Multiplication

Multiply across the top, and then across the bottom.

$$\frac{1}{4} \times \frac{1}{8} = \frac{1}{32} \qquad \frac{3}{5} \times \frac{7}{8} = \frac{21}{40}$$
$$7 \times 1\frac{15}{16} = \frac{7}{1} \times \frac{31}{16} = \frac{217}{16} = 13\frac{9}{16}$$

Important Definitions

Dividend: The number you're dividing *into*.

Divisor: The number you're dividing *by*.

Quotient: The result of division—the answer.

Division

For ÷, read "divided by." $8 \div 4 = 2$.

Invert the divisor and multiply.

$$\frac{15}{16} \div \frac{1}{2} = \frac{15}{16} \times \frac{2}{1} = \frac{30}{16} = 1\frac{14}{16} = 1\frac{7}{8}$$

$$1\frac{5}{8} \div \frac{2}{3} = \frac{13}{8} \times \frac{3}{2} = \frac{39}{16} = 2\frac{7}{16}$$

WORD PROBLEMS: 8 STEPS TO SUCCESS

People who have no difficulty at all with the actual arithmetic computations often have a struggle with word problems because they do not know how to attack a word problem. Here's an 8-step solution:

1. **Read and analyze** the problem through *carefully*.
2. **Classify:** Ask yourself, "What *type* of problem is this?"
3. **Set up:** You may need a picture or diagram.
4. **Label:** Save time in the long run.
5. **Eyeball estimate:** Is your answer *reasonable*? Or are you off two decimal points?
6. **Prove** or **check** your work the easiest way. Work back from the answer *if you have to.*
7. **Double check** that you answered the question that was asked for.
8. **Transpose** the answer to your answer sheet correctly. Don't be one number off all the way down!

WHAT YOU'RE GIVEN

Most word problems have three main parts:

- The information given—two facts
- The information asked for (the solution)

More Fraction Conversions

To work with fractions, you may need to convert a mixed fraction (such as $1\frac{1}{2}$ or $3\frac{1}{3}$) to an improper fraction ($\frac{3}{2}$ or $\frac{10}{3}$) and vice versa.

- To convert a mixed fraction, multiply the bottom number by the whole number; then add the top number:

$$1\frac{1}{2} = \frac{(2 \times 1) + 1}{2} = \frac{3}{2}$$

$$3\frac{1}{3} = \frac{(3 \times 3) + 1}{2} = \frac{10}{3}$$

- To convert an improper fraction, divide the top number by the bottom number. The quotient is the whole number, and the remainder is the top number of the fraction.

$\frac{3}{2}$—2 goes into 3 once, with a remainder of $1 = 1\frac{1}{2}$

$\frac{10}{3}$—3 goes into 10 three times, with a remainder of $1 = 3\frac{1}{3}$

Sometimes, however, the given information is not complete. Some function must be performed *before the fact can be used in the problem*. Look carefully to see if such a situation exists. If so, you must perform the needed function first.

Sometimes an *extra fact* is inserted into the problem that is not needed to solve the problem. Examine the problem if you seem to have too many facts, to see which ones should be used, or if you actually have a two-part problem to do.

MAGIC T FOR SUCCESS IN PERCENTAGE PROBLEMS

There are only a few kinds of word problems, most of them having to do with percents. The basic formula to use for all percentage problems, no matter what type, will always be the same, and the set-up will always be the same. Percentage problems—and many other kinds of problems—have three facts. If you know any two of these facts, you can solve the third. As soon as you have determined that you are dealing with a percentage problem, put down a Magic T and number to three.

#1 Part	
#2 Whole	#3 %

If there are four facts in the problem, one of two things is true:
- One fact is useless and should be ignored or crossed out, *or*
- The problem has two parts, and the solution of part one will be used *with* the fourth fact to solve the second part.

KINDS OF MAGIC T PROBLEMS							
Interest	**Brokerage**	**Capitalization**	**Profit**	**Loss**	**Taxes (A)**	**Taxes (B)**	**Insurance**
Interest	Commission	Return	Amount Gained	Amount Lost	Property Value	Amount of Taxes	Premium
Principal	Sales Price or Cost	Base Amount	Original Cost	Original Cost	Assessment	Assessed Value	Amount of Insurance
Interest Rate	Commission Rate	Rate of Return	% of Increase	% of Decrease	Assessment Ratio	Tax Rate	Insurance Rate

The types of percentage problems you can solve with the Magic T are *interest*, *brokerage*, *taxes*, *insurance*, *capitalization*, and even *scale* problems. *Profit* and *loss* problems are also solved by this formula.

HOW TO USE THE MAGIC T

Simply substitute the two facts you are given in the Magic T and proceed with the indicated function. The main difficulty in doing percentage problems is to know which piece of information to put where. And this is where the Magic T will simplify your life.

The horizontal line is read: "divided by"

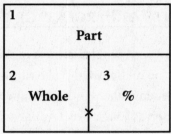

The vertical line is read: "multiply by"

- Always **put in the percent first** because it is easiest to recognize. (Rate and ratio are percents.) If the percent is the missing fact, just put the percent sign in your T in the lower right hand corner.

$$\frac{\qquad}{\Big|\ \%} \quad \begin{array}{l} 1. \\ 2. \\ 3.\ \% \end{array}$$

- You now have two empty places and two facts left. Simply put the smaller number at the top and the larger one at the bottom.

That's all there is to it. No agonizing over what to divide or multiply by what. Just follow the formula.

COMMISSION PROBLEMS

Let's take a simple commission problem to demonstrate.

1. Broker Jones sold the Smith house for $65,000. The total commission came to $4,000. What was the Jones' commission rate?
   a. .061%
   b. .6%
   c. 6%
   d. 6.5%

You see the word *rate* and decide this is a percentage problem. You set it up, writing down first your T and then your 1, 2, 3 facts.

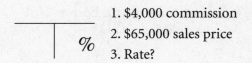

1. $4,000 commission
2. $65,000 sales price
3. Rate?

- The percent goes first.
- Now put the smaller of the remaining facts, $4,000, on the top of the T.
- Put $65,000 on the bottom.
- The horizontal line indicates *divide by*. So you have $4,000 divided by $65,000.

$$\frac{\$4000}{\$65,000} \Bigg| \quad \% \qquad 65,000 \overline{)4000.000}$$
$$\underline{3900\ 00}$$
$$100\ 000$$

Convert decimal to percent by moving the decimal point two places to right. .61 is the same as 6.1% Choice **c** is the correct answer. It has been rounded to the nearest percent.

How to Round

If the number after the one you need to round to is 5 or more, make the preceding number one higher. If it is less than 5, drop it and leave the preceding number the same. (Some testing services inform you when to round off. Consult your bulletin or application.)

$.0135 = .014$ or $.01$

INTEREST PROBLEMS

There are three basic kinds of interest problem, depending on which number is missing. First, try one in which you have to calculate the interest *rate* (percentage).

2. Mary Smith borrowed $5,000, for which she is paying $600 per year. What is the rate of interest being charged?

$$\frac{\$600}{\$5,000} \Bigg| \quad \%$$

1. $600 interest
2. $5,000 principal
3. % rate

$$\frac{\$600}{5,000} = .12 \text{ or } 12\%$$

Now here's a question in which you have to find the principal amount.

3. Mary's sister is paying $850 for a loan at the same rate. How much did she borrow?
Set up:

1. $850 interest
2. principal
3. 12% interest

Put the percent into the form of a decimal by moving the decimal point two places to the left.

.12 = 12%

Which is bigger, the interest or the principal? If the interest were bigger than the sum on which it is based, it would be over 100% of the loan. Obviously, the interest is less. Put it on the top.

$$\frac{\$850}{\text{Principal} \mid .12} = \frac{\$850}{.12} = \$7,083.3333$$

Next, try a problem in which you have to find the amount of interest (not the rate).

4. Her brother knew the rate his sisters were being charged. He wanted to borrow $10,300 and had no difficulty in calculating his annual payment. What was it?

$$\frac{\text{Interest}}{\$10,300 \mid .12}$$

1. Annual payment
2. $10,300 principal
3. 12%

The vertical line means multiply:

$10,300 × .12 = $1,236

MORE COMPLICATED PROBLEMS

Before going on to the other kinds of percentage problems, take a look at some questions that have more than three facts. Just stay clear-headed and keep asking yourself leading questions.

Too Much Information

Here's a percentage problem on commissions that has three numbers, but you only need two. What to do?

5. Betty Boor was curious about what her neighbor sold her house for. The neighbor was reticent about the price but let slip that the commission was a shocking $4,500. Betty knew that Realtor Raleigh's commission rate was 8%. She also knew that houses in the area were being assessed at 40% of their value. What was the selling price of the house?

You have three facts here. Do you need them all? In calculating the selling price, if you know the commission and you know the commission rate, what do you need the assessment rate for? You don't. This fact was just thrown in to confuse you, so ignore it.

Set up:

$$\begin{array}{c|c} & \text{1. } \$4,500 \text{ commission} \\ \hline .08 & \text{2. selling price?} \\ & \text{3. } 8\% \text{ commission rate} \end{array}$$

The percent goes in first; then, which is bigger, the selling price or the commission? Common sense says the selling price is bigger than the commission; otherwise, we'd all be in trouble. Fill them in and compute.

$$\frac{\$4,500}{.08} = \frac{\$4,500}{.08} = \$56,250$$

Two-Step Problems

Now, here is another kettle of fish. This one has some extra facts, but you need them.

6. A house listed for $60,000 is sold for 5/6 of the listed price. If a 7% commission was paid with a 50/50 split, how much did the selling broker receive?

This is essentially a percentage problem, but you need to figure out some of the facts to fill in your Magic T.

1. $60,000 $\times \frac{5}{6}$ = listed price
2. 7% $\times$ list price = commission
3. 50% $\times$ commission = broker's commission

Labeling helps in a case like this. Although there appear to be a great many extra facts in the problem, this is not the case. It is just that, in this case, some calculations have to be done in advance to get the three facts to use in the problem. Let's call these *derivable* facts.

Set up:

3,500 Commission		1. $\$60,000 \times \frac{5}{6} = \$50,000$ sale price
$50,000	.07	2. $7\% \times \$50,000 = $ total commission
Listed Price	Commission Rate	3. $50\% \times$ total commission = sales

$1,750 Broker's Commission		
		▪ First the %
$3,500 Total Commission	.50 Broker's split	▪ The larger figure on the bottom
		▪ Now the smaller figure on top

Maybe you didn't need the formula to do this part of the problem, because it is straight multiplication. Most people have trouble only when they have to divide, because they don't know which number to divide by which. But you can see how you used the solution of one problem to fill in for the solution of the second problem. Also, see how much labeling helps.

What Question Was Asked?

The final act in problem solving—especially when dealing with multi-step problems—is to ask yourself "Did I answer the question that was asked?" If you **always** take this last precaution, you can save yourself a lot of unnecessary mistakes. Take the following problem:

7. A salesman's total commission was $7,600. He received 6% on the first $100,000 sold and has received $2\frac{1}{2}\%$ on all sales over $100,000. What were his total sales?

This problem shows the difference between given and *derivable* information. It also illustrates how easy it is to forget where you are, unless you ask yourself the final question.

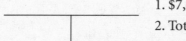

1. $7,600 = total commission
2. Total sales?
3. 6% × $100,000 plus $2\frac{1}{2}\%$ on all above = %

Long, Complicated Problems

A lot of the problems you will encounter are that not difficult; they are just long, and they are further complicated by small calculations that give you a maximum opportunity for careless error. Leave long, complicated problems until the end! All the problems are worth only one point each, and you might be doing ten or twelve short ones while you lug through a long one. If you have time, you can go back and do the long, complicated ones at your leisure—with no pressure to make careless error likely.

Fact #1 is no difficulty; it is given.

Fact #2 is the solution needed.

Fact #3 is derivable.

The first thing to do is turn the derivable fact into a fact.

- 6% × $100,000 = $6,000
- $7,600 − $6,000 = $1,600 (his remaining commission)

$2\frac{1}{2}$% of what = $1,600?

$$\frac{1,600}{\text{Sales} \mid .025}$$

1. $1,600
2. Remaining amount of sales
3. $2\frac{1}{2}$%

Proceed as always. Fill in the percent first. Is the commission going to be smaller or larger than the sales it is based on? Smaller, of course, or else the sellers will go broke.

Turn the $2\frac{1}{2}$% into a decimal so you can use it in the T. The solution is:

$$.025 \overline{)1600} = \$64,000$$

And here is where a lot of people stop. They have solved the two parts of the problem, and they find the answer in the choices listed. There it is in black and white, $64,000. The only trouble is, what was the question asked? It was: What were the salesman's total sales?

$$
\begin{array}{ll}
\$100,000 & (\text{6\% of first \$100,000}) \\
+ \ \$64,000 & (2\frac{1}{2}\% \text{ of the remainder}) \\
\hline
\$164,000 & \text{an answer which } also \text{ appears on the test}
\end{array}
$$

Proving

Now what about step #6 in problem solving, *prove?* How can you check the answer to the problem you just did? Reread the problem:

7. A salesman's total commission was $7,600. He received 6% on the first $100,000 sold and has received $2\frac{1}{2}$%
on all sales over $100,000. What were his total sales?

$$6\% \times \$100,000 = \$6,000$$
$$2\frac{1}{2}\% \times \ \ \$64,000 = \ \ 1,600$$
$$\overline{\ \ \ \ \ \ \ \ \ \ \$164,000 \ \ \ \ \$7,600}$$
$$\text{total sales} \ \ \ \ \text{commission}$$

The answer to your proof matches the information given in the question, so your answer is correct.

Now that you can do even complicated percentage problems, you're ready to tackle the three other types:
tax, insurance, and capitalization.

TAX PROBLEMS

8. You are curious about the value of the Jones' house and happen to know that houses in this area are assessed
at 40% of value. Mr. Jones mentioned to your husband that the house and land were assessed at $41,250.
What was the market value of the house?

Set up:

$$\frac{\$41,250}{\text{Market Value}} \ \Big|\ .40$$

1. $41,250 = amount of assessment
2. Market value?
3. 40% ratio of assessment to value

$$\frac{\$41,250}{.40} = \$103,125$$

Proof:
40% × $103,125 = $41,250   Correct

9. The tax rate in your county is $4.17 per hundred of assessed valuation, and Mr. Brown, a possible client,
has told you his taxes are $1,100. What is his property assessment?

$$\frac{\$1,100}{\text{Assessment}} \ \Big|\ .0417$$

1. $1,100 taxes
2. Assessment?
3. $4.17 per hundred is the tax rate (%)

The tax rate information is derivable. That is, you must do something to it before you can use it in an arithmetic computation. If you think of the word *per* as meaning "divided by," you can make the $4.17 per hundred
usable by moving the decimal point two places to the left to divide by 100. (.04.17)

$$\frac{\$1100}{.0417} = \$26,378.896 \text{ (or rounded up to \$26,378.90)}$$

Eyeball . . . Transpose

There are two other problem-solving steps:

Eyeball estimate: Is the answer reasonable?

Transposing: Is the answer in the right circle on the answer sheet?

This last one is particularly important if you have skipped a question. If you skip a question, mark it, and be sure the following question is put in the right place.

10. Mr. Brown knew his own taxes were $975 and his property assessment was $17,000 for the house and $6,000 for the land. He wanted to know the rate.

Set up:

$$\frac{\$975}{23{,}000} \Big| \% \qquad \begin{array}{l} \text{1. \$975 tax} \\ \text{2. \$17,000 plus \$6,000 or \$23,000 assessment} \\ \text{3. rate (\%)?} \end{array}$$

$$\frac{\$975}{23{,}000} = .0423913 \text{ (or } .04.239 \text{ or } \$4.24 \text{ per hundred)}$$

The answers on the test read as follows:

a. $4.24 per hundred (.04.24 ÷ 100)

b. $42.40 per thousand (.042. ÷ 1000)

c. 42 mills (same as ÷ 1000)

d. All of the above

First of all, you have to round the answer to .0424.

Secondly, if you want the per hundred or per thousand rate—and this is the way taxes are usually expressed—or if you want the mills ($\frac{1}{10}$ of a cent), which is another way taxes are expressed, you have to multiply by the required number. To multiply by 100, move two places to the right; by a thousand, three places. Since a mill is $\frac{1}{10}$ of a cent, you also have to multiply by 1,000 to get mills. You can see that **d** is the correct answer.

Now try one more problem: a two-part problem with too many facts for one.

11. The market value of Mr. Ipswitch's house was $85,000, and houses in his area are assessed at 42% of their market value. He called the courthouse and found the local tax rate is $3.50 per hundred of assessed evaluation. How much should Mr. Ipswitch's taxes be?

Since you have four parts to the problem—the market value, the ratio of assessed value to market value, the tax rate, and the solution—you realize you have a two-part problem. The trick is to find out which parts go in which calculation. After that, you simply apply your regular procedure. Put in the percent. Ask yourself which number is smaller and which is bigger, and work the calculation.

Set up Part I:

Assessment		Four facts means a two-part problem.
85,000	.42	1. $85,000 market value
		2. Assessment?
		3. 42% ratio (%)
		4. ($3.50 per $100 = tax rate)

$85,000 × .42 = $35,700

Set up Part II:

Taxes		1. Taxes?
Assessment	.0350	2. $35,700 assessment (see part I)
$35,700		3. $3.50 per hundred is rate (%)

$35,700 × .035 = $1,249.50—the answer.

INSURANCE PROBLEMS

12. Mr. Brewer wishes to insure his home for 80% of its market value of $92,000. The insurance agent informs him that homeowner insurance costs $3.50 per thousand dollars of the amount of insurance. How much will insurance cost him annually? How much monthly insurance escrow will be required?

Premium		1. Annual premium? Monthly premium?
$73,600	.0035	2. 80% × $92,000 = amount of insurance
		3. $3.50 per thousand rate (%)

Hot Tip

When trying to decide how many parts you have in a percentage problem, always consider the solution as one of the parts.

- The rate (%) is .003.50—move the decimal point three places to the left to divide by 1,000.
- Is the premium going to be more or less than the amount of insurance? If the premium is $73,600 a year, we should all go into insurance.

$73,600 × .0035 = $257.60 annual premium

257.60 ÷ 12 = $21.47 monthly escrow

13. Mr. Broadstreet bought his insurance ten years ago and he has forgotten how much he insured his house for. He wants to be sure it is insured for at least 80% of its present value of $100,000. He is paying a premium of $250 a year at a rate of $2.50 per thousand of amount of insurance. Is he carrying enough insurance?

	$250
Insurance	.0025
Amount	

1. $250 annual premium
2. Amount of present insurance?
3. $2.50 per thousand rate (%)

$$\frac{\$250}{.0025} = \$100,000$$

Since Mr. Broadstreet wanted to be insured for *at least* 80% of $100,000, the answer is yes, he is carrying enough insurance—more than enough.

CAPITALIZATION PROBLEMS

Capitalization problems are another kind of percentage problem. Use your Magic T.

14. Your mother calls you from Florida to say that she is getting $3,800 per year in interest from the insurance Dad left her. She is wondering if she has it invested wisely. Dad left $60,000. What rate is she earning on her investment?

	$3800
$60,000	%

$$\frac{\$3,800}{\$60,000} = .063 \text{ or } 6\%$$

Hot Tip

All calculations in the Magic T are on an annual basis—unless you convert to monthly by dividing by 12. Note that you may be asked for *monthly* amounts in insurance and capitalization problems.

15. An investor is considering the purchase of an income property generating a gross income of $350,000. Operating expenses constitute 70% of gross income. If the investor wants a return of 14%, what is the maximum he can pay?

This is a two-part problem. Set up your Magic T, but then stop to figure out net income.

Net Income			$350,000	gross income
Value	Rate of Return		$\times$ .70	expenses
			$245,000	expenses

$105,000		$ 350,000	
Value	.14	− 245,000	
		$ 105,000	net income

$105,000 \div .14 = $750,000$ maximum price

PERCENTAGES PLUS

Several kinds of questions mix percentages with fractions or with dollar amounts. If you diagram these questions, you can solve them easily. You may not even need to use the Magic T.

Percentages Plus Fractions

16. An agent received a 3% commission on $\frac{1}{4}$ of her total sales. On the remainder, she received a 6% commission. What was her average commission for all of her sales?
 a. 5.75%
 b. 4.25%
 c. 5.25%
 d. 4.5%

Start off by asking yourself: How many fourths (parts) were there? Four, naturally. Draw a diagram representing these fourths of the commission. Enter in each part the commission for that part.

3%	6%	6%	6%

You will see, then, that what the agent got was 3% plus 6% plus 6% plus 6% divided by 4 (the number of parts). So you just add all the percents together and divide by the number of parts. This will give you the average commission:

$$\frac{21}{4} = 5.25\%$$

Let's say the problem went on to say:

17. The agent had a total sales of $250,000. What was her commission on those sales?
$5.25\% \times \$250,000 = .0525 \times \$250,000 = \$13,125$

Prove: You can check your work by dividing her total sales by four ($62,500) and then multiplying by the percentages.

$3\% \times \$62,500 = \$1,875$
$6\% \times \$62,500 = \$3,750$
$6\% \times \$62,500 = \$3,750$
$6\% \times \underline{\$62,500} = \underline{\$3,750}$
$\$250,000 \quad \$13,125$

Now try a problem involving commission splits.

18. On a $54,000 sale, the rate of commission was 6%. If the salesperson and broker split the commission at a 2 to 3 ratio, how much did the salesperson get?

- Start off by asking yourself: How many parts were there, total?
- There were 2 plus 3 parts or 5 parts.
- Now divide the commission money into 5 parts.
  $\$54,000 \times .06 = \dfrac{\$3240}{5} = \$648$
- The salesperson gets 2 parts and the broker gets 3 parts.
  Salesperson: $2 \times \$648 = \$1,296$

This problem might call the division a 40/60 split. $\frac{40}{100}$ is $\frac{2}{5}$ and $\frac{60}{100}$ is $\frac{3}{5}$, when the fraction is reduced.

Percentages Plus Amounts

Another similar type is the subdivision problem.

19. Old MacDonald had a farm. He divided it into five parts and gave four of them to his four sons. Zeke got 13%, Rube got $12\frac{1}{2}$%, Elmer got 9%, and Buck got 90 acres. Old MacDonald kept 150 acres for himself. How large was the farm originally?

The trick here is to find the relationship between the size of the parcels and the portion of ownership. The best way to do this is to set it up in chart form.

Owner	Portion Owned	Size
Zeke	13%	
Rube	$12\frac{1}{2}$%	
Elmer	9%	
Buck		90 acres
Old MacDonald		150 acres
	$34\frac{1}{2}$%	240 acres

The five parcels all added together make up the original farm, or 100%.

$.13 + .125 + .09 = .345$ or $34\frac{1}{2}$% of the farm is owned by the three sons. Therefore, Buck and Old MacDonald together must own the remaining percentage. Subtracting from 100%, they own $65\frac{1}{2}$%.

Once you get to this point, you can solve with the Magic T.

240	
Whole	.655

1. 240 acres owned by Buck and Old MacDonald
2. Whole farm in acres?
3. .655 owned by Buck and Old MacDonald

Put in your percent. Naturally, the whole farm is larger than any part, so it is easy to substitute in the formula. Put the smaller number at the top, the larger at the bottom as usual.

$\frac{240}{.655} = 366.41$ acres

Another problem similar to this is a kind of commission problem which is a *must* for you to learn.

20. Salesman Oakes was trying to list a house. The owner said he wanted to clear (net) $12,000 from the sale of the house. The balance of the mortgage was $37,000. It would cost about $1,200 to fix the house up to sell. How much would the owner have to sell the house for if the 7% commission was included?

Here you have almost the same situation as with Farmer MacDonald, and use of a chart will clarify it.

Expenses	In Dollars	In Percents
Seller's net	12,000	
Loan balance	37,000	
Repairs	1,200	
Commission		7%
	50,200	7%

If the sales price is 100% and the commission is 7% of the sales price, all the remaining items added together must make 93% of the sales price. The place where most people go wrong is in not including the seller's net when they add the expenses. The seller's net has to *come out* of the sales price. (Where else would it come from?) Therefore, it is part of the remaining 93%. You now have a percentage problem. The sales price is obviously higher than any of the expenses, so it goes on the bottom of the T.

$$\frac{\$50,200}{\text{Sales Price}} \quad .93$$

1. $50,200 expenses
2. Sales price?
3. .93 percent

$$\frac{\$50,200}{.93} = \$53,978.494$$

Proof: $.07 \times \$53,978.494 = \$\ 3,778.4945$

$$+ \$50,200.00$$

$$\overline{\$53,978.494} \quad \text{(round down to \$53,978.49)}$$

MEASUREMENT PROBLEMS

AREA

Most of the measurement problems on the exam will ask you to figure the area of a piece of land, a building, or some other figure.

Rectangles

Area = length × width

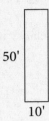

50'

10'

21. A man purchased a lot which is 50 feet by 10 feet for a garden. How many square feet of land does he have?

A = 50 × 10 or 500 square feet

That problem is not difficult, but suppose you were asked:

22. A man purchased 500 square feet of land for a garden. It is 10 feet wide. How long is it?

You can do this problem with your Magic T.

area	
length	width

$$\frac{500}{\text{Length} \mid 10} = 50$$

Try a couple of other questions like that one.

23. A man bought a lot that was 250 feet wide and 675 feet deep (length). How many acres does he have?

$$\frac{\text{Area}}{250 \times 675} = 168,750 \text{ sq. ft.}$$

Divide 168,750 sq. ft. by 43,560 sq. ft. per acre = 3.8739669 (or 3.87 rounded)

24. The Smiths bought a piece of land for a summer home that was 2.75 acres. The lake frontage was 150 feet. What was the depth of the lot?

2.75 × 43,560 = 119,790 sq. ft.

$$\frac{119,790}{150 \mid \text{Length}} = 798.6 \text{ feet}$$

MEASUREMENT TOOLS

Distance Equivalences

Linear measure along a straight line—1 dimension

12 inches (in. or ") = 1 foot (ft. or ')

3 feet or 36 inches = 1 yard (yd.)

1,760 yards = 1 mile

5,280 feet = 1 mile

Area Equivalences

Surface measurement—2 dimensions

144 square inches (sq. in. or in²) = 1 square foot (sq. ft. or ft.²)

9 square feet = 1 square yard

27 cubic feet = 1 cubic yard (3 dimensions)

43,560 square feet = 1 acre

640 acres = 1 square mile

Area Formulas

Area of a rectangle = length × width (or $a = l \times w$)

Area of a parallelogram = base × height (or $a = b \times h$)

Area of a triangle = $\dfrac{b \times h}{2}$ or $\dfrac{1}{2} bh$

Area of a circle = Πr^2 ($\Pi = 3.14$)

Triangles

$$\text{Area} = \frac{\text{Base} \times \text{Height}}{2} \quad \text{or} \quad \frac{1}{2}(\text{base} \times \text{height})$$

(The height or altitude is a perpendicular line, 90° to the base.)

25. The Rogers family is buying a triangular piece of land for a gas station. It is 200 feet at the base, and the side perpendicular to the base is 200 feet. The third side is 275 feet. The Rogers are paying $2.00 a square foot for the property. What will it cost?

$$\text{Area} = \frac{200 \times 200}{2} \text{ or } \frac{40,000}{2} \text{ or } 20,000 \text{ sq. ft.}$$

20,000 sq. ft. × $2 = $40,000

The length of the third side is unnecessary information.

Here again, if you know two factors, you can find the third.

$$\frac{\text{Area}}{\frac{1}{2}\text{Height} \mid \text{Base}} \quad \frac{20,000}{100 \mid \text{Base}} = 200$$

26. Mary and John Robinson have an outlot that a neighbor wants to buy. The side next to their property is 86 feet. The rear line is perpendicular to their side lot, and the road frontage is 111 feet. Their plat shows they own 3,000 sq. ft. in the outlot. What is the length of the rear line of the outlot?

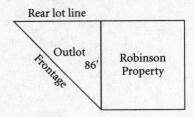

It helps to draw the figure to conceive shapes. The rear lot line is perpendicular to the side lot line. This makes the side lot line the base and the rear lot line the height (altitude).

Area of a triangle $= \frac{1}{2}$ base $\times$ height.

$\frac{1}{2}$ Base (86 feet) $= 43$

$$\frac{3,000}{43 \mid \text{Height}} \quad 3,000 \div 43 = 69.767 \; (69.8 \text{ rounded}) \text{ rear lot line}$$

Circles

Area $= \Pi r^2$

Π is the Greek letter pi ("pie"). Π is approximately equal to 3.14. The radius is $\frac{1}{2}$ the diameter, which is the distance through the center of the circle.

27. Murray Brodman, a contractor, has been awarded the job to put up a circular bandstand in the town square. The concrete base costs $16 per square foot. The diameter of the circular area for the bandstand is 30 feet. How much will the concrete cost?

Area $= \Pi r^2$
Area $= 3.14 \times 15 \times 15 = 706.5$ sq ft.
$706.5 \times \$16 = \$11,304$

28. A gardener has been asked to construct a flower bed in the shape of a semi-circle. The radius is to be 12 feet. What is the area to the nearest square yard?

Area of a circle $= \Pi r^2$

$A = 3.14 \times 12 \times 12$ or 452.16 sq. ft.

This is a semi-circle (half of a circle)

$\frac{452.16}{2} = 226.08$ sq. ft.

9 sq. ft. = 1 square yard

$\frac{226.08}{9} = 25.12$ sq. yrds. (25 sq. yards. rounded)

PERIMETERS

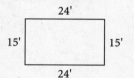

You may be asked to find the perimeter of a figure. Just add all the sides to find the sum.

$15 + 24 + 15 + 24 = 78$

FRONT FOOTAGE

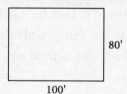

The first measurement given is a measurement facing the road. A *front foot* is one foot running the entire depth of the lot.

29. A lot is 100' $\times$ 80'. The frontage is 100'. If the lot is being sold at either \$65 per front foot, or 75¢ a square foot, which way would you rather buy it?

100' $\times$ \$65 = \$6,500

100' $\times$ 80' $\times$ .75 = \$6,000

MISCELLANEOUS REAL ESTATE QUESTIONS

In addition to the many kinds of percentage questions and the questions on measurement, you may also encounter a few arithmetic questions on a variety of real estate topics such as appraisal, financing, and proration. The kinds of arithmetic you'll have to do are varied, but none are very difficult.

APPRAISAL

Some of the math questions may deal with one of the methods of appraisal. If you need help with the appraisal methods, turn to Chapter 4, the Real Estate Refresher Course.

Market Data Approach

Appraisal problems based on the market data approach will typically be multi-step problems, but the math is very simple. You'll use measurements and other hypothetical features of the comparable property to arrive at a value. Just be sure to label your work.

30. If Building A measures 52' × 106' and Building B measures 75' × 85', how much will B cost if A costs $140,000 and both cost the same per square foot to build?

Area = Length × Width
Area of Building A = 52 × 106 = 5,512 sq. ft.
Area of Building B = 75 × 85 = 6,375 sq. ft.
Cost of Building A per sq. ft. = $\frac{140,000}{5,512}$ = $25.40
Cost of Building B = 6,375 × $25.40 = $161,925

31. Carson's house (B), which is being appraised, is an exact twin of the houses on either side of it, built by the same builder at the same time. House A was appraised for $45,000, but it has a 14 × 20 foot garage which was added at a cost of about $18 per square foot. House C was recently sold for $43,000, with central air valued at $3,000. What would be a fair estimate of the value of Carson's house?

Comparable C	$43,000	
— Air Conditioning	− 3,000	
	40,000	
Comparable A	$45,000	Garage: 14' × 20' = 280 sq. ft.
— Cost of Garage	− 5,040	280 sq. ft. × $18 = $5,040
	$39,960	

Answer: $40,000

Income Approach

The income or capitalization approach is a simple percentage problem and can be solved with the Magic T formula. The main thing to remember is to use, for the income figure, the annual net income: annual income minus all expenses except debt service (mortgage costs).

32. The Fosters plan to buy a piece of property and believe the capitalization rate should be 11%. The seller has produced a statement which shows the following figures:

        5 apartments rented at $150 per month each

        5 apartments rented at $200 per month each

        A vacancy rate of 2% per annum

        Taxes $2,000 semi-annually

        Utilities $75 per apartment per month

        Trash collection $2.50 per week

        Grass cutting $5.00 per week

        According to the income method of appraising, how much is this property worth?

                1. Net income—calculate from figures given.

    ? | .11   2. Value of property?

                3. Capitalization rate .11

Calculate *annual* income:

5 × 150 =   750 × 12 = $ 9,000

5 × 200 = 1,000 × 12 = $12,000

                    $21,000 gross annual income

Calculate *annual* expenses:

Vacancies: 2% × 21,000 $ 420

Taxes: $2,000 × 2   4,000

Utilities: 75 × 10 × 12   9,000

Trash & Grass: 7.50 × 52   390

                 $13,810

Now figure net income:

Gross Income $21,000

Less Expenses   13,810

Net Income $ 7,190

$7,190   1. Income is smaller than sales price, so it goes on top.

? | .11   2. ?

        3. .11

$7, 190 ÷ .11 = $65,363.363 (or 65,363.64 rounded)

Now you try one.

33. Solve the same problem for the capitalization rate if the Fosters paid $60,000 for the building.

Answer: approximately 12%

Cost Approach

The cost approach is by far the most complicated method of valuation. The cost formula is:

Land value + building replacement cost − depreciation = estimated value.

- **Land value.** Use current market value of the land alone, not including the value of improvements. This figure can be arrived at by analyzing comparable land now on the market in the same area. It is computed separately from improvements since land is not depreciable.
- **Building replacement cost.** What it would cost to build a similar building *today*. (Original cost is irrelevant.)
- **Depreciation.** You must calculate the difference in value between a new building of the same utility and the present condition of the building being appraised.

34. An appraiser estimates the value of a piece of land at $15,000 and the replacement cost of the building on that same land at $60,000. The depreciation has already been calculated at $6,500. What is the estimate of value based on the cost approach?

Take your formula and substitute:

Land Value + Building Replacement Cost − Depreciation
$15,000 + $60,000 − $6,500

The sequence of addition or subtraction does not matter—just remember to figure depreciation on the building *only*.

$15,000	$60,000
+ 60,000	− 6,500
75,000	53,500
− 6,500	+ 15,000
$68,500	$68,500

Sometimes when you are figuring the depreciation, you will add the land cost back at the end to arrive at a total value of the property.

In some problems, replacement cost of a building must be calculated by finding the area. Sometimes you are given the square feet (although it can also be calculated by cubic feet). Try your hand at this problem.

35. If the cost estimate is $30 a square foot, what is the value of the real estate in the following case? The land is estimated at $125,000. Depreciation estimates come in at $65,000, and the building has the following dimensions:

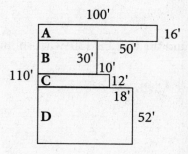

Compute area section by section:

A 100 × 16 = _____
B 50 × 30 = _____
C 60 × 12 = _____
D 78 × 52 = _____

_____ × _____ = _____
         Area   Cost per sq. ft.   Replacement Cost

_____ + _____ − _____ = _____
         Land   Building   Depreciation   Estimate of Value

Answer: $296,280

Gross Rent Multiplier (GRM)

Gross rent multiplier is sometimes used in valuing rental property. Use monthly rental income to compute GRM.

$$\frac{\text{Sale price}}{\text{rental income}} = \text{GRM}$$

For example, if a home sold for $90,000 and its monthly rental income was $600, the GRM would be:

$$\frac{\$90,000}{\$600 \mid GRM} = 150 \text{ GRM}$$

36. What would the estimated value of a property be if the average GRM for four similar properties was 130 GRM and the rental income was $750?

$$\frac{\text{Estimated Market Value}}{\text{Rental Income} \mid GRM} = \frac{\text{Value}}{\$750 \times 130} = \$750 \times 130 = \$97,500$$

37. If a property is worth $300,000 and the GRM is 130, what should the monthly rental be?

$$\frac{\$300,000}{\text{Rental} \mid 130} \qquad \frac{\$300,000}{130} = \$2,307.69$$

Depreciation

There are several methods of depreciation, but the only one you are likely to meet on the examination is the *straight line method*. This method spreads the total depreciation over the useful life of the building in equal annual amounts. It is calculated by dividing the replacement cost by the years of useful life left.

$$\frac{\text{Replacement cost}}{\text{years of useful life}} = \text{annual depreciation}$$

The depreciation rate may be given or may have to be calculated by the straight line method. This means dividing the total depreciation (100%) by the estimated useful life given for the building.

$$\frac{100\%}{\text{Years of useful life}} = \text{Depreciated rate}$$

If a building has 50 years of useful life left, the depreciation rate would be computed as follows:

$$\frac{100\%}{50} = 2\%$$

In other words, it has a 2% depreciation rate annually.

38. The replacement cost of a building has been estimated at $80,000. The building is 12 years old and has an estimated 40 years of useful life left. What can be charged to annual depreciation? What is the total depreciation for 12 years? What is the present value of this building?

Calculate the annual depreciation.

$$\frac{\text{Replacement}}{\text{useful life}} = \text{annual depreciation}$$

$$\frac{\$80,000}{40} = \$2,000$$

Find the total depreciation over the 12 years.

Annual depreciation of $2,000 × 12 years = $24,000

Find the current value: Replacement − depreciation = current value

$80,000 − $24,000 = $56,000

Now you try one.

39. If the building described above had been 10 years old, but still had 40 years of useful life, what would its estimate of current value be?

_____ × _____ =
_____ − _____ = _____

Answer: $60,000

Watch Out for the Booby Trap

Q: If the building described here had originally cost $50,000, what would it be worth today?

A: Same as before—previous value is *not relevant.*

FINANCING

There are five or six general categories of arithmetic problems which fall under the broad heading of financing. These categories include:

- Simple interest
- Principal, interest, and rate
- Points (loan discounting)
- Loan-to-value ratio
- Amortization problems asking for principal balances after one, two, or three payments

Interest

In doing arithmetic problems involving interest, remember that interest rates are always expressed as annual rates. If the time period is more or less than one year, the figures can be converted to annual terms by dividing the annual interest by the fraction of years. For example, if total interest paid equals $2,000, and the time involved is six months (or $\frac{1}{2}$ year), divide $2,000 by $\frac{1}{2}$.

$$\frac{\$2,000}{.5} = 4,000 \text{ annual interest}$$

If the time involved is 18 months (or $\frac{18}{12}$ or $\frac{3}{2}$ of a year), divide $2,000 by $\frac{3}{2}$. Remember, to divide fractions, invert and multiply.

$$\$2,000 \div \tfrac{3}{2} = \$2,000 \times \tfrac{2}{3} = \$1,333.33$$

Once the principal (amount borrowed), annual percentage (annualized rate of interest), and the amount of interest income in dollars are determined, simply use the Magic T.

40. Mr. Babcock pays $700 in interest on a loan over the course of one year. The interest rate is 7%. How much money did he borrow?

No problem about time, because it is an annual payment (one year). Put rate in the T first, as usual. The amount borrowed (the principal) is going to be bigger than the interest he pays, so the principal goes at the bottom and the interest at the top.

$700	1. $700 amount of interest
Principal	.07	2. Amount of principal?
	3. .07 annual percentage (rate)

$$\frac{\$700}{.07} = \$10,000$$

41. Suppose, however, that Mr. Babcock pays $700 interest, but only borrows the money for 6 months.

Now you divide $700 by $\frac{1}{2}$ year. So, the amount of interest you use is $700 × 2 or $1,400 annual interest.

$$\frac{\$1,400}{\text{Principal} \mid .07}$$
1. $1,400 interest per year
2. Principal?
3. .07 annual percentage

$$\frac{\$1400}{.07} = \$20,000$$

Balance, Interest, and Rate

Use this Magic T to solve balance, interest, and rate problems:

$$\frac{\text{Interest}}{\text{Loan Balance} \mid \text{Interest Rate}}$$

42. The interest rate on a loan is 13% and the monthly interest is $350. What is the loan balance?

$$\frac{\$350 \times 12}{\text{Loan Balance} \mid .13} = \frac{\$4,200}{.13} = \$32,307.69$$

43. The loan balance is $50,000 and the annual interest is $3,600. What is the interest rate?

$$\frac{3,600}{\$50,000 \mid \text{Rate}} = \frac{3,600}{50,000} = .072 = 7.2\%$$

44. The loan balance is $75,000 and the interest rate is 12%. What is the monthly interest?

$$\frac{\text{annual interest} \div 12}{\$75,000 \mid .12} = \$75,000 \times .12 = \frac{\$9,000}{12} = \$750 \text{ per month}$$

45. Rodgers borrowed $15,000 and gave the lender a straight note secured by a mortgage. He made monthly payments of interest at 14% annual rate for the full term of the note. The total interest was $5,250. How many months was the term of the note?

$$\frac{\text{Interest (for one year)}}{\$15,000 \mid .14} = \$2,100$$

$$\frac{\$5,250}{\$2,100 \mid 2.5} \quad 2.5 \times 12 = 30 \text{ months}$$

Note! The reason you put the *larger* number on *top* is that the result is going to be more than 100%: for example, $\frac{5}{2}$ rather than $\frac{2}{5}$. This sometimes happens in profit where the fraction is larger than 100%. For example, the original purchase price equals 100%, plus the profit is 25%. Then the percent is 125%, which is larger than 100%. In this case, the *larger* number goes in the top of your T.

Loan-to-Value

46. A mortgage loan for 10% is at a 75% loan-to-value ratio. The interest on the original balance for the first year is $6,590. What is the value of the property securing the loan?

First, find out the loan amount.

$$\frac{\$6,590}{\text{Loan} \mid 10\%}$$

$$\frac{\$6,590}{.10} = \$65,900 \text{ Loan Amount}$$

Then use the loan-to-value ratio to find the value.

$$\frac{\$65,900}{\text{Value} \mid .75}$$

$$\frac{\$65,900}{.75} = \$87,866.666 \text{ (or } \$87,866.67 \text{ rounded)}$$

Points (Loan Discounting)

Loan discounts are often called *points*, or loan placement fees, one point meaning one percent of the face amount of the loan. The service fee of one percent paid by buyers of government backed loans is called a *loan origination fee*.

47. A homebuyer may obtain a $50,000 FHA mortgage loan, provided the seller pays a discount of five points. What is the amount of the discount?

5 points = 5% of face of loan
= .05 × $50,000
= $2,500

48. A property is listed at $74,000. An offer is made for $72,000, provided the seller pays three points on a loan for 80% of the purchase price. The brokerage commission rate is 7%. How much less will the seller receive if he accepts the offer than he would have received if he sold at all cash at the original terms?

Sold for original terms—price	$74,000
Less 7% commission	5,180
Seller's net	$68,820

Sold at offered terms—price	$72,000
Less 7% Commission	5,040
Less discount	1,728
Seller's net	$65,232

$72,000	Sales price		Net at original	$ 68,820
.80	Loan-to-value ratio		Net at offered	−65,232
$57,600	Loan amount		Difference	$3,588
.03	Points			
$ 1,728	Discount			

Amortization

In computing monthly amortization, a fixed monthly payment is determined. Every month, the interest due is deducted from the payment and the remainder is credited to the principal. Each month the principal payment will be a little higher and the interest payment a little lower, but the monthly payment remains the same.

Since one of the recurring problems on the examination is a problem asking for the principal balance up to about the second or third month after a loan is made, practice this simple but long problem requiring mostly stamina and cool. (And remember, a complicated problem is worth no more than the simpler ones. Leave a problem like this until last, or skip it altogether if you're at all pressed for time.)

49. You purchase a home with a 25-year $25,000 mortgage at 9% interest. Monthly PI payments are $209.80. How much of the payment will be applied to the interest and how much to principal for each of the first two months?

Step 1: Compute the annual interest.

$25,000 × .09 = $2,250 interest per annum.

Step 2: Compute first month's interest.

$2,250 ÷ 12 = $187.50 interest

Step 3: Compute first month's principal repaid.

$209.80 total payment

−187.50 interest payment (from Step 2)

$ 22.30 applied to principal

Step 4: Compute second month's principal balance.

$25,000.00 mortgage

−   22.30 principal repaid 1st month

$24,977.70 Balance of principal second month

Step 5: Compute annual interest as of the second month.

$24,977.70 × .09 = $2,247.99

$2247.99 ÷ 12 = $187.33 interest

Step 6: Compute second month's principal paid.

$ 209.80 total payment

− 187.33 interest payment

$ 22.47 applied to principal

Principal	Interest	
$22.30	$187.50	first month
$22.47	$187.33	second month

Note that the length of the mortgage is immaterial when the monthly principal and interest payment is provided.

PRORATION

At the time of settlement, there must be a reconciliation or adjustment of any monies owed by either party as of that date. The important fact to bear in mind is that *the party who used the service pays for it*. If you will keep this firmly in mind you will not have any difficulty deciding who to credit and who to debit.

50. Mr. Seller's taxes are $1,200 a year paid in advance on a calendar year. He is settling on the sale of his house to Mr. Buyer on August 1. Which of them owes how much to the other?

Ask yourself some questions:

How many months has the seller paid for?	12	($1,200)
How many months has the seller used?	7	($700)
How many months should the seller be reimbursed for?	5	($500)
How many months will the buyer use?	5	($500)
How many months has he paid for?	0	($0)
How many months should he reimburse the seller for?	5	($500)

Credit Mr. Seller $500

Debit Mr. Buyer $500

What would the answer be if the taxes were paid in arrears? In other words, the seller has used the service for 7 months but hasn't paid anything. The buyer will have to pay it all at the end of the year. In that case, the seller owes the buyer for 7 months, or $700.

Computing Time

All computations are based on a 30-day month and a 360-day year, with the seller paying the day of settlement. An easy way to calculate large periods of time is to write down the later date, year, number of the month, and day. Then underneath put the earlier day and subtract (borrowing, as in any subtraction).

	2	38			14	
				7	2	38
1998	3	8	March 8, 1998	1998	3	8	One year,
−1996	10	17	October 17, 1996	−1996	10	17	four months
		21		1	4	21	21 days

Most proration problems will be short and easy. They cover taxes, utilities, interest, insurance, or rents.

51. The buyer of a rental unit will take possession on the July 15th closing date and the seller has already received the month's rent. Since the rent is $600 a month, how much will the seller owe the buyer?

Answer: The seller owes $\frac{1}{2}$ month's rent, or $300.

Hot Tip

In working proration problems, be sure you have the right dates when you subtract. Sometimes the termination date for the policy is not given, and the tendency is to subtract the date the policy was written from the date of settlement. This will not give you the unused portion. You must subtract the date of settlement from the date of termination of the policy, which will be exactly the same date, one, three, or five years after written, depending on the term of the policy. Most problems use either a one-or three-year term.

Remember!

Use a 30-day month and a 360-day year in all calculations unless you're told otherwise. Assume a calendar year, unless fiscal or school year is specified.

52. John Towle settles on his home on August 23 and has paid annual sewer charges of $150 a year. How much will the buyer have to reimburse him for those prepaid charges?

John has used 7 months and 23 days.

$$\frac{\$150}{12} = \$12.50 \text{ per month}$$

$$\frac{\$12.50}{30} = \$.42 \text{ per day}$$

Buyer will use 4 months and 7 days.
$12.50 \times 4 = \$50.00$
$.42 \times 7 = \underline{2.94}$
$52.94 credit to the seller

SUMMARY

Real estate "math" is really simple arithmetic. Once you conquer percentages—along with their cousins, decimals and fractions—and the basics of measurement, you will have no trouble with the math on your real estate exam. Review once more the steps for success on word problems (page 5.6), and you're all set!

C·H·A·P·T·E·R
REAL ESTATE GLOSSARY

CHAPTER SUMMARY

One of the most basic components in preparing for your real estate exam is making sure you know all the terminology. This glossary provides an alphabetical list of the most commonly tested real estate terms and their definitions.

A

Abandonment: the voluntary surrender of a right, claim, or interest in a piece of property without naming a successor as owner or tenant.

Abstract of Title: a condensed, chronological history of a title to property, showing all recorded instruments and proceedings affecting the title.

Abutting: sharing a common boundary; adjoining.

Acceleration Clause: a clause in a mortgage or deed of trust that permits the lender to declare the entire amount of principal and trust due and payable immediately in the event of default.

Acceptance: the indication by a party receiving an offer that they agree to the terms of the offer.

Accretion: the increase or addition of land resulting from the natural deposit of sand or soil by streams, lakes, or rivers.

Accrued Depreciation: (1) the amount of depreciation, or loss in value, that has occurred since initial construction; (2) the difference between the current appraised value and the cost to replace the building new.

Acknowledgment: a formal declaration before a public official, usually a notary public, by a person who has signed a deed, contract, or other document that the execution was a voluntary act.

Acre: an area of land consisting of 43,560 square feet.

Actual Eviction: the result of legal action brought by a landlord against a defaulted tenant, whereby the tenant is physically removed from rented or leased property by a court order.

Actual Notice: the actual knowledge that a person has of a particular fact.

Ad Valorem: Latin meaning "according to value;" usually used in reference to real estate tax, which is levied according to value (that is, on an *ad valorem* basis).

Administrator: a person appointed by a court to settle the estate of a person who has died without leaving a will.

Adverse Possession: a method of acquiring title to another person's property by taking actual, open, hostile, and continuous possession for a statutory period of time.

Affidavit: a written statement made under oath and signed before a public official, usually a notary public.

Agent: one who has the authority to act on behalf of another.

Agreement of Sale: a written agreement between a seller and a purchaser whereby the purchaser agrees to buy a certain piece of property from the seller for a specified price.

Air Rights: the right to use the open space above a particular property.

Alienation: the transfer of ownership of a property to another, either voluntarily or involuntarily.

Alienation Clause: the clause in a mortgage or deed of trust that permits the lender to declare all unpaid principal due and payable if the borrower transfers title to the property.

Allodial System: the type of land ownership system in which an individual may own property freely and completely.

Amenities: features or benefits of a particular property that enhance the property's desirability, such as a scenic view or a pool.

Amortization: the method of repaying a loan or debt by making periodic installment payments.

Annual Percentage Rate (APR): the total amount of interest charged on a loan expressed on a yearly basis.

Anti-Deficiency Law: used in some states to limit the claim of a lender on default on payment of a purchase money mortgage on owner-occupied residential property to the value of the collateral.

Anti-Trust Laws: laws designed to protect free enterprise and the open marketplace by prohibiting certain business practices that restrict competition. In reference to real estate, these laws would prevent such practices as price-fixing or agreements by brokers to limit their areas of trade.

Appraisal: an estimate or opinion of the value of a property.

Appreciation: an increase in the value of a property.

Appurtenance: something that transfers with the title to land even if not an actual part of the property, such as an easement.

Arbitration: the process of settling a dispute in which the parties submit their differences to an impartial third party, whose decision on the matter is binding.

ARELLO: the Association of Real Estate License Law Officials.

Assessed Value: the value of a property used to calculate real estate taxes.

Assessment: the process of determining the value of a property for the purpose of levying a tax on the property.

Assignment: the transfer of rights or interest from one person to another.

Assumption of Mortgage: the act of acquiring the title to a property that has an existing mortgage and agreeing to be personally liable for the payment of any debt still existing on that mortgage. The lender must accept the transfer of liability for the original borrower to be relieved of the debt.

Attachment: the process of a court taking custody of a debtor's property until the creditor's debt is satisfied.

Attest: to bear witness by giving a signature.

Attorney-in-Fact: a person who is authorized under a power of attorney to act on behalf of another.

B

Balloon Mortgage: a loan in which the periodic payments do not fully amortize the loan, so that a final payment (a balloon payment) much larger than the amount of the periodic payments must be made to satisfy the debt.

Bargain and Sale Deed: a deed which conveys title, but does not necessarily carry warranties against liens or encumbrances.

Base Line: one of the imaginary east-west lines used as a reference point when describing property with the rectangular or government survey method of property description.

Bench Mark: a permanently marked point with a known elevation, used as a reference by surveyors to measure elevations.

Beneficiary: (1) one who benefits from the acts of another; (2) the lender in a deed of trust.

Bequest: personal property given by provision of a will.

Bilateral Contract: a contract in which each party promises to perform an act in exchange for the other party's promise also to perform an act.

Bill of Sale: a written instrument that transfers ownership of personal property. A bill of sale cannot be used to transfer ownership of real property, which is passed by deed.

Binder: an agreement, accompanied by an earnest money deposit for the purchase of a piece of real estate, to show the purchaser's good faith intent to complete a transaction.

Blanket Mortgage: a mortgage in which more than one parcel of real estate is pledged to cover a single debt.

Blockbusting: the illegal and discriminatory practice of inducing homeowners to sell their properties by suggesting or implying the introduction of members of a protected class into the neighborhood.

Bona Fide: Latin meaning "in good faith"; honest.

Branch Office: a place of business secondary to a principal office. The branch office is generally run by a licensed broker and is for the benefit of the broker running the principal office.

Breach of Contract: the failure to perform according to the conditions of a contract.

Broker: one who acts as an agent for another in a real estate transaction.

Brokerage: the business of bringing together buyers and sellers or other participants in a real estate transaction.

Building Codes: regulations mandated by local governments specifying minimum standards for building construction.

Building Line: a line located on a lot at a specific distance from the front and/or sides of the lot beyond which no structures may extend.

Building Restrictions: limitations listed in zoning ordinances or deed restrictions on the size and type of improvements allowed on a property.

Bundle of Rights: the concept that ownership of a property includes certain rights regarding the property, such as possession, enjoyment, control of use, and disposition.

C

Canvassing: the practice of searching for prospective clients by making unsolicited phone calls and/or visiting homes door-to-door.

Capital Gains Tax: a tax charged on the profit gained from the sale of a capital asset.

Capitalization: the process of estimating the present value of an income-producing piece of property by dividing anticipated future income by a capitalization rate.

Capitalization Rate: the rate of return a property will generate on an owner's investment.

Cash Flow: the net income produced by an investment property, calculated by deducting operating and fixed expenses from gross income.

Caveat Emptor: Latin meaning "let the buyer beware," representing the traditional view that a buyer is responsible for inspecting a property for defects before purchase.

Certificate of Sale: the document given to a purchaser of real estate that is sold at a tax foreclosure sale.

Certificate of Title: a report stating an opinion on the status of a title, based on the examination of public records.

Chain of Title: the recorded history of conveyances and encumbrances that affect the title to a parcel of land.

Chattel: personal property, as opposed to real property.

Chattel Mortgage: a loan in which personal property is pledged to secure the debt.

Closing: the point in a real estate transaction when the purchase price is paid to the seller and the deed to the property is transferred from the seller to the buyer.

Closing Statement: a written accounting of funds received and disbursed during a real estate transaction. Buyer and seller receive separate closing statements.

Cloud on the Title: a claim or encumbrance which, if valid, may affect or impair the title to a piece of property.

Codicil: a supplemental document to a will, that adds to or amends the original terms.

Coinsurance Clause: a clause in an insurance policy specifying the minimum percentage of value that must be insured in order to collect the full amount of loss.

Collateral: something of value hypothecated (real property) or pledged (personal property) by a borrower as security for a debt.

Color of Title: an instrument that appears to convey good title, but does not.

Commercial Property: property used to produce income, such as an office building or a restaurant.

Commingling: the illegal act of an agent mixing a client's monies, which should be held in a separate escrow account, with the agent's personal monies; it involves placing funds that are separate property in an account containing funds that are community property.

Commission: the fee paid to a broker for services rendered in a real estate transaction.

Common Law: the body of law derived from customs and judicial precedents developed in England.

Community Property: a system of property ownership in which each spouse has equal interest in property acquired during the marriage.

Comparable: a recently sold property that is substantially similar to a property being sold or appraised. Comparables are used to indicate fair market value of a subject property.

Competent Parties: persons legally qualified to enter a contract, usually meaning that they are of legal age and sound mind.

Condemnation: the judicial process by which the government exercises its power of eminent domain.

Condominium: a form of ownership in which an individual owns a specific unit in a multi-unit building and shares ownership of common areas with other unit owners.

Conformity: an appraisal principle that asserts that property achieves its maximum value when a neighborhood is homogeneous in its use of land; the basis for zoning ordinances.

Consideration: something of value that induces parties to enter into a contract, such as money or services.

Construction Mortgage: a short-term loan used to finance the building of improvements to real estate.

Constructive Eviction: action or inaction by a landlord that renders a property uninhabitable, forcing a tenant to move out with no further liability for rent.

Constructive Notice: notice of a fact given by making the fact part of the public record. All persons are responsible for knowing the information, whether or not they have actually seen the record.

Contract: an agreement between two or more legally competent parties to do or to refrain from doing some legal act in exchange for a consideration.

Contract for Deed: a contract for the sale of a parcel of real estate in which the buyer makes periodic payments to the seller and receives title to the property only after all, or a substantial part, of the purchase price has been paid, or regular payments have been made for one year or longer.

Conventional Loan: a loan that relies on the credit of the borrower and the property itself for security of the loan and is not insured or guaranteed by any government source.

Conveyance: the transfer of title from one person to another.

Cooperative: a form of property ownership in which a corporation owns a multi-unit building and stockholders of the corporation may lease and occupy individual units of the building.

Corporation: a legal entity with potentially perpetual existence that is created to conduct business or some other lawful activity.

Cost Approach: an appraisal method whereby the value of a property is calculated by estimating the cost of constructing a comparable building, subtracting depreciation, and adding land value.

Counteroffer: an offer submitted as a response to a previous offer, which has the effect of rejecting the previous offer.

Cul-de-sac: a dead-end street that widens at the end, creating a circular turnaround area.

Curtesy: the statutory or common law right of a husband to all or part of real estate owned by his deceased wife, regardless of will provisions, recognized in some states.

D

Damages: the amount of money recoverable by a person who has been injured by the actions of another.

DBA: the abbreviation for "doing business as."

Dedication: the donation of private property by its owner to a governmental body for public use.

Deed: a written document that, when properly signed and delivered, conveys title to real property from the grantor to the grantee.

Deed of Trust: a deed in which the title to property is transferred to a third party trustee to secure repayment of a loan; similar in effect to a mortgage.

Deed Restrictions: clauses in a deed that limit the use of the land.

Default: the failure to perform a contractual duty.

Defeasance Clause: a clause in a mortgage or deed of trust that overrides the lender's right to redeem property after the borrower defaults, usually provided the borrower pays the debt in full.

Deficiency Judgment: a personal claim against a borrower when mortgaged property is foreclosed and sale of the property does not produce sufficient funds to pay off the mortgage. Deficiency judgments may be prohibited in some circumstances by anti-deficiency protection.

Density Zoning: a zoning ordinance that restricts the number of houses that can be built per acre in a particular area, such as a subdivision.

Depreciation: a loss in the value of a parcel of real estate due to any cause, including physical deterioration, or functional or external obsolescence.

Descent: the transfer of property to an owner's heirs when the owner dies intestate.

Devise: the transfer of title to real estate by will.

Discount Points: an amount charged by a lender at closing to increase a loan's effective interest rate.

Dispossess: to remove a tenant from property by legal process.

Dominant Tenement: property that includes the right to use an easement on adjoining property.

Dower: the statutory or common law right of a wife to all or part of real estate owned by her deceased husband, regardless of will provisions, recognized in some states.

Duress: the use of unlawful means to force a person to act or to refrain from an action against his or her will.

E

Earnest Money: an amount of money put down by a buyer as a deposit to indicate good faith intention to complete the transaction.

Easement: the right of one party to use the land of another for a particular purpose, such as to lay utility lines.

Easement by Necessity: an easement, granted by law, that is deemed necessary for the full enjoyment of a parcel of land. An example would be an easement allowing access of land-locked property to a road.

Easement by Prescription: a means of acquiring easement by continued, open, and hostile use of someone else's property for a specified period of time.

Easement in Gross: an easement granted by an owner to an individual with no requirement that the individual own adjoining land.

Economic Life: the period of time in which an improved property will generate more income than it costs to operate.

Emblements: cultivated crops; generally considered to be personal property.

Eminent Domain: the power of the government to take private land for public use with compensation to the owner.

Encroachment: a trespass caused when a structure, such as a wall or fence, invades another person's property.

Encumbrance: a claim on or interest in a parcel of real estate that decreases the real estate's value.

Equitable Title: the interest in a piece of real estate held by a buyer who has agreed to purchase the property, but has not yet completed the transaction; the interest of a buyer under a contract for deed.

Equity: the amount of interest that an owner has in a parcel of real estate, equaling the fair market value of the property minus the amount of debt owed on the property.

Equity of Redemption: the right of a borrower to reclaim the title to foreclosed property by paying the debt and court costs in full.

Erosion: the gradual wearing away of land by wind, water, and other natural processes.

Escalation Clause: a clause in a lease allowing the lessor to charge more rent based on an increase in costs.

Escheat: the claim to property by the state when the owner dies intestate and no heirs can be found.

Escrow: the deposit of funds and/or documents with a disinterested third party for safekeeping until the terms of the escrow agreement have been met.

Estate for Years: a lease of property allowing possession for a definite period of time.

Estoppel: a legal doctrine that prevents a person from denying or contradicting statements that that person once acknowledged as true.

Estoppel Certificate: a legal document executed by a mortgagor or borrower certifying the balance due on a mortgage.

Et Al: abbreviation for the Latin phrase "et alius," meaning "and another."

Et Ux: abbreviation for Latin term "et uxor," meaning "and wife."

Eviction: a legal process instigated by a landlord to remove a tenant from leased property.

Evidence of Title: a document that proves ownership of property.

Exchange: a transaction in which property is traded for like-kind property, rather than sold for money or other consideration.

Exclusive Agency Listing: a contract between a property owner and one broker that only gives the broker the right to sell the property for a commission within a specified period of time. This type of contract does not obligate the owner to pay the broker a commission if the owner sells the property personally.

Exclusive Right to Sell: a contract between a property owner and a broker that gives the broker the right to collect a commission regardless of who sells the property during the specified period of time of the agreement.

Executed Contract: a contract in which all parties have performed their obligations, fulfilling the terms of the contract.

Execution: the signing of a contract.

Executor: a person named in a will to carry out the provisions of the will.

Executory Contract: a contract in which one or more of the obligations have yet to be performed.

Express Contract: an oral or written contract in which the terms are expressed in words.

External Obsolescence: a loss in value of a property due to factors outside the property, such as a change in surrounding land use.

F

Fair Housing Law: a term used to refer to federal and state laws prohibiting discrimination in the sale or rental of residential property.

Federal Housing Administration (FHA): an agency within the U.S. Department of Housing and Urban Development (HUD) that insures mortgage loans by FHA-approved lenders.

Federal National Mortgage Association: also known as "Fannie Mae," a privately-owned corporation that buys existing government-backed and conventional mortgages.

Federal Reserve System: the central banking system of the United States, which controls the monetary policy and, therefore, the money supply, interest rates, and availability of credit.

Fee Simple: most complete form of ownership of real estate.

FHA-Insured Loan: a loan insured by the Federal Housing Administration.

Fiduciary Relationship: a relationship with an obligation of trust, as that of agent and principal.

First Mortgage: a mortgage that has priority to be satisfied over all other mortgages.

Fixture: an article that was once considered personal property, but is now considered real property.

Foreclosure: the legal procedure of selling mortgaged property to satisfy mortgage debt when the borrower defaults on the loan.

Forfeiture: a loss of money or property due to failure to perform under a contract or as provided by law when property is used in the commission of an illegal act.

Fraud: a misstatement of material fact or an act or omission made with deliberate intent to deceive (active fraud) or gross disregard for the truth (constructive fraud).

Freehold Estate: an estate of ownership in real property.

Front Foot: a measurement of property taken by measuring the frontage of the property along the street line.

Functional Obsolescence: a loss in value of a property due to causes within the property, such as faulty design, outdated structural style, or inadequacy to function properly.

Future Interest: ownership interest in property that cannot be enjoyed until sometime in the future.

G

General Lien: a claim on all property, real and personal, owned by a debtor.

General Warranty Deed: an instrument in which the grantor guarantees the grantee that the title being conveyed is good and free of other claims or encumbrances.

Government National Mortgage Association (GNMA): an agency within the U.S. Department of Housing and Urban Development that assists with financing certain federally aided housing programs and participates in the purchase of government-backed loans.

Government Survey System: a method of land description in which meridians (lines of longitude) and base lines (lines of latitude) are used to divide land into townships and sections.

Graduated Lease: a lease that calls for periodic, stated changes in rent during the term of the lease.

Grant: the transfer of title to real property by deed.

Grant Deed: a deed that includes three warranties: (1) that the owner has the right to convey title to the property, (2) that there are no encumbrances other than those noted specifically in the deed, and (3) that the owner will convey any future interest he or she acquires in the property.

Grantee: one who receives title to real property.

Grantor: one who conveys title to real property; the present owner.

Gross Income: the total income received from a property before deducting expenses.

Gross Income Multiplier: a method of estimating the true value of an income property by dividing the sales price of a comparable property by its gross annual rent.

Gross Lease: a lease in which a tenant pays only a fixed amount for rental and the landlord pays all operating expenses and taxes.

Gross Rent Multiplier: a method of estimating the value of an income property by dividing the sales price of a comparable property by its gross monthly rent.

Ground Lease: a lease of land only on which a tenant already owns a building or is responsible for building his or her own improvements.

Guaranteed Sale Plan: an agreement between a broker and a seller that the broker will buy the seller's property if it does not sell within a specified period of time.

Guardian: one who legally responsible for the care of another person's rights and property.

H

Habendum Clause: the clause in a deed, beginning with the words "to have and to hold," that defines or limits the exact interest in the estate granted by the deed.

Heir: one who is legally entitled to receive property when the owner dies intestate.

Highest and Best Use: the legally permitted use of a parcel of land that will yield the greatest net income.

Holdover Tenant: a tenant who retains possession of a leased property after the term of the lease has expired.

Holographic Will: a will that is entirely handwritten, dated, and signed by the testator.

Homeowner's Insurance: an insurance policy specifically designed to protect residential property owners against financial loss from common risks such as fire, theft, and liability.

Homeowner's Warranty: an insurance policy that protects purchasers of newly-constructed homes against certain structural and mechanical defects.

Homestead: the parcel of land and improvements designated as the owner's principal residence.

HUD: an acronym for the Department of Housing and Urban Development, a federal agency that enforces federal fair housing laws and oversees agencies such as FHA and GNMA.

I

Implied Contract: a contract created through the actions of the parties, rather than by written or spoken words.

Improvement: alterations or additions to raw land that add to its value.

Income Capitalization Approach: a method of appraising the value of income-producing property by dividing the expected annual income of the property by a capitalization rate.

Incorporeal Right: intangible, nonpossessory rights in real estate, such as easements or rights of way.

Independent Contractor: one who is retained by another to perform a certain task and is subject to the control and direction of the hiring person with regard to the end result of the task. Individual contractors receive a fee for their services, but pay their own expenses and taxes and receive no benefits.

Industrial Property: buildings and land used for the manufacture and distribution of goods, such as a factory.

Installment Contract: see *Contract for Deed*.

Installment Sale: a transaction in which the sales price is paid to the seller in two or more installments over more than one calendar year.

Interest: a fee charged by a lender for the use of the money loaned.

Interim Financing: a short-term loan made during the building phase of a project; also known as a construction loan.

Intestate: having made no valid will.

Invalid: not legally binding or enforceable.

J

Joint Tenancy: ownership of real estate by two or more parties who each has equal rights of ownership and the right of survivorship.

Joint Venture: an agreement between two or more parties to engage in a specific business enterprise.

Judgment: a decision rendered by a court determining the rights and obligations of parties to an action or lawsuit.

Junior Mortgage: a mortgage that is subordinate to a prior mortgage and that will be satisfied only after the prior mortgage.

L

Laches: a doctrine used by a court to bar the assertion of a legal claim or right, enforceable because of the failure to assert the claim in a timely manner.

Land: the surface of the earth, extending down to the center of the earth, and upward including the air and sky above it, and anything permanently attached.

Landlocked: property surrounded on all sides by property belonging to another.

Lease: a contract between a landlord and a tenant wherein the landlord grants the tenant possession and use of the land for a specified period of time and for a consideration.

Leased Fee: the landlord's interest in a parcel of leased property.

Leasehold: a tenant's right to occupy a parcel of real estate for the term of a lease.

Legal Description: a description of a parcel of real estate specific and complete enough for an independent surveyor to locate and identify it.

Lessee: one who rents property under a lease.

Lessor: one who leases property to another.

Leverage: the use of borrowed funds to purchase an asset.

Levy: to assess or collect a tax.

License: (1) authorization to perform a particular act on another's property, (2) authorization granted by a state to act as a real estate broker or salesperson.

Lien: a claim on the property of another to secure repayment of a debt.

Life Estate: a freehold estate in real property limited in duration to the lifetime of the owner or another specified person. See *Pur Autre Vie*.

Life Tenant: one who holds a life estate.

Liquidity: the ability to convert an asset into cash.

Lis Pendens: Latin meaning "suit pending"; a public notice that a lawsuit has been filed that may affect the title to a particular piece of property.

Listing Agreement: a contract between a property owner and a real estate broker employing the broker to sell the owner's property within a specified period of time for a commission.

Listing Broker: the broker who originates a listing, who distributes it to other brokers in the attempt to find a buyer.

Littoral Rights: the rights of a landowner whose property borders on a nonflowing body of water, such as a lake or ocean.

Lot and Block Description: a method of describing a particular property by referring to a lot and block number within a subdivision recorded in the public record.

M

Management Agreement: a contract between the owner of an income property and a firm or individual who agrees to manage the property.

Market Data Approach: a method of estimating the value of a property by comparing it to similar properties recently sold and analyzing their sale prices.

Market Value: the most likely price that a willing buyer and willing seller will agree to for a property if both are knowledgeable about market conditions and neither are under any undue pressure to act.

Marketable Title: title to property that is free from encumbrances and reasonable doubts and that a court would compel a buyer to accept.

Mechanic's Lien: a statutory lien created to secure payment for those who supply labor or materials for the construction of an improvement to land.

Metes and Bounds: a method of describing a parcel of land using direction and distance.

Mill: one-tenth of one cent; used by some states to express or calculate property taxes.

Minor: a person who has not attained the legal age of majority.

Misrepresentation: a misstatement of fact, either deliberate or unintentional.

Money Judgment: a court order to settle a claim with a monetary payment, rather than specific performance.

Month-to-Month Tenancy: tenancy in which the tenant rents for only one month at a time.

Monument: a fixed, visible marker used to establish boundaries for a survey.

Mortgage: a written instrument used to create a lien on a property to secure payment of a promissory note.

Mortgage Lien: an encumbrance placed on a property to secure payment of a debt.

Mortgagee: a lender who holds title to a borrower's property as security for repayment of the debt.

Mortgagor: the owner of property who borrows money and pledges title to that property as security for repayment of the debt.

Multiple Listing System CMLS: method of marketing a property listing to all participants in the MLS.

Mutual Rescission: an agreement by all parties to a contract to release one another from the obligations of a contract.

N

Net Income: the income produced by a property, calculated by deducting operating expenses from gross income.

Net Lease: a lease that requires the tenant to pay maintenance and operating expenses, as well as rent.

Net Listing: a listing in which the broker's commission is established as anything above a specified amount received by the seller from the sale of the property.

Nonconforming Use: a use of land that is permitted to continue after a zoning ordinance is passed that prohibits that use.

Notarize: to attest or certify as a notary public.

Notary Public: a person who is authorized to administer oaths and take acknowledgments.

Note: a written instrument acknowledging a debt, with a promise to repay, including an outline of the terms of repayment.

O

Obsolescence: a loss in the value of a property due to functional or external factors.

Offer and Acceptance: two of the necessary elements for the creation of a contract.

Open-End Mortgage: a loan containing a clause that allows the borrower to borrow additional funds from the lender, up to a specified amount, without rewriting the mortgage.

Open Listing: a listing contract given to one or more brokers in which a commission is paid only to the broker who procures a sale. If the owner sells the house without the assistance of one of the brokers, no commission is due.

Opinion of Title: an opinion, usually given by an attorney, regarding the status of a title to property.

Option: an agreement that gives a prospective buyer the right to purchase a seller's property within a specified period of time for a specified price.

Optionee: one who receives or holds an option.

Optionor: one who grants an option; the property owner.

Ownership: the exclusive right to use, possess, control, and dispose of property.

P

Package Mortgage: a loan that finances the purchase of personal property as well as real property.

Participation Mortgage: a type of mortgage in which the lender receives a certain percentage of the income or resale proceeds from a property, as well as interest on the loan.

Partition: the division of property held by co-owners into individual shares.

Partnership: An agreement between two parties to go into business or to invest together. In a partnership, property is owned by the partnership, not the individual partners, so partners cannot sell their interest in the property without the consent of the other partners.

Party Wall: a common wall used to separate two adjoining properties.

Payee: one who receives payment from another.

Payor: one who makes payment to another; in a real estate loan, the property owner.

Percentage Lease: a lease in which the rental rate is based on a percentage of the property's gross income. This type of lease is most often used for retail space.

Personal Property: all items that are not considered real property; also known as *chattels*.

Physical Deterioration: a loss in the value of a property due to impairment of its physical condition.

Planned Unit Development (PUD): a type of zoning that provides for residential and commercial uses within a specified area.

Plat: a map of a specific area of subdivided land showing the boundaries of individual parcels or lots.

Plat Book: a group of maps located in the public record showing the division of land into subdivisions, blocks, and individual parcels or lots.

Point: equals one percent; a fee paid to a lender at closing for making a mortgage, also known as a *discount point*.

Point of Beginning: the starting point for a survey using the metes and bounds method of description.

Police Power: the right of the government to enact laws, ordinances, and regulations to protect the public health, safety, welfare, and morals.

Power of Attorney: a written instrument granting one person the authority to act on behalf of another.

Prepayment Penalty: a fee charged to a borrower by a lender for paying off a debt before the term of the loan expires.

Prescription: a method of acquiring an easement to property by unauthorized use.

Primary Mortgage Market: the financial market in which lenders make loans for property directly to borrowers.

Principal: (1) one who authorizes another to act on his or her behalf, (2) one of the main parties to a transaction, (3) the amount of money borrowed in a loan, separate from the interest charged on it.

Principal Meridian: one of the 36 longitudinal lines used in the rectangular survey system method of land description.

Probate: the judicial procedure of proving the validity of a will.

Procuring Cause: the action that brings about the desired result. For example, if a broker takes actions that result in a sale, the broker is the procuring cause of the sale.

Property Management: the operating of an income property for another.

Property Tax: a tax levied by the government on property, real or personal.

Prorate: to divide certain closing costs proportionately between buyer and seller.

Pur Autre Vie: a phrase meaning "for the life of another." In a life estate *pur autre vie*, the term of the estate is measured by the life of a person other than the person who holds the life estate.

Purchase-Money Mortgage: a mortgage given by a buyer to a seller to cover part or all of the purchase price; any loan used to pay part or all of the purchase price.

Q

Quitclaim Deed: a deed that conveys whatever interest a person may have in a property with no warranties.

R

Range: an area of land six miles wide, numbered east or west from a principal meridian in the rectangular survey system.

Ready, Willing, and Able: one who is able to pay the asking price for a property and is ready to complete the transaction.

Real Estate: land, the earth below it, the air above it, and anything permanently attached to it.

Real Estate Broker: a licensed person or organization who negotiates real estate transactions for others for a fee.

Real Estate Settlement Procedures Act (RESPA): a federal law that regulates lending procedures for mortgage loans on one-to-four unit residential properties.

Real Property: land, and anything permanently attached to the land; also called *real estate.*

REALTOR®: a registered trademark for use by members of the National Association of REALTORS® and affiliated state and local boards.

Recording: entering documents, such as deeds, into the public record.

Rectangular Survey System: a method of land description based on principal meridians (lines of longitude) and base lines (lines of latitude). Also called the *government survey system.*

Redemption Period: the period of time during which an owner can reclaim foreclosed property by paying the debt owed plus court costs.

Redlining: the illegal practice of lending institutions refusing to provide certain financial services, such as mortgage loans, to property owners in areas considered to be of high risk.

Regulation Z: a Federal Reserve regulation that implements the federal Truth-in-Lending Act.

Release Clause: a clause in a mortgage that releases a portion of the property upon payment of a portion of the loan.

Remainder: a future interest in an estate that takes effect upon the termination of a life estate.

Rent: a periodic payment paid by a lessee to a landlord for the use and possession of leased property.

Replacement Cost: the cost of constructing a building that is the functional equivalent of an existing structure.

Reproduction Cost: the cost of building an exact duplicate of a building at current prices.

Rescission: canceling or terminating a contract by mutual consent or by the action of one party on default by the other party.

Restriction: a limitation on the way a property can be used.

Reversion: the return of interest or title to grantor of a life estate.

Right of First Refusal: the right of a person to have the first opportunity to purchase property before it is offered to anyone else.

Right of Survivorship: the right of a surviving joint tenant to receive a co-owner's share of interest upon the death of the co-owner.

Riparian Rights: the rights of a landowner whose property is adjacent to a flowing waterway, such as a river, to access and use the water.

S

Safety Clause: a contract provision that provides a time period following expiration of a listing agreement during which the agent will be compensated if there is a transaction with a buyer initially contacted by the agent during the listing period.

Sale and Leaseback: a transaction in which an owner sells his or her property and, as part of the sales agreement, leases the property from the new owner.

Sales Contract: a contract between a buyer and a seller outlining the terms of the sale.

Salesperson: one who is licensed to perform real estate activities while under the supervision of a licensed broker.

Salvage Value: the value of a property at the end of its economic life.

Satisfaction: an instrument acknowledging that a debt has been paid in full.

Second Mortgage: a mortgage that is second in priority for repayment behind a first mortgage.

Section: an area of land under the rectangular survey system, measuring one square mile, or 640 acres.

Selling Broker: the broker who secures a buyer for a listed property.

Separate Property: property owned individually by a spouse, as opposed to community property.

Servient Tenement: property on which an easement or right-of-way for an adjacent (dominant) property passes.

Setback: the amount of space between the lot line and the building line, usually established by a local zoning ordinance.

Severalty: ownership of property by a single individual.

Special Assessment: a tax levied against only the specific properties that will benefit from a public improvement, such as a street or sewer.

Special Warranty Deed: a deed in which the grantor guarantees the title against only the defects that occurred during the grantor's ownership, not defects prior to that time.

Specific Lien: a lien, such as a mortgage, that attaches only to a particular piece of property.

Specific Performance: a legal action in which a court compels a defaulted party to a contract to perform according to the terms of the contract, rather than awarding damages.

Statute of Frauds: the state law that requires certain contracts to be in writing to be enforceable.

Statute of Limitations: the state law that requires that certain actions be brought to court within a specified period of time.

Steering: the illegal practice of directing prospective homebuyers to or away from particular areas.

Straight-Line Depreciation: a method of computing depreciation by decreasing value by an equal amount each year of useful life.

Subdivision: a tract of land divided into lots according to a publicly recorded plat that complies with state and local regulations.

Sublet: the act of a lessee transferring part of his or her lease to a third party.

Subordinate: lower in priority, such as a subordinate lien.

Substitution: the principle in appraising that a buyer will be willing to pay no more for the property being appraised than the cost of purchasing an equally desirable property.

Subrogation: the substitution of one party into another's legal role as the creditor for a particular debt.

Suit for Possession: a lawsuit filed by a landlord to evict a tenant who has violated the terms of the lease or retained possession of the property after the lease expired.

Suit for Specific Performance: a lawsuit filed for the purpose of compelling a party to perform particular acts to settle a dispute, rather than pay monetary damages.

Survey: the process by which the boundaries of a parcel of land are measured and its land areas are determined.

Syndicate: a group formed by a syndicator to combine funds for real estate investment.

T

Tax Deed: an instrument that conveys title to property that has been seized by the government for unpaid taxes and is then sold to satisfy the delinquent taxes.

Tax Lien: a lien placed against a property for failure to pay taxes.

Tax Rate: the rate applied to the assessed value of a property to determine the property taxes.

Tax Sale: the court-ordered sale of a property after the owner fails to pay taxes owed on the property.

Tenancy at Sufferance: the tenancy of a party who unlawfully retains possession of a landlord's property after the term of the lease has expired.

Tenancy at Will: an indefinite tenancy that can be terminated by either the landlord or the tenant.

Tenancy by the Entirety: ownership by a married couple of property acquired during the marriage with right of survivorship.

Tenancy in Common: a form of co-ownership wherein two or more persons hold an undivided interest in the property without the right of survivorship.

Tenant: one who holds or possesses property by any kind of title.

Tenement: anything that may be occupied by a tenant under the terms of a lease.

Testate: leaving a valid will.

Time is of the Essence: a phrase in a contract that requires strict adherence to the dates listed in the contract as deadlines for the performance of specific acts.

Title Insurance: an insurance policy that protects the holder from defects in a title, subject to the exceptions noted in the policy.

Torrens System: a system of registering titles to land with a public authority, who is usually called a *registrar*.

Township: a division of land, measuring six miles square (36 square miles), in the government survey system.

Trade Fixtures: an item of personal property installed by a commercial tenant and removable upon expiration of the lease.

Trust: an arrangement whereby title to property is transferred from a grantor to a trustee, who holds the property for a third party, a beneficiary.

Trust Deed: see *Deed of Trust*.

Trustee: a person who holds title to property for another person designated as the beneficiary.

Truth in Lending Law: also known as *Regulation Z*; requires lenders to make full disclosure regarding the terms of a loan.

U

Undivided Interest: the interest of co-owners to use of an entire property despite the fractional interest owned.

Unilateral Contract: a one-sided contract in which one party is obligated to perform a particular act, but the other party is not bound to act.

Urban Renewal: the process of purchasing property in dilapidated areas for the purpose of redevelopment.

Useful Life: the period of time a property is expected to have economic utility.

Usury: the practice of charging interest at a rate higher than that allowed by law.

V

VA-Guaranteed Loan: a mortgage loan made to a qualified veteran that is guaranteed by the Department of Veteran Affairs.

Valid Contract: an agreement that is legally binding on all parties.

Variance: permission to construct or use a structure in a way contrary to current zoning ordinances.

Vendee: a buyer.

Vendor: a seller; the property owner.

Void Contract: a contract that is not legally enforceable.

Voidable Contract: a contract that appears to be valid but is subject to cancellation by one or both of the parties.

W

Waiver: the surrender of a known right or claim.

Warranty Deed: a deed in which the grantor fully guarantees that a title is good and clear.

Waste: the improper use of a property by a party with the right to possession, such as the holder of a life estate.

Will: a written document that describes the distribution of a deceased person's property, real and personal.

Wraparound Mortgage: a second and subordinate mortgage, granted by a different lender and exceeding the amount of the first loan.

Writ of Execution: a court order to the sheriff or other officer to sell the property of a debtor to satisfy a previously rendered judgment.

Z

Zoning Ordinances: local laws regulating the uses of property.

C·H·A·P·T·E·R 7

ASI REAL ESTATE SALES EXAM 2

CHAPTER SUMMARY

This is the second of the four practice tests in this book based on the ASI Real Estate Sales Exam. Having taken one test before, you should feel more confident in your ability to choose the correct answers. Use this test to see how knowing what to expect can make you feel better prepared.

L ike the first exam in this book, this test is based on the ASI Real Estate Sales Exam. It should not, however, look to you just like the first test you took, because you know more now about how the test is put together and how the different types of questions are presented.

If you're following the advice in this book, you've done some studying between the first exam and this one. This second exam will give you a chance to see how much you've improved.

The answer sheet follows this page, and the test is followed by the answer key. Pay attention to the answer explanations in the key, especially for the questions you have missed.

1.	ⓐ	ⓑ	ⓒ	ⓓ
2.	ⓐ	ⓑ	ⓒ	ⓓ
3.	ⓐ	ⓑ	ⓒ	ⓓ
4.	ⓐ	ⓑ	ⓒ	ⓓ
5.	ⓐ	ⓑ	ⓒ	ⓓ
6.	ⓐ	ⓑ	ⓒ	ⓓ
7.	ⓐ	ⓑ	ⓒ	ⓓ
8.	ⓐ	ⓑ	ⓒ	ⓓ
9.	ⓐ	ⓑ	ⓒ	ⓓ
10.	ⓐ	ⓑ	ⓒ	ⓓ
11.	ⓐ	ⓑ	ⓒ	ⓓ
12.	ⓐ	ⓑ	ⓒ	ⓓ
13.	ⓐ	ⓑ	ⓒ	ⓓ
14.	ⓐ	ⓑ	ⓒ	ⓓ
15.	ⓐ	ⓑ	ⓒ	ⓓ
16.	ⓐ	ⓑ	ⓒ	ⓓ
17.	ⓐ	ⓑ	ⓒ	ⓓ
18.	ⓐ	ⓑ	ⓒ	ⓓ
19.	ⓐ	ⓑ	ⓒ	ⓓ
20.	ⓐ	ⓑ	ⓒ	ⓓ
21.	ⓐ	ⓑ	ⓒ	ⓓ
22.	ⓐ	ⓑ	ⓒ	ⓓ
23.	ⓐ	ⓑ	ⓒ	ⓓ
24.	ⓐ	ⓑ	ⓒ	ⓓ
25.	ⓐ	ⓑ	ⓒ	ⓓ
26.	ⓐ	ⓑ	ⓒ	ⓓ
27.	ⓐ	ⓑ	ⓒ	ⓓ

28.	ⓐ	ⓑ	ⓒ	ⓓ
29.	ⓐ	ⓑ	ⓒ	ⓓ
30.	ⓐ	ⓑ	ⓒ	ⓓ
31.	ⓐ	ⓑ	ⓒ	ⓓ
32.	ⓐ	ⓑ	ⓒ	ⓓ
33.	ⓐ	ⓑ	ⓒ	ⓓ
34.	ⓐ	ⓑ	ⓒ	ⓓ
35.	ⓐ	ⓑ	ⓒ	ⓓ
36.	ⓐ	ⓑ	ⓒ	ⓓ
37.	ⓐ	ⓑ	ⓒ	ⓓ
38.	ⓐ	ⓑ	ⓒ	ⓓ
39.	ⓐ	ⓑ	ⓒ	ⓓ
40.	ⓐ	ⓑ	ⓒ	ⓓ
41.	ⓐ	ⓑ	ⓒ	ⓓ
42.	ⓐ	ⓑ	ⓒ	ⓓ
43.	ⓐ	ⓑ	ⓒ	ⓓ
44.	ⓐ	ⓑ	ⓒ	ⓓ
45.	ⓐ	ⓑ	ⓒ	ⓓ
46.	ⓐ	ⓑ	ⓒ	ⓓ
47.	ⓐ	ⓑ	ⓒ	ⓓ
48.	ⓐ	ⓑ	ⓒ	ⓓ
49.	ⓐ	ⓑ	ⓒ	ⓓ
50.	ⓐ	ⓑ	ⓒ	ⓓ
51.	ⓐ	ⓑ	ⓒ	ⓓ
52.	ⓐ	ⓑ	ⓒ	ⓓ
53.	ⓐ	ⓑ	ⓒ	ⓓ
54.	ⓐ	ⓑ	ⓒ	ⓓ

55.	ⓐ	ⓑ	ⓒ	ⓓ
56.	ⓐ	ⓑ	ⓒ	ⓓ
57.	ⓐ	ⓑ	ⓒ	ⓓ
58.	ⓐ	ⓑ	ⓒ	ⓓ
59.	ⓐ	ⓑ	ⓒ	ⓓ
60.	ⓐ	ⓑ	ⓒ	ⓓ
61.	ⓐ	ⓑ	ⓒ	ⓓ
62.	ⓐ	ⓑ	ⓒ	ⓓ
63.	ⓐ	ⓑ	ⓒ	ⓓ
64.	ⓐ	ⓑ	ⓒ	ⓓ
65.	ⓐ	ⓑ	ⓒ	ⓓ
66.	ⓐ	ⓑ	ⓒ	ⓓ
67.	ⓐ	ⓑ	ⓒ	ⓓ
68.	ⓐ	ⓑ	ⓒ	ⓓ
69.	ⓐ	ⓑ	ⓒ	ⓓ
70.	ⓐ	ⓑ	ⓒ	ⓓ
71.	ⓐ	ⓑ	ⓒ	ⓓ
72.	ⓐ	ⓑ	ⓒ	ⓓ
73.	ⓐ	ⓑ	ⓒ	ⓓ
74.	ⓐ	ⓑ	ⓒ	ⓓ
75.	ⓐ	ⓑ	ⓒ	ⓓ
76.	ⓐ	ⓑ	ⓒ	ⓓ
77.	ⓐ	ⓑ	ⓒ	ⓓ
78.	ⓐ	ⓑ	ⓒ	ⓓ
79.	ⓐ	ⓑ	ⓒ	ⓓ
80.	ⓐ	ⓑ	ⓒ	ⓓ

1. Of the following, which lien has the lowest priority?
   a. property taxes
   b. a mortgage or trust deed
   c. an unpaid water bill
   d. a special assessment

2. The provisions of the Real Estate Settlement Procedures Act (RESPA) apply to
   a. all residential mortgage loans
   b. one- to four-family residential mortgage loans
   c. all mortgages except home equity loans
   d. installment contracts

3. The business of maintaining escrows, collections, and processing of tax records related to mortgage loans is called
   a. servicing
   b. origination
   c. warehousing
   d. brokering

4. In an agency relationship, the client is also known as the
   a. customer
   b. fiduciary
   c. subagent
   d. principal

5. A disabled tenant must be allowed to make necessary alterations at his or her own expense, but the landlord has a legal right to
   a. determine who performs the work
   b. require the tenant to restore the property to its original state when leaving
   c. collect a security deposit from the tenant to ensure compensation for any damage
   d. increase the tenant's rent

6. All of the following are required to create a valid mortgage EXCEPT a
   a. legal description of the property being pledged
   b. signature by the mortgagor
   c. signature by the mortgagee
   d. credit life policy

7. Ownership of a property by only one person is known as
   a. entirety
   b. remainder interest
   c. reversionary interest
   d. severalty

8. Simon Burke took out a $125,000 loan to buy his home. Five years later he sold the house to Richard DeSantos, and the lender agreed that Richard could take the remaining mortgage debt along with the house. Simon will have the most protection if Richard
   a. assumes the loan
   b. takes title subject to the loan
   c. assigns the loan
   d. substitutes his eligibility by novation

9. Sam Brown is suing Linda Green for an unpaid debt. If he wins in court, he'll file a judgment against her home. If Linda should try to sell her home before legal action is resolved, Sam can inform prospective buyers of a potential claim to the property by entering into the public records
a. a mortgage lien
b. an estoppel certificate
c. an alienation clause
d. a lis pendens

10. The lender's underwriting criterion is a maximum payment to income ratio of 35% of gross monthly income. If the applicant proves annual earnings of $75,000 in the previous year, and that salary rate is continuing, the maximum monthly PITI would be
a. $2,187.50
b. $2,625.00
c. $6,250.00
d. $2,571.42

11. The penalty for a first violation of federal fair housing laws can be as much as
a. $1,000
b. $5,000
c. $10,000
d. $100,000

12. How many acres are contained in a parcel 121 feet wide and 240 yards deep?
a. 1
b. 1½
c. 2
d. 2½

13. Jim Fox is 17 when he signs a contract to lease a small house. After the property manager accepts his offer, the lease contract is
a. void
b. voidable
c. valid
d. unenforceable

14. At a closing, items such as property taxes and water bills are divided fairly between buyer and seller in the procedure known as
a. payoff
b. proration
c. price fixing
d. performance

15. An assessment is a special type of appraisal used for
a. property tax purposes
b. income tax returns
c. estate tax returns
d. divorce settlements

16. A cap rate is used in what type of appraisal?
a. reproduction
b. income approach
c. tax assessment
d. competitive market analysis

17. Ed Klein has a large lake on his property. He sells a permit to his friend Phil, allowing him to fish in Ed's lake at any time for one year. Phil's right to use Ed's property is known as
a. a license
b. an encroachment
c. an easement by necessity
d. a prescriptive right

18. Which of the following would best be handled by a property manager of commercial property?
  a. a single-family home
  b. a condominium
  c. a townhouse complex
  d. a shopping center

19. In defining the purpose of the appraisal, the appraiser considers all of the following EXCEPT
  a. the type of value to be arrived at
  b. the date of the valuation
  c. the nature of the real estate involved
  d. recent sales prices

20. The Real Estate Settlement Procedures Act (RESPA) applies to
  a. all residential financing
  b. land contracts
  c. first mortgages only
  d. financing of one- to four-family residences

21. With a VA mortgage, the highest possible loan-to-value ratio is
  a. 10%
  b. 80%
  c. 90%
  d. 100%

22. Jack Logan is informed by the owner of the apartment building he lives in that when his lease expires at the end of the month, it cannot be renewed because the owner's sister is going to need a place to live in 3 months. The owner tells Jack that he may stay in the apartment until a few days before his sister is scheduled to arrive. After Jack's lease expires, but before he moves out, Jack is a
  a. tenant at will
  b. tenant at sufferance
  c. holdover
  d. trespasser

23. The Equal Credit Opportunity Act prohibits discrimination in credit lending based on
  a. political affiliation
  b. dependence on public assistance
  c. criminal record
  d. occupation

24. Repair or remodeling of a property generally adds to its worth. In recognition of the role contractors play in increasing the value of a property, in many states they are assured payment for their goods and services by being able to file a
  a. declaratory judgement against the owner
  b. lis pendens against the title insurance company
  c. mechanics lien against the property
  d. registration with the new owner

25. The most profitable way in which a particular property can be utilized is known as its
  a. plottage value
  b. highest and best use
  c. increasing return
  d. principle of progression

26. Paul and John Mitchell are brothers who own a chain of auto shops. Paul Mitchell is also a real estate broker, and he's been authorized to find a buyer for their business. Paul has
   a. an ostensible agency
   b. a designated agency
   c. an agency by ratification
   d. an agency coupled with an interest

27. In a real estate office, salespersons are generally considered the principal broker's
   a. subagents
   b. delegates
   c. clients
   d. designees

28. Which of the following items should NOT be included in a manager's budget for a property?
   a. utilities
   b. cleaning services and supplies
   c. purchase of adjacent property for expansion of parking lot
   d. debt service

29. In the government survey system of land measurement, how many square miles does a township contain?
   a. 1
   b. 6
   c. 16
   d. 36

30. Under what circumstances, if any, might a broker collect a commission from both buyer and seller?
   a. under no circumstances
   b. only with approval from the state licensing authorities
   c. if both parties give informed consent
   d. if doing so does not violate company policy

31. Which of the following describes the function of mortgage bankers?
   a. They use depositors' money to make mortgage loans.
   b. They are intermediaries who bring borrowers and other lenders together.
   c. They make mortgage loans and sell them on the secondary market.
   d. They often keep loans in their own portfolios.

32. A legal description that includes phrases such as "starting at the intersection of Smith and Baird roads and proceeding westerly 150 feet to a stream" is referred to as
   a. metes and bounds
   b. rectangular survey
   c. lot and block
   d. recorded plat

33. The best method for appraising an apartment building would be the
   a. sales comparison approach
   b. cost approach
   c. income approach
   d. narrative report

34. A customer goes into a restaurant and orders dinner. At the end of the meal, is the customer legally obligated to pay the check?
a. No, because strictly speaking, the customer did not promise to do so.
b. Yes, because when the customer ordered, the customer entered into an implied contract to pay for the meal.
c. Yes, but only if the customer is over the age of 17.
d. Yes, because the customer is liable through the process of novation.

35. When property is appraised as part of the loan application process, a copy of the appraisal
a. belongs to the buyer who paid for it
b. is confidential and for the lender's use only
c. is furnished to the seller only upon written request
d. must be shared with all the parties

36. The amount of tax placed on real estate that is based on the property's assessment is known as
a. a special assessment
b. an ad valorem tax
c. an attachment
d. a general lien

37. Most multiple-listing systems distribute information only on members'
a. exclusive right to sell listings
b. open listings
c. net listings
d. multiple listings

38. On January 1, Fred Gillespie buys a small rental property for $300,000, with the land accounting for 20% of the value. The IRS allows him to depreciate the property over a period of 27.5 years, with land not depreciable. How much can Fred deduct as a charge for depreciation on this year's income tax return?
a. $6,000
b. $8,727.27
c. $10,909.09
d. $24,000

39. Neighbors are allowed input through public hearings when someone applies for a zoning
a. variance
b. amendment
c. nonconforming use
d. conditional use

40. The party most likely to sue for specific performance in the purchase of real estate is the
a. buyer
b. seller
c. broker
d. mortgage insurance company

41. If a person dies leaving no will and no natural heirs, his or her property passes to
a. local charities
b. the state
c. the Internal Revenue Service
d. the Department of Housing and Urban Development

42. The acronym that represents the elements of value is
a. NCAA
b. RUST
c. DUST
d. SPCA

43. Miriam Shepherd lists her house for sale through Quality Realty, with the provision that if she finds a buyer herself, she won't owe any commission. She has given Quality Realty
a. an open listing
b. an exclusive right to sell
c. an exclusive agency
d. a net listing

44. In return for a $100,000 loan, Julia Lawrence gave her bank both a mortgage and a
a. lien
b. lease
c. note
d. check

45. The seller's agent must make diligent efforts to market the property because of the fiduciary duty of
a. notice
b. care
c. loyalty
d. accounting

46. A rectangular tract of land measures 860 feet by 560 feet. Approximately how many acres is this?
a. 11
b. 10.5
c. 8.6
d. 12.8

47. The Sherman Antitrust Law prohibits real estate brokers from
a. selling each other's listings
b. agreeing to set standard commission rates
c. advertising the amount of down payment needed on a property
d. discriminating on the basis of race or religion

48. Before a closing, a buyer will want to make a final
a. survey
b. walk-through
c. inspection
d. assessment

49. When the Taylors finally paid off their 30-year mortgage, their mortgage company was required to send them the document known as
a. a satisfaction piece
b. an alienation clause
c. an acceleration statement
d. an hypothecation

50. Property on the shore of Lake Pleasant is selling for $250 a front foot. If Mary Akerman buys a lot 300 feet wide by 500 feet deep, how much will it cost her?
a. $12,500
b. $15,000
c. $75,000
d. $125,000

51. The function of the Federal Housing Administration (FHA) is to
a. make loans
b. insure loans
c. guarantee loans
d. buy loans

52. The Civil Rights Act of 1866 prohibits discrimination in real estate based on
a. race
b. race and gender
c. handicap and country of origin
d. gender and religion

53. One of the newer developments in mortgage
lending is the use of
a. adjustable rate mortgages
b. wraparound mortgages
c. regional reserve banks
d. computerized loan origination

54. The investor criteria for a home mortgage is
an uninsured loan to value ratio of 75% of the
appraisal. The sales agreement and appraisal is
in the amount of $180,000. Following under-
writing guidelines, the buyer qualifies for a loan
of $145,000. How much of the purchase will be
financed by this investor?
a. $180,000
b. $145,000
c. $108,750
d. $135,000

55. In order to reach the lake, the Browns have a permanent right of way across their neighbor's lake-
front property. The Browns own
a. an easement appurtenant
b. a license
c. a deed restriction
d. a lien

56. All of the following are purposes of the secondary
mortgage market EXCEPT to
a. circulate the flow of money in all markets
b. standardize loan requirements
c. counteract disintermediation
d. set minimum and maximum interest rates

57. A quitclaim deed is often used for transfers
a. to clear title defects
b. for arms length transactions
c. when the grantee requires full assurances
d. that must go into effect immediately

58. The seller has agreed to pay three points to the
lending institution, to help the buyers obtain a
mortgage loan. The house was listed for $200,000
and is being sold for $180,000. The buyers will pay
10% in cash and borrow the rest on a mortgage.
How much will the seller owe to the lender for
points?
a. $1,620
b. $4,860
c. $5,400
d. $6,000

59. Mills are often used in calculating
  a. mortgage interest
  b. property tax rates
  c. real estate commissions
  d. fire insurance premiums

60. A homeowners association decides that the neighborhood community center should be sold for economic reasons. Before attempting to find an investor to purchase the property, the association decides it needs guidance on an appropriate asking price and hires an appraiser. Which approach will the appraiser find most accurate to appraise this property?
  a. the sales comparison approach
  b. the income approach
  c. the gross rent multiplier approach
  d. the cost approach

61. Rita Morgan has $86,576 left on her 8.5% mortgage. Her monthly payment is set at $852.56 for principal and interest (she pays her own taxes and insurance). How much of her next payment will go to reduce the principal?
  a. $116.76
  b. $239.31
  c. $613.25
  d. $735.80

62. When tenant Heather Grayson opened her ice cream shop in the mall, she installed counters and special freezers. When Heather closes the shop, can she remove them?
  a. It depends on whether her lease specifically states that she can.
  b. No, because as a tenant she gives up the right of possession.
  c. Yes, if she repairs any damage caused by their removal.
  d. No, because as fixtures they have become part of the real estate.

63. After estimating the cost to reconstruct a hospital, the appraiser deducts a figure for depreciation, which represents
  a. the amount of IRS deductions
  b. the loss of value from all causes
  c. an adjustment for today's construction techniques
  d. an analysis of the income stream

64. John Fitzpatrick holds $800 in security deposits from the six tenants in his apartment building when he sells the building to Helen Baker. The tenants can expect a return of their security deposits from
  a. John at closing
  b. Helen upon termination of the lease
  c. the person who conducted the closing
  d. John upon completion of the tenancy

65. The approach to value that includes adjustments for depreciation is
a. the cost approach
b. the sales comparison approach
c. the income approach
d. gross rent multiplier approach

66. In inflationary times, a property manager would NOT want a long-term lease based on
a. graduated payments
b. the consumer price index
c. a fixed rate
d. a cost-of-living index

67. In general, the lien with first claim on the real estate is the one first
a. agreed upon
b. signed
c. recorded
d. foreclosed

68. A tenant in a strip mall pays a monthly rental that includes all property maintenance charges, utilities, and cleaning services. This is known as a
a. net lease
b. percentage lease
c. ground lease
d. gross lease

69. Real estate salespersons are most likely to work as
a. independent contractors
b. employees
c. associate brokers
d. listing agents

70. For a lease to be valid, all of the following are required EXCEPT
a. signatures
b. property description
c. term
d. a lease option

71. A deed is the instrument used in most states to convey ownership of
a. personal property
b. short-term use of real estate
c. real property
d. crops and other produce

72. A property manager may legally attract prospective tenants to a building by doing all of the following EXCEPT
a. offering generous concessions
b. removing troublesome tenants
c. undertaking an extensive remodeling effort
d. paying referral fees to salespersons

73. Who can give advice to a prospective buyer on how much to offer for a property?
a. the seller's broker
b. the buyer's broker
c. the facilitator only
d. either the seller's broker or the buyer's broker

74. Key components of an adjustable rate mortgage include all of the following EXCEPT
a. a lower initial rate
b. an index identification
c. a payment to income ratio
d. an adjustment interval

75. Sally Moss, a salesperson associated with broker Ben Deihl, is serving as a buyer's agent for the Whites. After the Whites have bought the Brown's house, Sally can expect payment of a commission from
a. the Whites
b. the Browns
c. either the Whites or the Browns, depending on the wording of the sales agreement
d. Ben

76. Tom Jones asks Sarah Smith, a real estate salesperson, to help him set the right asking price for his home. Sarah's broker will help her prepare
a. a reconciliation of value
b. an assessment analysis
c. a competitive market analysis
d. a limited appraisal

77. Consideration to bind a contract may be in the form of
a. cash or cash equivalent only
b. anything that the parties agree upon as long as it has monetary value
c. money, promises, or services
d. thoughtful treatment of the other party's feelings

78. For a property to bring fair market value, it is necessary that
a. the buyer and seller have never met
b. the seller offers to finance the purchase
c. the property be exposed on the open market
d. a buyer's market exists in the community

79. A new contract may be substituted for an existing one through the process known as
a. assignment
b. delegation
c. execution
d. novation

80. When a borrower defaults on a mortgage, the lender proceeds to cure the default by invoking the
a. default clause
b. acceleration clause
c. prepayment penalty
d. power of sale clause

ANSWERS

1. **c.** Property taxes, special assessments, and recorded liens have priority over all others.
2. **b.** RESPA covers federally related one-to four-family mortgage loans, including equity loans.
3. **a.** The loan servicing organization maintains escrow accounts from which property taxes and insurance premiums are paid. It also initiates appropriate collection procedures in the event of default by the borrower.
4. **d.** The person who retains an agent is known as the client, or principal.
5. **b.** The tenant has the right to adapt the property but the landlord may require the premises restored to their original state when the tenant leaves.
6. **d.** A valid mortgage must be in writing, signed by all parties having capacity to contract, and have a valid debt (note), legal description, and mortgaging clause.
7. **d.** The word "severalty" comes from "sever," and implies that all other persons are severed, or cut off, from any share of ownership.
8. **d.** Simon will still be liable even if Richard assumes the loan. He will be completely free only if Richard's qualifications allow him to substitute his liability for Simon's. The process is called novation.
9. **d.** A lis pendens gives the public notice that a lien may be placed on the property, dating back to the time the lis pendens was recorded.
10. **a.** $75,000 ÷ 12 × .35 = $2,187.50
11. **c.** HUD's penalty for a first offense can be $10,000. (The Justice Department may fine for a pattern of repeat violations up to $100,000.)

12. **c.** 240 yards = 720 feet (240 × 3 feet in a yard). 121 feet × 740 feet = 87,120 square feet. 87,120 square feet divided by 43,560 square feet in an acre = 2 acres.
13. **b.** The lease contract appears to be valid, but if it is not completed when Jim turns 18, he may disavow it, thus making it voidable.
14. **b.** Proration assigns credits and debits for various expenses to buyer and seller during the settlement process.
15. **a.** Assessors set the value at which real estate will be taxed.
16. **b.** The capitalization rate is an analysis of how much investors are willing to spend in a certain neighborhood in return for a certain amount of income.
17. **a.** A license is a privilege to use the land of another for a specific purpose. It may not be assigned, and ends upon expiration, revocation, or withdrawal.
18. **d.** Income-producing properties are generally classified as commercial.
19. **d.** Recent sales prices are a part of the data the appraiser will collect later.
20. **d.** RESPA sets requirements for all federally related mortgages and home equity loans on one- to four-family residences.
21. **d.** A VA mortgage is possible with no down payment, making the loan-to-value ratio 100%.
22. **a.** If the tenant agrees to an offer to remain in the property until a date uncertain, the estate is a tenancy at will.
23. **b.** In 1976, the ECOA was amended to add income from public assistance and age to race, color, religion, and national origin as protected classes for loan applicants.

24. **c.** Contractors are permitted to file a mechanics lien against the improved property, and the encumbrance remains on the property until removed.

25. **b.** Analyzing a parcel's highest and best use (in terms of money) is a standard part of the appraisal process.

26. **d.** Paul is not only an agent, but also has an interest (part ownership) in the property, and should disclose this to potential buyers.

27. **a.** In most cases, associated licensees in an office are the supervising broker's subagents.

28. **c.** Purchase of adjacent property may be an objective of the owner but is not a part of the manager's job.

29. **d.** A township is six miles on each side and contains 36 one-square-mile sections.

30. **c.** Particularly in commercial transactions, payment by both parties does occur; the requirement is that each agrees and approves.

31. **c.** Mortgage bankers are in the business of originating, selling, and servicing loans.

32. **a.** The intersection and the stream are known as monuments, which mark the corners of a metes and bounds legal description.

33. **c.** Real estate used for the production of income is best appraised by analyzing the amount of income that may be expected.

34. **b.** A valid contract can be implied by the action of the parties.

35. **a.** The Equal Credit Opportunity Act provides that the borrower is entitled to a copy of the appraisal if the buyer paid for it.

36. **b.** *Ad valorem* means "according to the value." More expensive real estate will pay a higher ad valorem tax than its neighbor.

37. **a.** An exclusive right to sell agreement is the type preferred by most multiple-listing systems.

38. **b.** Fred can claim depreciation only on the cost of the building, which represents 80% of his purchase price. The building costs $240,000 (.80 × $300,000). He may deduct that amount as depreciation over a period of $27\frac{1}{2}$ years. $240,000 divided by 27.5 = $8,727.27 depreciation each year.

39. **a.** The landowner who wants to use property in a manner forbidden by local zoning restrictions applies for a variance. It may or may not be granted following a public hearing.

40. **a.** While a seller's problems might be solved with money damages, a buyer might prefer forcing the seller to sell, because each parcel of real estate is unique.

41. **b.** The state becomes owner of a deceased person's property in the absence of a will or natural heirs, through the power of escheat.

42. **c.** The acronym stands for Demand, Utility, Scarcity, Transferability

43. **c.** With an exclusive agency, the property owner retains the right to sell on his or her own without paying commission.

44. **c.** The mortgage serves as security for the debt, which the borrower promises to repay by signing a note.

45. **b.** The agent's obligation to exercise due diligence comes from the fiduciary duty of care.

46. **a.** 860 feet × 560 feet ÷ 43,560 sq. ft. per acre = 11.05 acres.

47. **b.** In the past, brokers have suffered large fines for conspiring to set commission rates beyond their own offices.

48. **b.** The buyer will want to make sure the property is still in good condition.

49. **a.** The *satisfaction piece* is sometimes known as a mortgage discharge or release of mortgage.

50. **c.** Each front foot along the lake costs $250, so the total value is $75,000 ($250 times 300 feet).

51. **b.** The FHA does not lend any money; it administers an insurance program that allows home-buyers to borrow almost the full purchase price with a low down payment.

52. **a.** The law that followed the close of the Civil War extended equal rights in real property to members of all races.

53. **d.** The use of CLO, computerized loan origination systems, shortens approval time and is growing in popularity.

54. **d.** $180,000 times .75 = $135,000 maximum uninsured loan.

55. **a.** An easement appurtenant allows the owner a particular use of an adjoining parcel's land. The Browns do not have a license, because they have a permanent right, while a license may be withdrawn or canceled.

56. **d.** The secondary mortgage market does not set rates, but it does assure that money is available to purchase qualifying mortgages from anywhere in the country.

57. **a.** The signer of a quitclaim deed makes no guarantee of ownership and transfers only what interest he or she may have. Besides clearing a cloud (possible or partial claims), quitclaim deeds are often used for transfers within a family or during a divorce.

58. **b.** Points are paid on the amount borrowed, not the selling price. The buyers are borrowing 90% of the sale price, or $162,000. Each point is one percent of that figure, so three points are .03 times $162,000 is $4,860.

59. **b.** Mills, each one-tenth of a cent, are sometimes used to express the tax rate per dollar of assessed value.

60. **d.** Unique properties are most accurately appraised by employing the cost approach to value.

61. **b.** A year's interest on the present debt would be $7,358.96 ($86,576 × .085). A month's interest is $613.25 ($7,358.96 ÷ 12). The principal portion of her payment is $239.31 ($852.56 − 613.25).

62. **c.** Trade fixtures, installed for use in a trade or business, may be removed by the tenant prior to the expiration of the lease if the premises are returned to their original condition.

63. **b.** Depreciation includes loss of value from physical, economic, and functional obsolescence.

64. **b.** The new landlord is responsible for the return of the security deposits, which should have been credited to him when the sale was settled.

65. **a.** In the cost approach, the property's depreciated value is estimated.

66. **c.** With a fixed-rate lease, the property manager would not have the ability to raise the rent as the market dictates.

67. **c.** The general rule is that the lien first recorded takes priority.

68. **d.** A gross lease is one that includes all expenses within the rental price.

69. **a.** Few licensees are hired as employees; in most cases, they work as independent contractors.

70. **d.** An option is only used if that is the intent of the parties.

71. **c.** A deed conveys ownership of real property; all other matter is conveyed by lease, bill of sale, or title.

72. **d.** It is illegal to pay referral fees to anyone except a principal broker.

73. **b.** Only the buyer's own broker, if one is involved, should advise on the proper offering price.

74. **c.** Capacity to repay is not a consideration. The important components are initial rate, adjustment interval, and rate caps.

75. **d.** A salesperson may never accept payment from anyone except his or her own supervising broker.

76. **c.** The CMA, competitive market analysis, is a simple form intended to estimate possible sale price.

77. **c.** If the parties agree, consideration need not be valuable in order to be considered "good" enough.

78. **c.** Wide exposure on the open market is a part of the definition of fair market value.

79. **d.** The substitution of a new contract in place of the original one is known as novation.

80. **b.** The acceleration clause empowers the lender to call the loan, making it payable immediately. If the borrower fails to cure the default or pay off the balance, the lender begins foreclosure proceedings.

SCORING

Evaluate how you did on this second practice exam by again counting only the number of questions you got right; remember that questions you skipped or got wrong don't count. Divide the number of questions you got right by 80, the total number of questions in the test, to find your percentage. The table at the end of Practice Exam 1 will help you to check your math. If you achieve a score of at least 70 to 75 percent, you will most likely pass the ASI Real Estate Sales Exam.

Keep in mind that how you did on each of the basic areas tested by the exam is more important, at this point, than your score. Your percentage scores in conjunction with the EasySmart Test Preparation System in Chapter 2 of this book will help you revise your study plan if need be. After your study plan is revised, turn again to the Real Estate Refresher Course and the Real Estate Math Review in Chapters 4 and 5, and to the Real Estate Glossary in Chapter 6.

Use the table below to see where your strengths and weaknesses lie so that you can concentrate your efforts as you continue to prepare. After working more on your problem areas, take the third practice exam in Chapter 8 to see how much you've improved.

FOR REVIEW	
QUESTION SUBJECT AREA	**QUESTION NUMBERS**
Real Property	1, 7, 9, 12, 17, 24, 29, 32, 36 39, 41, 46, 55, 57, 67, 71
Valuation and Appraisal	15, 16, 19, 25, 33, 38, 42, 60, 63, 65, 76, 78
Contracts, Agency, Federal Requirements	2, 4, 20, 23, 26, 27, 30, 34, 35, 37, 40, 43, 45, 47, 52, 69, 73, 75, 77, 79
Financing	3, 6, 8, 10, 14, 21, 31, 44, 48, 49, 50, 51, 53, 54, 56, 58, 59, 61, 74, 80
Leases, Rents, Property Management	5, 11, 13, 18, 22, 28, 62, 64, 66, 68, 70, 72

C·H·A·P·T·E·R
ASI REAL ESTATE SALES EXAM 3
8

CHAPTER SUMMARY
This is the third of the four practice tests in this book based on the ASI Real Estate Sales Exam. Use this test to identify which types of questions are still giving you problems.

You are now beginning to be very familiar with the content of the ASI Real Estate Sales Exam and most likely feel more confident than you did at first. However, your practice test-taking experience will help you most if you have created a situation as close as possible to the real one.

For this third exam, simulate a real test. Find a quiet place where you will not be disturbed. Have with you two sharpened pencils and a good eraser. Complete the test in one sitting, using a timer or stopwatch set for three hours. You should have plenty of time to answer all of the questions when you take the real exam, but you'll want to practice working quickly without rushing.

As before, the answer sheet you should use is on the next page. After the exam is an answer key, with all the answers explained. These explanations will help you see where you need further study. When you've finished the exam and scored it, look at the table at the very end of this practice exam to see areas you may have had trouble with; then you'll know which areas to concentrate on before you take the fourth exam.

1. (a) (b) (c) (d)
2. (a) (b) (c) (d)
3. (a) (b) (c) (d)
4. (a) (b) (c) (d)
5. (a) (b) (c) (d)
6. (a) (b) (c) (d)
7. (a) (b) (c) (d)
8. (a) (b) (c) (d)
9. (a) (b) (c) (d)
10. (a) (b) (c) (d)
11. (a) (b) (c) (d)
12. (a) (b) (c) (d)
13. (a) (b) (c) (d)
14. (a) (b) (c) (d)
15. (a) (b) (c) (d)
16. (a) (b) (c) (d)
17. (a) (b) (c) (d)
18. (a) (b) (c) (d)
19. (a) (b) (c) (d)
20. (a) (b) (c) (d)
21. (a) (b) (c) (d)
22. (a) (b) (c) (d)
23. (a) (b) (c) (d)
24. (a) (b) (c) (d)
25. (a) (b) (c) (d)
26. (a) (b) (c) (d)
27. (a) (b) (c) (d)

28. (a) (b) (c) (d)
29. (a) (b) (c) (d)
30. (a) (b) (c) (d)
31. (a) (b) (c) (d)
32. (a) (b) (c) (d)
33. (a) (b) (c) (d)
34. (a) (b) (c) (d)
35. (a) (b) (c) (d)
36. (a) (b) (c) (d)
37. (a) (b) (c) (d)
38. (a) (b) (c) (d)
39. (a) (b) (c) (d)
40. (a) (b) (c) (d)
41. (a) (b) (c) (d)
42. (a) (b) (c) (d)
43. (a) (b) (c) (d)
44. (a) (b) (c) (d)
45. (a) (b) (c) (d)
46. (a) (b) (c) (d)
47. (a) (b) (c) (d)
48. (a) (b) (c) (d)
49. (a) (b) (c) (d)
50. (a) (b) (c) (d)
51. (a) (b) (c) (d)
52. (a) (b) (c) (d)
53. (a) (b) (c) (d)
54. (a) (b) (c) (d)

55. (a) (b) (c) (d)
56. (a) (b) (c) (d)
57. (a) (b) (c) (d)
58. (a) (b) (c) (d)
59. (a) (b) (c) (d)
60. (a) (b) (c) (d)
61. (a) (b) (c) (d)
62. (a) (b) (c) (d)
63. (a) (b) (c) (d)
64. (a) (b) (c) (d)
65. (a) (b) (c) (d)
66. (a) (b) (c) (d)
67. (a) (b) (c) (d)
68. (a) (b) (c) (d)
69. (a) (b) (c) (d)
70. (a) (b) (c) (d)
71. (a) (b) (c) (d)
72. (a) (b) (c) (d)
73. (a) (b) (c) (d)
74. (a) (b) (c) (d)
75. (a) (b) (c) (d)
76. (a) (b) (c) (d)
77. (a) (b) (c) (d)
78. (a) (b) (c) (d)
79. (a) (b) (c) (d)
80. (a) (b) (c) (d)

1. A landlord is NOT allowed to charge a tenant extra rent because the tenant has a
   a. dog
   b. second car
   c. child
   d. RV

2. A contingency in a purchase contract is
   a. something that must happen before the buyer can be required to complete the purchase
   b. a listing of personal property that is to be left by the seller
   c. a statement making time of the essence in the performance of the contract
   d. the seller's promise to prove clear title to the buyer's satisfaction

3. The Franks receive two offers on their house, which is listed for $140,000. Anne Hill offers to pay $138,000 cash for the house. Bob Stone offers $141,000, putting 20% down, if the Franks will pay three points to their lender for the mortgage loan the buyers need. What is the monetary difference between the two offers?
   a. $384
   b. $3,000
   c. $2,000
   d. $1,128

4. Under the regulations of the Real Estate Settlement Procedures Act (RESPA),
   a. a broker may collect a fee for referring the buyer to a lending institution
   b. the seller may require that the buyer purchase title insurance from a certain title company
   c. the lender must provide the borrower a good-faith estimate of settlement costs at least an hour before closing
   d. controlled business arrangements are permitted as long as the consumer is informed and notified about the availability of other providers

5. A residential property was built 75 years ago. Two of the five bedrooms have no closets, the basement floor is unpaved, and the original slate roof needs repairs. To the appraiser, the most important consideration is
   a. the sale price of a nearby similar property
   b. how much it would cost to finish the basement floor
   c. how the bedrooms could be reconfigured to provide some storage
   d. the life-expectancy of the roof

6. In the event the landlord fails or refuses to provide essential services, the tenant is permitted to
   a. refuse to make further lease payments
   b. file an injunction for recovery
   c. arrange for those services
   d. redeem the property

7. An article of personal property that is permanently attached and becomes part of the real estate is known as
   a. an emblement
   b. an accretion
   c. a chattel
   d. a fixture

8. The veteran who receives a VA loan is borrowing the money from
   a. the state veterans' agency
   b. the Department of Veterans Affairs
   c. Fannie Mae
   d. a local lending institution

9. A subdivider must place in the public records a map of the property known as a
   a. plan
   b. zone
   c. plot
   d. plat

10. A property manager may legally deny leasing an apartment to a prospect if
   a. the tenant is handicapped and requires the assistance of a guide dog
   b. the applicant has more than 3 children
   c. the prospective tenants are being evicted from their present dwelling because of continual late payment of rent
   d. one of the applicants is of foreign descent and has objectionable religious practices

11. The amount of commission a salesperson receives is set by
   a. state law
   b. negotiation between lister and seller
   c. agreement between broker and associate
   d. the Department of Commerce

12. Depreciation is classified as curable if it can be
   a. lived with
   b. recovered
   c. deducted on an income tax return
   d. fixed

13. Tim and Bonnie Hill are most likely to borrow the money to buy their dream home from
   a. a credit union
   b. an investment group
   c. a pension fund
   d. a secondary market company

14. An abstract of title contains
   a. the summary of a title search
   b. an attorney's opinion of title
   c. a registrar's certificate of title
   d. a quiet title lawsuit

15. When determining replacement costs, the appraiser may use any of the following EXCEPT
   a. price-per-square-foot method
   b. cubic-foot method
   c. unit-in-place method
   d. consumer-price-index method

16. Any buyer or seller should be informed at first contact whom the agent represents, so that they will know
   a. who is responsible for the commission
   b. whether they need a lawyer
   c. whom to ask about hidden defects
   d. whether their disclosures will be held in confidence

17. The seller of a house built before 1978 is required by law to furnish the buyer with a
   a. good-faith estimate of settlement costs
   b. lead paint information booklet
   c. reduction certificate
   d. proof of flood insurance

18. At closing, the lending institution may ask the buyer to
   a. pay the state transfer tax
   b. sign a disclosure of property condition
   c. deposit money in an escrow account
   d. reimburse the seller for prepaid property taxes

19. In some states, the instrument used instead of a mortgage is a
   a. deed of trust
   b. negotiable instrument
   c. promissory note
   d. release deed

20. Which of the following approaches would an appraiser most likely use to appraise a church?
   a. market data approach
   b. cost approach
   c. income approach
   d. gross rent multiplier approach

21. Unless otherwise stated in the sales agreement, the buyer accepts the property in its condition at the time of the
   a. settlement
   b. walk-through inspection
   c. contract
   d. possession

22. In determining the market value of the subject property, which of the following would be of most importance?
   a. market value less depreciation
   b. market price of comparable properties
   c. market value of recently sold properties
   d. adjustment between market value and market price

23. When adjusting for differences, the appraiser should base the value of the feature on
   a. their personal feeling about the worthiness of the feature
   b. the cost of removing or adding the feature
   c. their opinion of what the feature adds to or detracts from the property
   d. what a knowledgeable buyer would pay or penalize for the feature

24. The term PITI refers to
    a. the designation of a graduate of the Property Insurance Training Institute
    b. a participation mortgage
    c. a broker's proof of procuring cause
    d. the various sums that make up a monthly mortgage payment

25. Tenancy by the entirety differs from other forms of co-ownership in that
    a. neither owner can force a sale
    b. each owner is free to devise his or her share to chosen heirs
    c. shares may be acquired at different times
    d. the property must be a principal residence

26. A lease would NOT be terminated in which of the following situations?
    a. The tenant becomes the owner.
    b. The property is destroyed by fire.
    c. The landlord has the tenant removed from the property.
    d. The tenant defaults in lease payments.

27. The amount of commission to be paid to a broker is determined by
    a. the Federal Trade Commission
    b. negotiation between agent and client
    c. the Sherman Anti-Trust Act
    d. the local Association of Realtors

28. An acre contains approximately
    a. 5,270 square yards
    b. 40,000 square feet
    c. one quarter square mile
    d. 43,560 square feet

29. When the Franks bought their first home, some of their costs included payment of points, establishment of an escrow account, premium for title insurance, and commission to their own buyers' agent. On that year's income tax return they may deduct the
    a. points
    b. title insurance
    c. commission
    d. escrowed amount

30. Prices are likely to rise when there is a
    a. buyer's market
    b. seller's market
    c. thin market
    d. broad market

31. Kelly Adams lists her house and tells her listing agent, Sheila Fabris, "I'm listing for $150,000 but I might take less." Sheila may properly
    a. advertise the property for "$150,000 or less"
    b. explain Kelly's position to prospective buyers in an effort to obtain an offer
    c. share Kelly's statement only with the buyer's broker
    d. keep the information to herself

32. Land consisting of a quarter section is sold for $1,850 per acre. The total sale price is
    a. $296,000
    b. $592,000
    c. $1,184,000
    d. $1,850,000

33. The Smiths offer to buy the Browns' house for $125,000, with the closing scheduled for June 15. The Browns sign a written acceptance, with the provision that the closing is to be on June 16. At this point, which of the following can occur?
- a. The Smiths can back out of buying the house with no penalty.
- b. The Browns can hold the Smiths to a June 15 closing.
- c. The Browns can hold the Smiths to a June 16 closing.
- d. The Smiths can sue for specific performance on June 15.

34. Each party is bound to a specific date for performance if a real estate sales contract contains
- a. an exact date for transfer of title
- b. a time limit for the buyer to secure mortgage financing
- c. a provision that time is of the essence
- d. a meeting of the minds

35. Which of the following is an example of voluntary alienation of real property?
- a. a condemnation sale
- b. a foreclosure auction
- c. a deed of trust
- d. a transfer by escheat

36. Information gathered when the agent lists property should include data on
- a. the racial makeup of the neighborhood
- b. the seller's motivation
- c. current property tax exemptions
- d. any past murders or suicides on the property

37. Land and the buildings on it can be owned separately under the arrangement known as a
- a. net lease
- b. life estate
- c. reversion
- d. ground lease

38. Which of the following statements is NOT true of an FHA loan?
- a. The loan is insured up to certain limits.
- b. The funds for the loan are provided by FHA.
- c. The down payment requirements are much lower than for conventional loans.
- d. A mortgage insurance premium is included in the monthly payment.

39. After a purchase contract is accepted, the parties may later make additional agreements without changing the original document by use of
- a. an addendum
- b. a codicil
- c. a revision
- d. a contingency

40. A contract owner of a property suspects that the seller is considering selling the property to another buyer. To preserve her rights, the contract owner should
- a. immediately begin suit for specific performance
- b. file a lis pendens in the public records of the jurisdiction in which the property is located
- c. post a warning sign in the front yard
- d. declare the deposit to be forfeited

41. The house on Summit Street is up for sale because last year an ax murder took place in an upstairs bedroom. In real estate circles the house is now considered
   a. latently defective
   b. environmentally unsound
   c. functionally obsolescent
   d. stigmatized

42. The alienation clause found in most mortgages states that the full amount will be immediately due and payable if the
   a. borrower is late with three monthly payments
   b. property is sold to a new owner
   c. hazard insurance policy is allowed to lapse
   d. homeowner borrows more money on the property

43. The Flynns have lost their jobs, fallen behind on mortgage payments, and are about to lose their home to foreclosure proceedings, which have already started. At the last minute, Bob Flynn's father agrees to give them all the money they owe plus legal costs. The Flynns can stop the foreclosure using their
   a. equitable right of redemption
   b. deed in lieu of foreclosure
   c. defeasance clause
   d. deficiency judgment

44. If a comparable property has a $15,000 garage and the subject property has no garage, the appraiser would
   a. subtract $15,000 from the sale price of the comparable property
   b. add $15,000 to the appraised price of the subject
   c. add $15,000 to the sale price of the comparable property
   d. subtract $7,500 from the estimated price of the subject

45. The definition of land includes all of the following EXCEPT
   a. the bundle of legal rights
   b. minerals below the surface
   c. planted vegetation
   d. space above the surface

46. One example of an easement in gross is the right of
   a. owners to cut across their neighbor's property in order to reach their lot
   b. a roofing company working on repairs to store some of their equipment in the neighbor's yard
   c. owners to use the neighbor's backyard for their summer office party
   d. utility companies to access a property in order to maintain wires or pipes

47. Lenders across the country are likely to offer a certain type of mortgage plan after an announcement that mortgages with certain specifications will be purchased by
a. the Office of Thrift Supervision
b. the Federal Deposit Insurance Corporation
c. Fannie Mae
d. HUD

48. The main obligation the principal owes a real estate agent is
a. confidentiality
b. compensation
c. obedience
d. accounting

49. The borrower who carries private mortgage insurance is allowed a loan-to-value ratio as high as
a. 80%
b. 90%
c. 95%
d. 100%

50. The term "comps" refers to
a. operating expense ratios
b. recent nearby sales
c. reserves for replacement
d. reproduction cost

51. The large organizations that influence the mortgage market by purchasing mortgages in the secondary market include
a. HUD
b. FIRREA
c. GNMA
d. RESPA

52. The buyer at a foreclosure auction is usually required to
a. pay all cash within a short period of time
b. bring proof of pre-approval for a mortgage
c. assume the defaulted mortgage
d. recompense the lending institution for any loss on the sale

53. The best way for a broker acting as a dual agent to minimize his or her risk is to
a. negotiate a win/win transaction from which each party walks away satisfied
b. obtain written acknowledgment from each party that they consent to the agent acting for both sides
c. obey each party's instructions even if they are in conflict
d. give notice to each party of any information useful in negotiation

54. The Bakers have a gross income of $60,000. The lender will let them spend no more than 28% of their income on a monthly mortgage payment. A house they can buy for $140,000 has $4,000 in annual property taxes. Homeowners insurance would cost about $400 a year. At today's interest rates, monthly payments would be $8.56 per $1,000 borrowed on a 30-year mortgage. What is the smallest amount they can expect to spend for a cash down payment?
   a. $10,334
   b. $12,717
   c. $14,000
   d. $19,283

55. Real estate agents are licensed by
   a. the United States Attorney General's office
   b. their state
   c. their local Association of Realtors
   d. the Federal Trade Commission

56. Five covenants that protect the grantee are found in a
   a. quitclaim deed
   b. bargain and sale deed
   c. sheriff's deed
   d. warranty deed

57. FHA mortgage insurance premium is calculated at a rate of one-half percent annually. How much is the premium for the month in which the remaining principal owed is $92,347?
   a. $.05
   b. $12
   c. $38.48
   d. $46.17

58. A real estate listing is usually an example of
   a. a universal agency
   b. a special agency
   c. a general agency
   d. an ostensible agency

59. A buyer contracts for a property and negotiates a purchase price of $250,000. With a 20% down payment, he has no problem obtaining a 30-year conventional loan for the balance. At 8% the table calls for a monthly payment at the rate of $7.34 per thousand. If the lender adds another $250 per month for escrows, what will the buyer pay each month?
   a. $1,835.00
   b. $1,468.00
   c. $2,085.00
   d. $1,718.00

60. The first step in the appraisal process is to
   a. establish the fee
   b. determine the purpose of the appraisal
   c. collect data
   d. estimate the value of the land

61. To secure a loan, the borrower conveys legal title to the property to a disinterested third party for safekeeping. In this situation, the title is known as a
   a. general warranty deed
   b. trust deed
   c. involuntary conveyance
   d. mortgage

62. Common covenants found in a mortgage could be any of the following EXCEPT a promise to
   a. keep the property in good repair
   b. pay all real estate taxes as they come due
   c. provide unlimited access to the mortgagee
   d. not destroy or remove any improvements securing the loan

63. A lien against all property of an individual for an IRS debt is referred to as
   a. specific and voluntary
   b. general and involuntary
   c. specific and involuntary
   d. general and voluntary

64. The borrower negotiates with the lender to cure a default by assigning title to the lender in exchange for a release from further indebtedness. This agreement is called a
   a. non-judicial foreclosure
   b. power of sale transfer
   c. deed in lieu of foreclosure
   d. strict foreclosure

65. A conventional fully amortized loan features
   a. equal payments of principal and interest
   b. fixed principal payment with interest deferred to a future date
   c. interest payments only with principal due at a future date
   d. constant payments with earned interest collected and any remainder applied to principal

66. When a licensee knows a statement is false and makes it in order to take advantage of someone, the licensee is guilty of
   a. negligent misrepresentation
   b. puffing
   c. fraud
   d. undue influence

67. The federal ban on discrimination based on familial status is intended to provide equal access to rentals for
   a. unmarried couples
   b. people with children
   c. single tenants
   d. the elderly

68. The land between a large factory and a residential neighborhood has been zoned for use as a park or playground. This is an example of a
   a. buffer zone
   b. spot zone
   c. variance
   d. nonconforming use

69. A shoe store in the Town Mall pays a base rent each month plus additional rent based on the amount of business it does. It is operating under a
   a. ground lease
   b. percentage lease
   c. net lease
   d. holdover lease

70. The difference between replacement cost and reproduction cost results from the different
   a. lots on which the properties are placed
   b. times when the structures are built
   c. handbooks used to estimate labor and materials
   d. materials and techniques used for construction

71. The term "APR" stands for
   a. annual percentage rate
   b. appraisal procedure regulations
   c. associate property reviewer
   d. average purchase ratio

72. No federal fair housing laws are violated if a landlord refuses to rent to
   a. children
   b. Vietnamese
   c. deaf persons
   d. students

73. Don Bottelli's family has run a little corner grocery store for 50 years in a neighborhood that has been newly zoned for single family homes only. Don may continue to operate the store as a
   a. variance
   b. conditional use
   c. nonconforming use
   d. buffer zone

74. In order to find out if fair housing laws are being followed, real estate offices are sometimes visited by
   a. Human Rights Commission supervisors
   b. undercover testers
   c. Equal Credit Opportunity lenders
   d. families with children

75. A tenant with a commercial lease pays, on a monthly basis, $1,000 base rental plus $\frac{1}{12}$ of the $18,000 annual tax bill and 3% of his gross receipts. If the tenant takes in $75,000 in the month of May, what is the rental payment for June?
   a. $4,750
   b. $3,750
   c. $3,250
   d. $7,400

76. Martha James lives in one side of a two-family house. She wants to advertise the other side as non-smoking. Can she legally do so?
   a. Yes, because the right to smoke is not protected by law.
   b. Yes, because she occupies part of the house herself.
   c. No, because a property owner cannot advertise discriminatory practices.
   d. No, because she can only legally discriminate on the basis of credit and income.

77. The relationship of a property manager with the owner is a
a. special agency
b. general agency
c. limited partnership
d. dual agency

78. The Simons have defaulted on their loan payments and are behind in paying the rest of their bills, so their home is being sold in a foreclosure auction. Of the many liens against it, which will have first claim on the proceeds of the sale?
a. the first mortgage recorded
b. the mechanics lien
c. the unpaid real estate taxes
d. the home equity loan

79. Robin Smith's neighbor had no room to store his RV, so Robin gave him permission to park it in Robin's backyard. The neighbor's right to use Robin's backyard is known as
a. an easement by necessity
b. a license
c. a leasehold estate
d. a driveway agreement

80. The task of the appraiser is to
a. establish market price
b. guess at the final contract price
c. estimate market value
d. evaluate the property for tax purposes

ANSWERS

1. **c.** The Fair Housing Amendments Act of 1988 added the presence of children in a family as a protected class.

2. **a.** The most common contingencies are for the buyer's securing the necessary financing, the sale of the buyer's present home, and the buyer's approval of a home inspector's report.

3. **a.** Bob will get a mortgage for $112,800 ($141,000 × 80%). Each point will cost $1,128 (1% of $112,800). Three points will cost $3,384 ($1,128 × 3). The Franks will end up with $141,000 less $3,384, or $137,616. This is $384 less than Anne would give them ($138,000 − $137,616).

4. **d.** RESPA allows controlled business arrangements with sufficient notice to the consumer. (That good-faith estimate in choice **c** must be provided no later than three days after the loan application.)

5. **a.** In appraising residential real estate, the subject property is compared with similar properties that have recently sold.

6. **c.** The tenant may arrange for those services and sue the landlord for damages.

7. **d.** A fixture is the correct response. *Emblements* are annual crops, *accretion* refers to land built up by soil deposits, and *chattel* is another word for personal property.

8. **d.** The VA guarantees the loan, which is obtained from a regular lending institution.

9. **d.** The subdivision map, which shows lots, blocks, streets, and the like, is known as a plat. It is filed in a plat book, open to the public, and sometimes designated as a liber.

10. **c.** Applicants may only be rejected because of financial qualification or past record problems.

11. **c.** Each real estate company has its own policy on how commissions are split between the office and the salesperson.

12. **d.** Curable depreciation can be remedied at reasonable cost.

13. **a.** Credit unions are increasingly entering the primary mortgage market. The other lenders mentioned deal mainly in large commercial loans.

14. **a.** An abstract reports the results of a title search of the public records.

15. **d.** Reliable methods of determining replacement costs are the square-foot method (most common), cubic-foot method, unit-in-place method, and quantity-survey method.

16. **d.** The question of confidential information is the main reason for all the new state laws on agency disclosure.

17. **b.** Tenants must receive lead paint information before a lease is signed, if the house was built before 1978.

18. **c.** If the lender is to handle the homeowner's insurance premiums and property tax bills, the escrow account is established at closing.

19. **a.** A deed of trust differs from a mortgage in that it simplifies the process of foreclosure in case of default.

20. **b.** Unique property that does not produce income is appraised by estimating reproduction or replacement cost.

21. **c.** Properties are generally accepted in the condition as of the time of contract. That is why it is important that a thorough inspection be made by the buyer or designee prior to the contract being ratified. The seller is responsible for any changes to the condition of the property between contract and closing.

22. **b.** The market price of the comparable (recently sold) properties is used to determine market value for the subject property.

23. **d.** Appraisers estimate reactions to features by buyers when adjusting for features.

24. **d.** PITI stands for the principal, interest, taxes, and insurance payments often included in a monthly mortgage payment.

25. **a.** When a married couple buys any real estate as tenants by the entirety, neither can obtain a court order for partition.

26. **d.** A default would not terminate a lease; all other listed options would.

27. **c.** Anti-trust legislation forbids any community-wide standard for fees, which must be set by agreement between the parties.

28. **d.** Students should memorize the size of an acre, which some estimate at "somewhat more than 200 feet by 200 feet."

29. **a.** Points paid for a purchase money mortgage on one's own home are immediately deductible as prepaid interest.

30. **b.** In a seller's market, buyers are competing for the few homes on the market and are likely to offer more for them.

31. **d.** The duty of confidentiality forbids Sheila's sharing any information that might damage her client's bargaining position.

32. **a.** A quarter section contains 160 acres. (160 times $1,850 is $296,000).

33. **a.** When the Browns made a counteroffer, it constituted a rejection of the original offer. The Smiths are now free and may accept or reject the counteroffer.

34. **c.** When time is of the essence, the party that is not ready to perform is liable for breach of contract.

35. **c.** Only the trust represents the owner's own decision; the other transfers would be involuntary.

36. **c.** The broker should be sure the data reflects the true tax figure. Seller's motivation should be kept confidential. Disclosure of stigmas is covered by state law in most areas.

37. **d.** A ground lease, usually for a long period of years, allows the tenant to erect and own buildings on rented land.

38. **b.** FHA insures the lenders against loss in the event of foreclosure. It does not provide funds for loans.

39. **a.** Any provision later added to a contract is known as an addendum. It identifies the original contract and must be signed by all parties.

40. **b.** A lis pendens gives notice to the world of a person's potential interest in a property and is the proper action to take in this situation.

41. **d.** State laws and court decisions vary on whether potential buyers are entitled to notification of past murders, suicides, and other "stigmas."

42. **b.** The term *alienation* means transfer of title. The lender reserves the right to call in the loan if the property is sold.

43. **a.** The equitable right of redemption allows the borrower to avoid foreclosure by coming up with all the money due plus costs.

44. **a.** When the comparable property has a better feature, the value of that feature is subtracted from its sale price to bring the comparable property equal to the subject property.

45. **a.** The bundle of legal rights is included in the definition of real property, not of land.

46. d. Public utility companies are given access over properties for the purpose of maintenance and repair of necessary lines, pipes, etc.

47. c. Fannie Mae buys large packages of mortgages that meet its particular specifications and has great influence on the primary mortgage market.

48. b. The principal's monetary obligation in an agency agreement is usually limited to payment of the agreed-upon commission.

49. c. Private mortgage insurance, required when a conventional loan involves less than 20% down, can cover mortgages made with down payments as low as 5%.

50. b. *Comps* is the term for recent nearby sales of comparable properties, whose prices are analyzed in the market sales approach to appraisal.

51. c. The Government National Mortgage Association buys packages of mortgages. The other initials stand for the Department of Housing and Urban Development; the Financial Institutions Reform, Recovery and Enforcement Act; and the Real Estate Settlement Procedures Act.

52. a. Foreclosure sales usually require cash payments.

53. b. A dual agent should make sure each party realizes the situation and gives written consent.

54. d. The Bakers' monthly gross income is $5,000 ($60,000 ÷ 12). The lender allows them a monthly mortgage payment no higher than 28% of $5,000 = $1,400. From that $1,400 must be subtracted a month's property taxes ($4,000 ÷ 12 = $333.33) and a month's homeowner insurance premium ($400 ÷ 12 = $33.33). That leaves $1,033.34 to pay for the mortgage itself, principal and interest. At $8.56 per thousand dollars, $1,033.34 will pay for $120,717 borrowed on a mortgage ($1,033.34 ÷ $8.56 × $1,000 = $120,717). If they buy for $140,000 and borrow $120,717, the Bakers will need $19,283 as a cash down payment ($140,000 − $120,717).

55. b. Each state sets its own requirements for real estate licensing.

56. d. A full warranty deed contains covenants that warrant the new owner's undisturbed and clear title.

57. c. The annual premium on $92,347 would be $461.74 ($92,347 × .005). One month's premium is $38.48 ($461.74 ÷ 12).

58. b. A special agent is authorized to perform one particular act, as in finding a ready, willing, and able buyer for a piece of property.

59. d. $250,000 × .80 ÷ 1,000 = $200 × 7.34 = $1,468 + $250 escrow = $1,718 monthly payment

60. b. The process begins with defining the purpose. The plan is then laid out before determining what data is needed.

61. b. A trust deed scenario involves three persons: the borrower, the lender, and a trustee who holds title for the benefit of the lender. The trustee also will reconvey ownership after the borrower has satisfied the debt.

62. c. The mortgagee must follow all rules about entering the property. Other covenants might be prompt payment and maintaining adequate hazard and casualty insurance coverage.

63. b. A claim against all property, real and personal, brought about by a default in an obligation is described as general and involuntary.

64. c. In a "friendly foreclosure," the lender accepts the property in full settlement and satisfaction of the debt.

65. d. Amortized loans pay out over a period of time, with interest collected from the periodic payment and any surplus applied to reduction of principal.

66. **c.** As opposed to negligent misrepresentation, in which the licensee merely should have known the statement was inaccurate, a fraudulent statement is made by someone who knows the statement is false.

67. **b.** Familial status refers to a parent or guardian who lives with one or more children under the age of 18.

68. **a.** A buffer zone is often used to soften the transition between residential and other uses.

69. **b.** The store will pay as additional rent a percentage of its receipts each month.

70. **d.** Reproduction of a building uses the original materials and techniques for an exact duplicate of the original; replacement uses modern methods for an equivalent building that will serve the same purpose as the original.

71. **a.** Regulation Z requires that borrowers be notified of their annual percentage rate, which takes into account not only the simple interest rate but also other financing costs, such as points.

72. **d.** Occupation and source of income are not protected classes under federal laws.

73. **c.** A use that was in existence before a zoning ordinance was enacted is allowed to continue as a nonconforming use.

74. **b.** Testers are individuals or organizations who pose as buyers and record and report the treatment they receive.

75. **a.** $1,000 + $1,500 + $2,250 = $4,750.

76. **●** No law offers equal protection for smoking.

77. **b.** Since the property manager makes decisions on behalf of the owner, such as tenant selection, budget preparation, and employee relations, the property manager is a general agent.

78. **c.** Whether entered in the public records or not, real property taxes automatically take priority over all other liens.

79. **b.** Personal permission that may be withdrawn is known as a license and gives the neighbor no interest in the real estate.

80. **c.** An appraisal is an estimate of market value through an analysis of data. This is the likely purchase price, given knowledgeable buyer and seller.

SCORING

Again, evaluate how you did on this practice exam by finding the number of questions you got right, disregarding for the moment the ones you got wrong or skipped. Divide the number you got right by 80 to find your percentage score. If need be, use the table at the end of Chapter 3 to check your math. Keep in mind that if you achieve a score of 70 to 75 percent, you will most likely pass the ASI Real Estate Sales Exam.

If you didn't score as well as you would like, ask yourself the following: Did I run out of time before I could answer all the questions? Did I go back and change my answers from right to wrong? Did I get flustered and sit staring at a difficult question for what seemed like hours? If you had any of these problems, be sure to go over the EasySmart test preparation system in Chapter 2 to review how best to avoid them.

You probably have seen improvement between your first two practice exam scores and this one; but if you didn't improve as much as you'd like, following are some options:

- **If you scored below 60 percent,** you should seriously consider whether you're ready for the ASI Real Estate Sales Exam at this time. You should try some brush-up courses, or at least hit your real estate course materials *hard,* maybe with the help of a friend.

- **If your score is in the 60 to 70 percent range,** you need to work as hard as you can to improve your skills. Besides reviewing the Real Estate Refresher Course in Chapter 4, go back to your textbooks and study your weak areas. If you need help with math, the LearningExpress book, *Practical Math Success in 20 Minutes a Day* (order information at the back of this book) will undoubtedly help with the items that involve math.

- **If your score is between 70 and 85 percent,** you could still benefit from additional work by going back to Chapters 4, 5, and 6 and by doing another quick review of your weakest areas before the exam.

- **If you scored above 85 percent,** that's great! You should have no trouble passing your licensing exam. Don't lose your edge, though; keep studying right up to the day before the exam.

Now, revise your study schedule according to the time you have left, emphasizing those parts that gave you the most trouble this time. Use the table below to see where you need more work, so that you can concentrate your preparation efforts. After working more on the subject areas that give you problems, take the fourth practice exam in Chapter 9 to see how much you've improved.

FOR REVIEW

Question Subject Area	Question Numbers
Real Property	7, 9, 14, 25, 28, 32, 35, 40, 45, 46, 56, 63, 68, 73, 78, 79
Valuation and Appraisal	5, 12, 15, 20, 22, 23, 30, 44, 50, 60, 70, 80
Contracts, Agency, Federal Requirements	2, 4, 11, 16, 27, 29, 31, 33, 34, 36, 39, 41, 48, 53, 55, 58, 66, 71, 74, 76
Financing	3, 8, 13, 18, 19, 24, 38, 42, 43, 47, 49, 51, 52, 54, 57, 59, 61, 62, 64, 65
Leases, Rents, Property Management	1, 6, 10, 17, 21, 26, 37, 67, 69, 72, 75, 77

C·H·A·P·T·E·R

ASI REAL ESTATE SALES EXAM 4

9

CHAPTER SUMMARY

This is the last of the four practice tests in this book based on the ASI Real Estate Sales Exam. Using all of the experience and strategy that you gained from taking the other three exams, take this exam to see how far you've come.

This is the last practice exam in this book, but it is not designed to be any harder or any trickier than the other three. It is simply another representation of what you might expect for the real test. Just as when you go to take the real test, there shouldn't be anything here to surprise you. In fact, you probably already know what's in a lot of it! That will be the case with the real test, too—you will be prepared, so you won't be surprised.

For this last test, pull together all the tips you've been practicing since the first one. Give yourself the time and the space to work. Since you won't be taking the real test in your living room, it might be best to take this one in an unfamiliar location such as a library. In addition, draw on what you've learned from reading the answer explanations on previous practice tests. Remember the types of questions that tripped you up in the past, and when you are unsure, try to consider how those answers were explained.

Most of all, relax. You have worked hard and have every right to be confident.

1.	ⓐ	ⓑ	ⓒ	ⓓ
2.	ⓐ	ⓑ	ⓒ	ⓓ
3.	ⓐ	ⓑ	ⓒ	ⓓ
4.	ⓐ	ⓑ	ⓒ	ⓓ
5.	ⓐ	ⓑ	ⓒ	ⓓ
6.	ⓐ	ⓑ	ⓒ	ⓓ
7.	ⓐ	ⓑ	ⓒ	ⓓ
8.	ⓐ	ⓑ	ⓒ	ⓓ
9.	ⓐ	ⓑ	ⓒ	ⓓ
10.	ⓐ	ⓑ	ⓒ	ⓓ
11.	ⓐ	ⓑ	ⓒ	ⓓ
12.	ⓐ	ⓑ	ⓒ	ⓓ
13.	ⓐ	ⓑ	ⓒ	ⓓ
14.	ⓐ	ⓑ	ⓒ	ⓓ
15.	ⓐ	ⓑ	ⓒ	ⓓ
16.	ⓐ	ⓑ	ⓒ	ⓓ
17.	ⓐ	ⓑ	ⓒ	ⓓ
18.	ⓐ	ⓑ	ⓒ	ⓓ
19.	ⓐ	ⓑ	ⓒ	ⓓ
20.	ⓐ	ⓑ	ⓒ	ⓓ
21.	ⓐ	ⓑ	ⓒ	ⓓ
22.	ⓐ	ⓑ	ⓒ	ⓓ
23.	ⓐ	ⓑ	ⓒ	ⓓ
24.	ⓐ	ⓑ	ⓒ	ⓓ
25.	ⓐ	ⓑ	ⓒ	ⓓ
26.	ⓐ	ⓑ	ⓒ	ⓓ
27.	ⓐ	ⓑ	ⓒ	ⓓ

28.	ⓐ	ⓑ	ⓒ	ⓓ
29.	ⓐ	ⓑ	ⓒ	ⓓ
30.	ⓐ	ⓑ	ⓒ	ⓓ
31.	ⓐ	ⓑ	ⓒ	ⓓ
32.	ⓐ	ⓑ	ⓒ	ⓓ
33.	ⓐ	ⓑ	ⓒ	ⓓ
34.	ⓐ	ⓑ	ⓒ	ⓓ
35.	ⓐ	ⓑ	ⓒ	ⓓ
36.	ⓐ	ⓑ	ⓒ	ⓓ
37.	ⓐ	ⓑ	ⓒ	ⓓ
38.	ⓐ	ⓑ	ⓒ	ⓓ
39.	ⓐ	ⓑ	ⓒ	ⓓ
40.	ⓐ	ⓑ	ⓒ	ⓓ
41.	ⓐ	ⓑ	ⓒ	ⓓ
42.	ⓐ	ⓑ	ⓒ	ⓓ
43.	ⓐ	ⓑ	ⓒ	ⓓ
44.	ⓐ	ⓑ	ⓒ	ⓓ
45.	ⓐ	ⓑ	ⓒ	ⓓ
46.	ⓐ	ⓑ	ⓒ	ⓓ
47.	ⓐ	ⓑ	ⓒ	ⓓ
48.	ⓐ	ⓑ	ⓒ	ⓓ
49.	ⓐ	ⓑ	ⓒ	ⓓ
50.	ⓐ	ⓑ	ⓒ	ⓓ
51.	ⓐ	ⓑ	ⓒ	ⓓ
52.	ⓐ	ⓑ	ⓒ	ⓓ
53.	ⓐ	ⓑ	ⓒ	ⓓ
54.	ⓐ	ⓑ	ⓒ	ⓓ

55.	ⓐ	ⓑ	ⓒ	ⓓ
56.	ⓐ	ⓑ	ⓒ	ⓓ
57.	ⓐ	ⓑ	ⓒ	ⓓ
58.	ⓐ	ⓑ	ⓒ	ⓓ
59.	ⓐ	ⓑ	ⓒ	ⓓ
60.	ⓐ	ⓑ	ⓒ	ⓓ
61.	ⓐ	ⓑ	ⓒ	ⓓ
62.	ⓐ	ⓑ	ⓒ	ⓓ
63.	ⓐ	ⓑ	ⓒ	ⓓ
64.	ⓐ	ⓑ	ⓒ	ⓓ
65.	ⓐ	ⓑ	ⓒ	ⓓ
66.	ⓐ	ⓑ	ⓒ	ⓓ
67.	ⓐ	ⓑ	ⓒ	ⓓ
68.	ⓐ	ⓑ	ⓒ	ⓓ
69.	ⓐ	ⓑ	ⓒ	ⓓ
70.	ⓐ	ⓑ	ⓒ	ⓓ
71.	ⓐ	ⓑ	ⓒ	ⓓ
72.	ⓐ	ⓑ	ⓒ	ⓓ
73.	ⓐ	ⓑ	ⓒ	ⓓ
74.	ⓐ	ⓑ	ⓒ	ⓓ
75.	ⓐ	ⓑ	ⓒ	ⓓ
76.	ⓐ	ⓑ	ⓒ	ⓓ
77.	ⓐ	ⓑ	ⓒ	ⓓ
78.	ⓐ	ⓑ	ⓒ	ⓓ
79.	ⓐ	ⓑ	ⓒ	ⓓ
80.	ⓐ	ⓑ	ⓒ	ⓓ

1. The buyers who sign a statement about the price and terms on which they are ready to purchase property have created
   a. a purchase offer
   b. an option
   c. a contract of sale
   d. a listing contract

2. Michael Brown refuses to sell his farm to the state, which needs it to complete the route for a new highway. The state may go to court and ask that his farm be condemned, allowing the state to purchase the land using its right of
   a. laches
   b. adverse possession
   c. easement by necessity
   d. eminent domain

3. Which of the following is NOT necessary in order for a property to have value?
   a. The property has a useful purpose.
   b. Somebody wants to own the property.
   c. The property is unique.
   d. The owner of the property is unknown.

4. The listing broker's commission is earned when
   a. the property is listed
   b. an offer has been accepted
   c. financing has been arranged
   d. the property is finally closed

5. The Veteran's Administration sets a limit on the amount of the
   a. loan
   b. down payment
   c. guarantee
   d. monthly payment

6. The owner of Highland Apartments has determined that his vacancy rate is less than five percent. What, if any, action should he take?
   a. He should spend less money on advertising.
   b. He should renovate the lobby.
   c. He should raise the rents.
   d. He should do nothing.

7. Mary White and Elizabeth Brown, widowed sisters, are buying a home together. To ensure that if one dies her share will go to her children, they should purchase the property as
   a. tenants in severalty
   b. tenants by the entirety
   c. tenants in common
   d. joint tenants with right of survivorship

8. The management agreement does all of the following EXCEPT
   a. identify the parties
   b. authorize the manager to make personal deals resulting in outside compensation by suppliers
   c. describe the manager's responsibilities and authorities
   d. state the owner's overall goals for the property

9. The furnace at 39 State Street doesn't work properly. However, because the prospective buyers inspect the house in July, there is no indication of this. The condition of the furnace is known as
   a. an encumbrance
   b. a cloud on title
   c. a latent defect
   d. an economic obsolescence

10. The new owner who agrees to pay an existing mortgage but does not officially take personal responsibility for it is
    a. assuming the mortgage
    b. taking the property subject to the mortgage
    c. subordinating the mortgage
    d. alienating the mortgage

11. Homeowners who wish to shorten the time left on their fixed-rate mortgages can do so by sending in extra payments to
    a. interest
    b. principal
    c. escrow
    d. interest and principal

12. Jessie Petersen makes a written offer to buy Sam Lewis's house for $120,000. She confides in Sam's agent, George Everly, that if necessary she'd pay $10,000 more, but she doesn't want Sam to know that. George should
    a. present the offer to Sam but respect Jessie's confidentiality
    b. warn Jessie that he must pass on to Sam anything useful he knows
    c. refuse to convey the lower offer to Sam
    d. explain to Jessie why the house isn't worth more than $120,000

13. Deed restrictions that forbid future sale of the property to members of certain ethnic groups cannot be enforced because they
    a. violate the law
    b. prevent free transfer of property
    c. are unrelated to the construction of a building
    d. are inconsistent with most local zoning ordinances

14. The manager who sets rental rates should take into consideration the
    a. price the owner paid for the property
    b. income the property must produce
    c. going rates elsewhere in the neighborhood
    d. owner's total expenses including debt service

15. The investor criteria for a home mortgage is an uninsured loan to value ratio of 75% of the appraisal. The sales agreement and appraisal is in the amount of $180,000. Following underwriting guidelines, the buyer qualifies for a loan of $145,000. The buyer agrees to purchase private mortgage insurance. How much of the purchase will the investor finance?
a. $180,000
b. $145,000
c. $108,750
d. $135,000

16. In order to appraise property valued over $1,000,000, the person performing the appraisal would need to be
a. state licensed
b. federally licensed
c. certified by the bank
d. approved by the government

17. The buyer gives his agent a check for $5,000 to serve as earnest money accompanying a purchase offer. He asks that the agent not deposit the check until the end of the month and also asks him not to tell the seller about this. When the agent presents the offer he should
a. say nothing to the seller but inform his supervising broker of the situation
b. say nothing to the buyer but tell the seller the exact status of the check
c. mention nothing about the check to anyone and wait to deposit it as requested
d. explain to the buyer that he has a fiduciary duty to inform the seller about the check

18. A building permit may be issued even if the proposed structure violates existing
a. zoning laws
b. deed restrictions
c. building codes
d. setback requirements

19. While Dana Nelson spends six months in Europe, she continues to pay rent to her landlord, but actually collects rent from her friend Tim Baylor, who is living there while she is gone. The situation is known as
a. an assignment of lease
b. a sublet
c. a lease option
d. a right of reverter

20. George Brown owns 150 acres of farmland and has posted "No Trespassing" signs on the fence surrounding the property. He can enforce this notice by virtue of his
a. constitutional privilege
b. right to exclude
c. obligation of disposition
d. surface rights

21. Joanna Bruno bought a house for $120,000, putting 20% down and borrowing the rest on a mortgage. At the end of the first year, her principal had been paid down by $480 and property values in that neighborhood had risen by 5%. Her equity at the end of that first year was
a. $6,000
b. $23,512
c. $30,480
d. $96,000

22. Simon Hersch, a salesperson associated with broker Bob King, lists a house for sale for $120,000, with 6% commission due at closing. Three weeks later the owner accepts an offer for $115,000, brought in by Simon. Bob's practice is that 45% of commissions go to the office and the rest to the salesperson. How much will Simon make on the sale?
a. $3,105
b. $3,240
c. $3,795
d. $3,960

23. A tax bill computed by a cost-per-front-foot is a
a. personal property tax
b. special assessment
c. license
d. use permit

24. The manager protects the owner from financial loss in all of the following ways EXCEPT by
a. being discriminatory in the selection of tenants
b. aggressively enforcing reasonable policies and rules
c. being overly attentive to insurance coverages
d. paying close attention to maintenance problems

25. Jeff and Alexandra Clancey have paid a total of $10,500 in mortgage interest and $1,500 in property taxes in this tax year. If they are in the 28% tax bracket, their tax savings is
a. $12,000
b. $1,000
c. $294
d. $3,360

26. An appraiser arrives at a gross rent multiplier by analyzing the
a. building's amount of depreciation from all causes
b. income and recent sale prices of nearby properties
c. vacancy rates in the overall community
d. cost of constructing an equivalent building on a similar lot today

27. The term "commingling" refers to
   a. looking for real estate business at community social events
   b. mixing funds held for other persons with one's own money
   c. the same office acting as buyer's broker and seller's broker for the same property
   d. one office finding a buyer for another office's listing

28. The house being appraised has no garage, but it does have a fireplace, and the appraiser estimates that a fireplace contributes $5,000 to the value of a home in that neighborhood. A nearby house that recently sold for $128,500 is similar except that it has a garage but no fireplace. The appraiser values a garage as worth $8,000 to buyers. The adjusted sale price of the comparable house is
   a. $125,500
   b. $128,500
   c. $131,500
   d. $141,500

29. The federal government requires a leaflet about possible lead paint contamination to be given to any potential purchaser or tenant of a residence built before
   a. 1995
   b. 1987
   c. 1981
   d. 1978

30. How may FHA and VA loans be assumed?
   a. freely only
   b. with qualification by the buyer only
   c. under no circumstances
   d. either freely or with qualification from the buyer, depending on the date of the loan

31. A single-family property located in an industrial area has minimum value because of the principle of
   a. diminishing returns
   b. contribution
   c. competition
   d. conformity

32. The Sinclairs needed two different loans to buy their first home. The mortgage that will have first claim on the value of the house in case of foreclosure is the one that was first
   a. negotiated
   b. signed
   c. recorded
   d. satisfied

33. The correct formula for estimating value using the cost approach is
   a. cost to replace + depreciation − value of land = value
   b. depreciation + value of land − cost to replace = value
   c. cost to replace − depreciation + value of land = value
   d. value of land + cost to replace + depreciation = value

34. A broker would not be violating a law for making the statement "I think this is the most beautiful view in the state," because it is considered harmless
   a. showmanship
   b. puffing
   c. advertising
   d. fibbing

35. Building codes define the
   a. architectural style of the improvement
   b. location of highways and utilities
   c. approved use of the property
   d. minimum standards for the materials used in the construction

36. The cost approach is best suited for estimating the value of
   a. a large tract of land
   b. the income generated by a commercial property
   c. a historic building
   d. a condominium apartment

37. Which of the following is most likely to be used as a legal description to identify a parcel of real estate in a deed?
   a. the tax assessment number
   b. the street address
   c. a description of existing structures
   d. the recorded plat numbers

38. Any federally related loan may require the borrower to carry special insurance if the property is located in
   a. an earthquake area
   b. a flood zone
   c. an ocean hazard district
   d. a desert

39. An owner is planning to build on newly purchased property. Zoning laws state that no improvement may exceed 50 feet in height, a restrictive covenant limits improvements to 45 feet in height, and the deed restriction states the maximum height to be 30 feet. What is the tallest building the owner can legally construct?
   a. 50 feet
   b. 45 feet
   c. 30 feet
   d. The new building can be any size the owner wants.

40. A property manager's compensation may be based on any of the following EXCEPT
   a. finder's fees from suppliers of goods and services
   b. a flat fee
   c. a percentage of gross income
   d. a fee per unit

41. The Truth in Lending Act (Regulation Z) applies to lender's practices
a. if the loan is for $25,000 or more
b. if the loan is secured by a residence
c. if the loan is for commercial or agricultural use
d. for all business loans

42. An appraiser predicts that a commercial property, if fully leased, would produce $250,000 in rent on a monthly basis. A vacancy factor of 9% is applied, and by using a capitalization rate of 12%, a value of the property is estimated at
a. $22,750,000
b. $25,000,000
c. $189,583
d. $2,777,777

43. In a real estate transaction, fiduciary duties are owed to the
a. broker
b. customer
c. principal
d. agent

44. Construction costs are usually estimated by the
a. overall project
b. square foot method
c. replacement method
d. income approach

45. The broker who is sued for an unintentional mistake can expect court costs to be paid by his
a. seller in the transaction involved
b. local Association of Realtors
c. errors and omissions policy
d. company's own funds

46. A mini-ranch is being established on a newly acquired 25-acre parcel of land. The new owner plans to enclose the property with a split-rail fence. The rectangular lot has 1,000 feet of frontage on the state road. How many feet of fencing will be needed?
a. 2,090 feet
b. 4,178 feet
c. 4,270 feet
d. 4,595 feet

47. At settlement, unpaid bills of the seller's that will eventually be paid by the buyer (water bills, interest on a mortgage that's being assumed) are known as
a. prorations
b. interims
c. impounds
d. closing costs

48. Under RESPA regulations, fees in connection with a sale of real estate may be paid to brokers for
   a. directing buyers or sellers to certain providers of settlement services
   b. arranging for property inspections
   c. referring of prospects by another licensed broker
   d. obtaining the necessary insurance policies

49. The form of simple appraisal that takes into account the prices of houses that failed to sell is a
   a. competitive market analysis
   b. limited appraisal
   c. reconciliation report
   d. cost approach

50. Ken Laughton's house is up "for sale by owner." Robert Hall falls in love with it during an open house, tells Ken he'll pay the full asking price, and writes an earnest money check for $5,000 then and there. Ken says he'll accept and takes the check. The contract between them is
   a. enforceable by court action if either tries to back out
   b. invalid because it lacks consideration
   c. valid only if there were witnesses
   d. unenforceable

51. Encroachments, liens, licenses, and other claims against an owner's full title are known as
   a. encumbrances
   b. restrictions
   c. easements
   d. mortgages

52. The Millers put their house on the market, the Blacks made a written purchase offer, and the Millers accepted the offer in writing. When is the contract valid?
   a. immediately
   b. as soon as the signatures are notarized
   c. when the Blacks are notified of the acceptance
   d. when it is placed in the public records

53. One example of a periodic estate is
   a. a month-to-month tenancy
   b. an estate at will
   c. a net lease
   d. a sublet

54. When several real estate brokers are invited to list a property, with commission due only to the one who produces the first acceptable buyer, the owner is offering
   a. an open listing
   b. an exclusive right to sell
   c. an exclusive agency
   d. a multiple listing

55. No one seems to own the vacant lot next to Henry's house, so he has used it for a garden for many years now. He may have a good chance of going to court and obtaining ownership by
   a. escheat
   b. condemnation
   c. adverse possession
   d. remainder

56. Which of the following is the most important factor for a lender in determining credit-worthiness?
a. age
b. race
c. credit history
d. gender

57. The blueprint for the final transfer of title is found in the
a. listing contract
b. buyer broker agreement
c. sales contract
d. multiple listing

58. Charging more than the legally allowed rate of interest is known as
a. discounting points
b. alienation
c. hypothecation
d. usury

59. Which of the following changes in zoning should result in compensation to the owner?
a. spot zoning
b. down-zoning
c. buffer zoning
d. "taking"

60. Which of the following is true about discount points?
a. They allow for cut-rate lending.
b. They are based on the purchase price of the property.
c. They are charged when a mortgage is resold.
d. They increase the effective yield to the lender.

61. The Federal Civil Rights Act of 1968, including the later amendments, prohibits discrimination in real estate based on
a. source of income
b. political affiliation
c. handicap
d. criminal record

62. The lender's right to call in the loan in case of default and put the property up for sale is based on the mortgage document's
a. alienation clause
b. acceleration clause
c. defeasance clause
d. equity of redemption

63. With an amortized loan, each month
a. the amount of principal and interest in each payment remain the same
b. interest and principal payments each increase
c. interest decreases and principal portion increases
d. interest increases and principal decreases

64. An appraiser adjusts the sale price of a comparable property for date of sale if
a. the transaction occurred on a holiday
b. market conditions have changed since the sale
c. the sale occurred within the past month
d. the transaction included a delayed settlement

65. A junior mortgage is a mortgage placed
   a. by a person who is technically still a minor
   b. on property that already has a first mortgage on record
   c. as security for a loan of less than $25,000
   d. on property by a lender who pledges not to enter the document in the public records

66. With an adjustable rate mortgage, the term "margin" applies to the
   a. initial teaser rate
   b. percentage added to the index
   c. national average rate used for adjustments
   d. highest rate possible during the life of the loan

67. Although the term "purchase money mortgage" applies to any loan that finances the purchase of real estate, it is commonly used to refer specifically to a
   a. loan taken back as part of the sales price by the seller
   b. refinance loan
   c. loan on property already owned that is used to finance the purchase of a second property
   d. loan that is packaged for sale on the secondary market

68. Steering, prohibited by fair housing laws, is the practice of
   a. inducing panic-selling because a neighborhood is changing
   b. refusing to make loans in certain inner city areas
   c. subtly guiding buyers to areas that match their race or religion
   d. denying membership in a brokers' organization because of the applicant's race or other protected class

69. A house is valued at $185,000, in a community that assesses property at 85% of value. If the tax rate is $24.85 per thousand, how much is the property tax bill?
   a. $1,480
   b. $1,850
   c. $3,907.66
   d. $4,597.25

70. The difference between the value of a property and the sum of the liens against it is called
   a. equity
   b. leverage
   c. cash asset
   d. pledge

71. Local building codes require any fence to be built at least ten feet in from the property lines. Tim Noh has a small yard on the corner of two busy highways. He wants to build a fence, to protect his small children, right on the property line. He should ask his zoning board for a
   a. building permit
   b. spot zoning
   c. certificate of occupancy
   d. variance

72. Anna Jamison rents a small building for her boutique. In addition to rent, she also pays property taxes, utility bills, and insurance on the property. She must have a
   a. net lease
   b. percentage lease
   c. variable lease
   d. ground lease

73. Linda has a three-year lease on her apartment. At the end of the three years
   a. the landlord must notify her if he wants her to vacate
   b. she must give the landlord one month's notice that she is leaving
   c. she may remain because an estate for years automatically renews
   d. neither party need give the other any notice that she is leaving

74. An owner's objectives for the property may be any of the following EXCEPT to
   a. increase value by elevating net operating income
   b. introduce undesirables into the neighborhood to cause property values to decline
   c. clean up the rent rolls and cause change in the quality of life in the neighborhood
   d. provide clean, safe, affordable shelter for low-income families

75. By mistake of the general contractor, a new building was constructed so that it extends over the property line onto an adjacent lot owned by another individual. Which of the following is NOT true in this situation?
   a. The owner of the new building has created a nuisance.
   b. The adjacent owner may require that the new building be reconstructed to remove the offending portion.
   c. The owner of the new building may acquire authority to maintain the building through the right to an easement by necessity.
   d. Title may be considered unmarketable unless the encroachment is removed or otherwise dealt with.

76. Office space is usually rented by the
   a. cubic foot
   b. square foot
   c. percentage of business done
   d. cost of living index

77. Tenancy by the entirety is a special form of ownership available only to
   a. sole owners
   b. corporations
   c. married couples
   d. limited partners

78. If a foreclosure sale fails to bring enough to pay off a lien, the lender may in most cases seek a
   a. release deed
   b. promissory note
   c. deficiency judgment
   d. right of redemption

79. Which of the following does an appraisal take into consideration?
   a. various conditions in the neighborhood
   b. the owner's financial situation
   c. the sentimental value of the property
   d. IRS depreciation claimed or available

80. The Federal Reserve influences the real estate market by its control of
   a. interest rates
   b. FHA mortgages
   c. discount points
   d. secondary markets

ANSWERS

1. a. Until it is accepted by a seller, the document remains simply a purchase offer.

2 d. The government's right of eminent domain is enforced through condemnation.

3. d. Property is valueless unless title can be passed.

4. b. Although most commissions may not be paid until the closing, the listing agent's assignment has actually been completed when a buyer is produced who is willing and able to purchase on the seller's terms.

5. c. The VA offers to guarantee a certain amount of the loan; lenders are free to determine their own lending limits.

6. c. A five percent vacancy rate is considered normal; anything lower means rents are too low.

7. c. Tenants in common have the right to devise their shares to any chosen heirs. "Severalty" applies to single ownership, and the other two answers involve automatic inheritance by one owner if the other dies.

8. b. The manager must avoid conflicts of interest by refusing to accept gratuities from suppliers.

9. c. Latent or hidden defects are those that cannot be seen by a normal prudent inspection.

10. b. Taking title to property subject to an existing mortgage acknowledges the existence of the debt but does not incur personal liability.

11. b. Any extra payment to principal shortens the time remaining on the loan. It does not lower monthly payments.

12. b. Jessie is entitled to honest treatment, so George should explain that he owes her no confidentiality and that he does owe a duty of notice to Sam.

13. a. Restrictive covenants cannot be used for illegal purposes. If they are, the courts will not enforce them.

14. c Rental rates are set by supply and demand.

15. b. The income to payment ratio indicates a maximum loan of $145,000. If the buyer's income and other financial data were adequate, this loan could be as high as 95% of the purchase price.

16. a. Under FIRREA, appraisers need to be licensed by the state.

17. d. The seller has a right to full information before making a decision about the offer. The buyer has a right to honest and straightforward treatment, which includes notice that his instructions will not be obeyed.

18. b. Deed restrictions are private and non-governmental, set by previous owners of the property. They are enforced through neighbors' lawsuits, not by local building authorities.

19. b. With a sublet, Dana remains responsible for the rent.

20. b. The right to exclude is one of the rights contained in the bundle of legal rights of ownership.

21. c. Her equity is the sum of three parts: $24,000, the cash she paid as down payment (20% of $120,000); $6,000, the year's increase in value (5% of $120,000); and $480, the amount by which her mortgage had been paid down.

22. c. Total commission is $6,900 (6% of sale price $115,000). Simon receives $3,795 (55% of $6,900). Note: to find 6%, multiply by .06; to find 55%, multiply by 0.55.

23. b. Special assessments are generally for repayment of the government for the cost of installing utilities, or curbs and gutters. Each owner is billed for their share of the expense calculated by their proportion of the benefit to their property.

24. a. Discrimination in the review of lease applications is not good business and will cause a great deal of trouble for the manager and owner alike.

25. d. The taxpayer is permitted to deduct $12,000 from earned income. At the 28% tax rate, the savings would be $3,360. ($10,500 + $1,500) $\times$ .28 = $3,360.

26. b. A gross rent multiplier estimates how much investors seem willing to pay for property yielding a given amount of income. This is only a rough estimate, as it does not consider some important factors, such as vacancies and expenses.

27. b. Commingling, prohibited by state license laws, refers to the mixing of other people's money (earnest deposits, for example) with the broker's own funds.

28. c. To compare the two houses, the appraiser subtracts the value of the fireplace from the comparable house and adds the value of the garage that is found in the subject property. $128,500 − $5,000 + $8,000 = $131,500.

29. d. Lead-based paint has not been manufactured since 1978.

30. d. Older FHA and VA loans are freely assumable; newer ones require the next borrower to prove financial qualification.

31. d. The principle of conformity states that to retain value the property should be located within an area of similar properties.

32. c. Liens, including mortgages, take priority from the order in which they were entered in the public records.

33. c. The formula is: cost to replace − depreciation + value of land = value

34. b. As opposed to potentially fraudulent misrepresentation, obvious exaggeration is considered acceptable puffing.

35. d. By setting building codes, the minimum standards for health, safety, and welfare of the public are provided by local, state, and municipal governments. This is an example of police power.

36. c. The cost approach is applicable when appraising unique properties.

37. d. Over the years, tax assessment numbers and street addresses can change. Structures are seldom mentioned in deeds, which transfer the land. The plat, however, is a surveyor's or engineer's map, with complete boundaries and numbers for each lot, entered in the public records.

38. b. The government issues flood hazard maps, and for mortgage loans within those areas, borrowers must carry flood insurance, which is available from the federal government.

39. c. When there is a conflict in limitations on the development of property, the most restrictive applies.

40. a. A property manager may not solicit or accept gratuities from suppliers of goods or services.

41. b. The Truth in Lending Act (Regulation Z) must be followed whenever a residence is pledged as security for a loan.

42. a. $250,000 $\times$ 12 $\times$ .91 ÷ .12 = $22,750,000

43. c. Specific fiduciary duties are owed to the agent's principal.

44. b. Construction handbooks estimate the current cost of building in a particular area by the square foot.

45. **c.** An E&O insurance company will defend the broker and pay legal costs and judgments where the mistake was not deliberate.

46. **b.** 25 acres × 43,560 square feet per acre ÷ 1,000 front feet = 1,089 feet deep. (1,000 feet × 2 sides) + (1,089 feet × 2 sides) = 4,178 feet.

47. **a.** The seller gives the buyer credit at closing for unpaid prorations.

48. **c.** A broker is not permitted to receive fees for merely referring business, except from a licensed broker who refers a prospect for real estate service.

49. **a.** The CMA, which assists sellers in setting an asking price, analyzes nearby properties that failed to sell, as well as competing property presently on the market and recently sold properties.

50. **d.** According to the statute of frauds, all contracts for the sale of real estate must be in writing to be enforceable.

51. **a.** The word *encumbrances* includes all the other types of claims on the property.

52. **c.** Acceptance of an offer must be communicated to the offeror.

53. **a.** A periodic estate automatically renews itself (for example, month after month) until either landlord or tenant gives notice to terminate it.

54. **a.** An open listing may be given to any number of firms, with only the one producing an acceptable buyer due a commission.

55. **c.** Adverse possession can sometimes give the use of title after occupancy of a parcel of land without permission or objection for a long period, the number of years varying from state to state.

56. **c.** Of this list, credit history is the only criterion the lender can evaluate. To look at the others critically would be a violation of the Equal Credit Opportunity Act.

57. **c.** The sales contract should anticipate and settle all questions about each party's rights and duties at closing.

58. **d.** Penalties for usury in some states prohibit the lender from collecting even the original loan amount.

59. **d.** When property is rezoned so that it destroys or severely limits its use, it is the same as being condemned or *taken*. This is usually a political, legal issue.

60. **d.** Each point is one percent of the amount being borrowed and serves as extra interest income to the lender.

61. **c.** Some state laws may add additional protected classes, but only *handicap* is included in the federal list.

62. **b.** The acceleration clause allows the lender to declare the whole debt immediately due and payable in case of default.

63. **c.** As the principal debt is paid down, the interest due each month becomes smaller, and more of the payment is available to be applied to the principal.

64. **b.** If economic conditions have changed since the sale, the appraiser adjusts the sale price accordingly.

65. **b.** A junior mortgage takes priority behind a first mortgage already on the property.

66. **b.** The lender calculates adjustments to the interest rate by adding a margin, typically of two or three percent, to an index of current rates.

67. **a.** Seller financing is often referred to as a purchase money mortgage.

68. **c.** Steering occurs when the licensee channels buyers either to or away from certain neighborhoods based on race, religion, or some other characteristic.

69. **c.** Assessed value is $157,250 (85% of $185,000). Tax is $3,907.66 ($24.85 tax rate times 157.25, the number of thousands).

70. **a.** The difference between value and debt is equity.

71. **d.** A variance, if granted, allows a use that will violate present zoning ordinances.

72. **a.** Anna's is actually a triple net lease, because she pays all the expenses on the building.

73. **d.** An estate for years automatically terminates and requires no notice from either party.

74. **b.** Causing property values to fall by introducing undesirables into a neighborhood would be a violation of the spirit and intent of fair housing laws.

75. **c.** An easement by necessity requires that crossing adjacent property is the only way to access another property.

76. **b.** It's common to quote office space prices by the square foot rent per year.

77. **c.** Tenancy by the entirety, available in most states, is automatically assumed when a married couple purchases real estate together unless they specify some other form of ownership.

78. **c.** Except where state law prohibits it, the lender who does not receive full payment after foreclosure may seek a deficiency judgment against the borrower.

79. **a.** An appraiser analyzes physical, political, and social conditions in the neighborhood of the subject property.

80. **a.** When the Fed raises the discount rate at which banks borrow from district reserve banks, the change is soon reflected in mortgage rates across the country, making it harder for borrowers to afford to buy real estate.

SCORING

Once again, in order to evaluate how you did on this last practice exam, find the number of questions you got right. Divide by 80 to find your percentage score. If you scored 70 to 75 percent, you will probably pass the exam, but most likely you've done better than that by now. Take a look at the table below to see what problem areas remain.

There's an ancient joke that goes like this: In New York City, a man stops a second man on the street and asks, "How do I get to Carnegie Hall?" The second man answers, "Practice."

The key to success in almost any pursuit is to prepare for all you're worth. By taking the practice exams in this book, you've made yourself better prepared than other people who may be taking the exam with you. You've diagnosed where your strengths and weaknesses lie and learned how to deal with the various kinds of questions that will appear on the test. So go into the exam with confidence, knowing that you're ready and equipped to do your best.

FOR REVIEW	
QUESTION SUBJECT AREA	**QUESTION NUMBERS**
Real Property	2, 7, 13, 18, 20, 23, 35, 37, 39, 46, 51, 55, 59, 71, 75, 77
Valuation and Appraisal	3, 16, 26, 28, 31, 33, 36, 42, 44, 49, 64, 79
Contracts, Agency, Federal Requirements	1, 4, 9, 12, 17, 25, 27, 29, 34, 38, 41, 43, 45, 48, 50, 52, 54, 57, 61, 68
Financing	5, 10, 11, 15, 21, 30, 32, 47, 56, 58, 60, 62, 63, 65–67, 69, 70, 78, 80
Leases, Rents, Property Management	6, 8, 14, 19, 22, 24, 40, 53, 72–74, 76

HOW TO USE THE CD-ROM

So you think you're ready for your exam? Here's a great way to build confidence and know you are ready: using LearningExpress's Real Estate Licensing Tester AutoExam CD-ROM software developed by Pearsoft Corporation of Cambridge, Massachusetts. The disk, included inside the back cover of this book, can be used with any PC running Windows 3.1 or Windows 95. (Sorry, it doesn't work with Macintosh.) The following description represents a typical "walk through" the software.

To install the program:

1. Insert the CD-ROM into your CD-ROM drive.

2. From Windows, select **File** (or **Start** in Windows 95), and then choose **Run.**

3. Type D:/Setup (using the letter of your CD-ROM drive for "D").

4. Click **OK.**

The screens that appear subsequently will walk you right through the installation procedure.

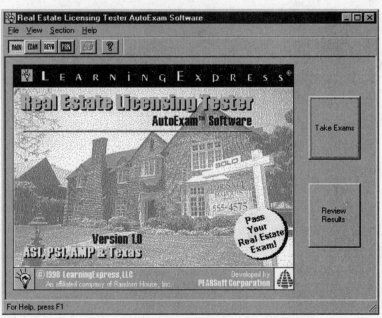

From the Main Menu, select **Take Exams.** (You can use **Review Results** after you have taken at least one exam, in order to see your scores.)

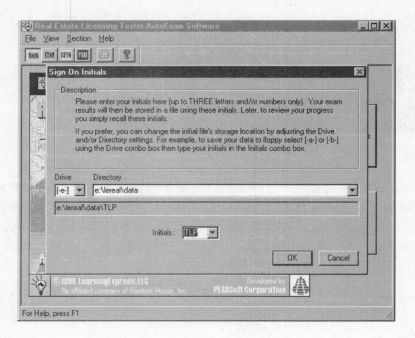

Now enter your initials. This allows you a chance to record your progress and review your performance for as many simulated exams as you'd like. Notice that you can also change the drive where your exam results are stored. If you want to save to a floppy drive, for instance, click on the arrow next to the **Drive** window and then choose the letter of your floppy drive.

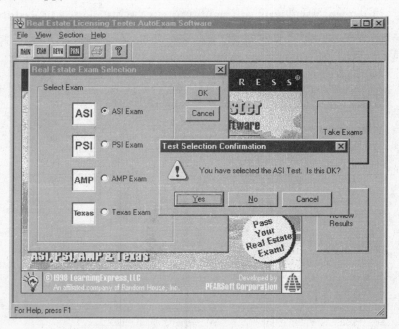

Now, since this CD-ROM supports four different real estate exams, you need to select your exam of interest. Let's try ASI, as shown above.

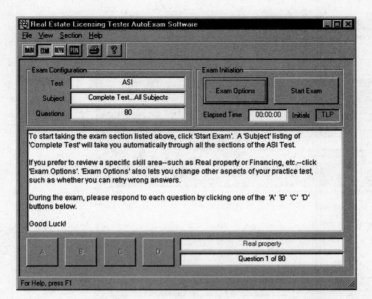

Now you're into the **Take Exams** section, as shown above. You can choose **Start Exam** to start taking your test, or **Exam Options.** The next screen shows you what your **Exam Options** are.

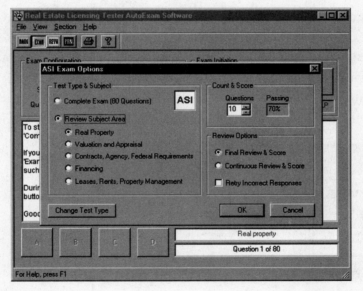

Choosing **Exam Options** gives you plenty of options to help you fine tune your rough spots. You can take a **Complete Exam** or **Review Subject Area.** If you choose **Review Subject Area,** a list of the subjects on your exam becomes active. Chose a subject area, and then, on the right, how many questions in that area you would like to review. On the right you can choose whether to wait until you've finished to see how you did (**Final Review & Score**) or have the computer tell you after each question whether your answer is right (**Continuous Review & Score**). Choose **Retry incorrect responses** to get a second chance at questions you answer wrong. (This option works best with **Review Skill Area** rather than **Complete Test.**) If you've chosen the wrong exam, you can click **Change Test Type** to go back and choose your exam. When you finish choosing your options, click **OK.** Then click the **Start Exam** button on the main exam screen.

Questions come up one at a time, just as they will on the real exam, and you click on A, B, C, or D to answer. When you've finished your exam or subject area, you'll have the option of switching to **Review Results.** (If you don't want to review your results now, you can always do it later by clicking on the **REV** button on the toolbar.) When you **Review Results,** you'll see your score and whether you passed. The questions again come up one at a time. Under **Options,** you can choose whether to look at all the questions or just the ones you missed. You can also choose whether you want a window with the **Explanation** of the correct answer to come up automatically.

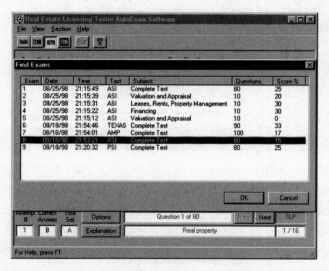

When you're in the **Review Results** section, click on the **Find** button to look at all the exams you've taken. By default, your exam results are listed from newest to oldest, but you can sort them by any of the headings. For instance, if you want to see your results arranged by score, you can click on the **Score** heading. To go to a particular exam you've taken, double click on it.

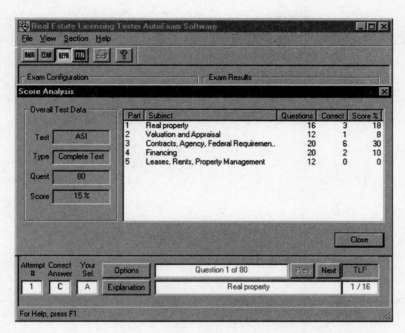

In the **Review Results** section, if you click on the **Score** button, you'll get a breakdown of your score on the exam you're currently reviewing. This section shows you how you did on each of the subject areas on the exam. Once again, you can sort the subject areas by any of the column headings. For instance, if you click on the **Score** heading, the program will order the subject areas from your highest percentage score to your lowest. You can see which areas are your strong and weak points, so you'll know what to review.

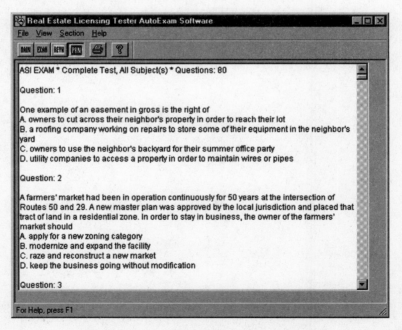

What's that? No time to work at the computer? Click the **Print Exams** menu bar button and you'll have a full-screen review of an exam that you can print out, as shown above. Then take it with you to the game.

For technical support, call (212) 995-2566.

NOTES

NOTES

FIVE WAYS TO MASTER THE BASICS!

IT ISN'T LUCK!

Anyone who wants to get good grades in school, pass entry-level or other job-related exams, or perform well on the job, must master basic skills: Reading Comprehension, Math, Vocabulary and Spelling, Writing, and basic Reasoning Skills.

What's the best way to master these skills?

With LearningExpress **SKILL BUILDERS**! Each book is designed to help you learn the important skills you need in the least amount of time.

Arranged in 20 quick and easy lessons, each guide:

- Pinpoints the areas where you need the most help
- Gives you hundreds of exercises with full answer explanations
- Provides you with tips on scoring your best on school and job-related tests

Skill Builders also feature:

- Specially designed "Before and After" tests to quickly pinpoint strengths, weaknesses *and* chart your progress
- "Skill Building Until Next Time": inventive ways to continue learning on the go

GIVE YOURSELF THE EXCLUSIVE LearningExpress ADVANTAGE!

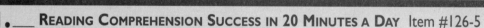

1. ___	READING COMPREHENSION SUCCESS IN 20 MINUTES A DAY	Item #126-5
2. ___	WRITING SKILLS SUCCESS IN 20 MINUTES A DAY	Item #128-1
3. ___	VOCABULARY/SPELLING SUCCESS IN 20 MINUTES A DAY	Item #127-3
4. ___	PRACTICAL MATH SUCCESS IN 20 MINUTES A DAY	Item #129-X
5. ___	REASONING SKILLS SUCCESS IN 20 MINUTES A DAY	Item #116-8

SPECIFICATIONS: 8 1/2 x 11 • 192-240 PAGES • $16.00 EACH (PAPERBACK)

ORDER THE LEARNINGEXPRESS SKILL BUILDERS YOU NEED TODAY:

Fill in the quantities beside each book and mail your check/money order*
for the amount indicated (please include $6.95 postage/handling
for the first book and $1.00 for each additional book) to:

LearningExpress, Dept. A040, 20 Academy Street, Norwalk, CT 06850

Or call, TOLL-FREE: **1-888-551-JOBS, Dept. A040,** to place a credit card order.

Also available in your local bookstores

Please allow at least 2-4 weeks for delivery. Prices subject to change without notice   **NY, CT, & MD residents add appropriate sales tax*

Order Form

CALIFORNIA EXAMS

___ @ $35.00   CA Allied Health
___ @ $35.00   CA Corrections Officer
___ @ $35.00   CA Firefighter
___ @ $20.00   CA Law Enforcement Career Guide
___ @ $35.00   CA Police Officer
___ @ $30.00   CA Postal Worker
___ @ $35.00   CA State Police
___ @ $17.95   CBEST (California Basic Educational
                         Skills Test)

NEW JERSEY EXAMS

___ @ $35.00   NJ Allied Health
___ @ $35.00   NJ Corrections Officer
___ @ $35.00   NJ Firefighter
___ @ $20.00   NJ Law Enforcement Career Guide
___ @ $35.00   NJ Police Officer
___ @ $30.00   NJ Postal Worker
___ @ $35.00   NJ State Police

TEXAS EXAMS

___ @ $17.95   TASP (Texas Academic Skills Program)
___ @ $32.50   TX Allied Health
___ @ $35.00   TX Corrections Officer
___ @ $35.00   TX Firefighter
___ @ $20.00   TX Law Enforcement Career Guide
___ @ $35.00   TX Police Officer
___ @ $30.00   TX Postal Worker
___ @ $29.95   TX Real Estate Exam
___ @ $30.00   TX State Police

NEW YORK EXAMS

___ @ $30.00   New York City Firefighter
___ @ $25.00   NYC Police Officer
___ @ $35.00   NY Allied Health
___ @ $35.00   NY Corrections Officer
___ @ $35.00   NY Firefighter
___ @ $20.00   NY Law Enforcement Career Guide
___ @ $30.00   NY Postal Worker
___ @ $35.00   NY State Police
___ @ $30.00   Suffolk County Police Officer

MASSACHUSETTS EXAMS

___ @ $30.00   MA Allied Health
___ @ $30.00   MA Police Officer
___ @ $30.00   MA State Police Exam

ILLINOIS EXAMS

___ @ $25.00   Chicago Police Officer
___ @ $25.00   Illinois Allied Health

FLORIDA EXAMS

___ @ $32.50   FL Allied Health
___ @ $35.00   FL Corrections Officer
___ @ $20.00   FL Law Enforcement Career Guide
___ @ $35.00   FL Police Officer
___ @ $30.00   FL Postal Worker

REGIONAL EXAMS

___ @ $29.95   AMP Real Estate Sales Exam
___ @ $29.95   ASI Real Estate Sales Exam
___ @ $30.00   Midwest Police Officer Exam
___ @ $30.00   Midwest Firefighter Exam
___ @ $17.95   PPST (Praxis 1)
___ @ $29.95   PSI Real Estate Sales Exam
___ @ $25.00   The South Police Officer Exam
___ @ $25.00   The South Firefighter Exam

NATIONAL EDITIONS

___ @ $20.00   Allied Health Entrance Exams
___ @ $14.95   ASVAB (Armed Services Vocational Aptitude
                         Battery): Complete Preparation Guide
___ @ $12.95   ASVAB Core Review
___ @ $17.95   Border Patrol Exam
___ @ $12.95   Bus Operator Exam
___ @ $15.00   Federal Clerical Exam
___ @ $12.95   Postal Worker Exam
___ @ $12.95   Sanitation Worker Exam
___ @ $17.95   Treasury Enforcement Agent Exam

NATIONAL CERTIFICATION & LICENSING EXAMS

___ @ $20.00   Cosmetology Licensing Exam
___ @ $20.00   EMT-Basic Certification Exam
___ @ $20.00   Home Health Aide Certification Exam
___ @ $20.00   Nursing Assistant Certification Exam
___ @ $20.00   Paramedic Licensing Exam

CAREER STARTERS

___ @ $14.95   Administrative Assistant/Secretary
___ @ $14.00   Civil Service
___ @ $14.95   Computer Technician
___ @ $14.95   Cosmetology
___ @ $14.95   EMT
___ @ $14.95   Firefighter
___ @ $14.95   Health Care
___ @ $14.95   Law Enforcement
___ @ $14.95   Paralegal
___ @ $14.95   Real Estate
___ @ $14.95   Retailing
___ @ $14.95   Teacher

To Order, Call TOLL-FREE: 1-888-551-JOBS, Dept. A040

Or, mail this order form with your check or money order* to:
LearningExpress, Dept. A040, 20 Academy Street, Norwalk, CT 06850

Please allow at least 2-4 weeks for delivery. Prices subject to change without notice

*NY, CT, & MD residents add appropriate sales tax

LEARNINGEXPRESS®

An Affiliate Company of Random House, Inc.